Sources of Non-Official UK Statistics

Sources of Non-Official UK Statistics

Sixth Edition

Compiled by
DAVID MORT

GOWER

Published by
Gower Publishing Limited
Gower House
Croft Road
Aldershot
Hampshire
GU11 3HR
England

Gower Publishing Company
Suite 420
101 Cherry Street
Burlington
VT 05401-4405
USA

David Mort has asserted his moral right under the Copyright, Designs and Patents Act, 1988, to be identified as the editor of this work.

British Library Cataloguing in Publication Data
  Sources of non-official UK statistics. – 6th ed.
  1. Great Britain – Statistical services – Directories
  I. Mort, David
  016.3'141

ISBN-10: 0 566 08715 4
ISBN-13: 978-0-566-08715-8

Library of Congress Control Number: 2006927402

Printed and bound in Great Britain by MPG Books Ltd. Bodmin, Cornwall.

Contents

Introduction

Published statistical series and marketing data play an important role in the provision of information for business, industry, economic analysis, academic and other research. In the United Kingdom as in most major economies, central government and its departments are the main suppliers of statistical information. These statistics are usually referred to as 'official statistics' and details of the range of official statistics available can be obtained from the National Statistics website at www.statistics.gov.uk.

As well as central government, there are many other organisations involved in compiling and disseminating statistics and these include trade associations, professional bodies, market research organisations, banks, other financial services companies, chambers of commerce, economic research and forecasting organisations, consultants, academic institutions and commercial publishers. Sources from these publishers form the basis of the entries in this directory, and these resources are usually referred to as 'non-official statistics' to differentiate them from data published by government. They may also be referred to as 'non-governmental statistics'.

Traditionally, the two areas of statistical publishing – official and non-official – have been largely separate from each other, although some trade association data have been used in selected official series, and various non-governmental bodies often lobby and advise government statisticians on statistical series and issues. In recent years, however, the line between official and non-official sources has become increasingly blurred with some official data being distributed and sold through private sector sources, and more data from non-governmental sources being incorporated in government series and services.

This sixth edition of *Sources of Non-Official UK Statistics* provides details of almost 900 non-official titles and services, and is a unique and well-established source of information on an important area of business information.

Non-official statistics

Although central government is the major producer of statistics, there are various reasons why these statistics do not always provide sufficient detail on specific markets, sectors, and products. Non-official sources can cover product areas and sectors excluded from central government data, and they may also cover different types of data not usually included in official sources. Examples of the latter include end-user statistics covering the consumption of specific products and services rather than just total sales, salary surveys, opinion surveys, product price information and forecasts. In some cases, non-official sources simply repackage and comment on official data but these commentaries often provide a useful analysis of the major trends in official series. New markets, such as e-commerce and mobile technologies, are often covered in more detail by non-official sources. Many of the private sector companies now selling detailed time series from central government sources are also adding value to the data with commentaries, ratios, and further analysis based on the original figures.

Prices of non-official statistics can vary from a few pounds to thousands of pounds for detailed research, but a considerable proportion of the UK titles included here – almost a third – are available free of charge. More publishers are beginning to put some or all of their statistical output on their websites and offering the data as a freely accessible feature.

One disadvantage of non-official statistics is that, in some cases, the material is not available generally. Many trade associations and professional bodies, for example, only circulate material to members while other organisations limit access to clients, survey participants, or others specific groups. However, the percentage of the total non-official output restricted to only a limited group of users is relatively small and, even where detailed statistics are confidential, an executive summary or synopsis of data may be available generally. Another problem is that the reliability and accuracy of the data can vary considerably from one non-official source to the next. The amount of resources devoted to statistical activity, and the level of statistical expertise, can vary from one organisation to another and this is likely to have an effect on the statistics produced. Only a few sources give details on how the figures have been compiled and the specific methodologies used.

Most of the items included in the directory are clearly statistical publications but non-statistical sources, such as trade journals and yearbooks, are included if they contain a regular statistical series or feature. This edition of the directory also has a separate section in each entry for web-based sources of statistics where these are available.

SOURCES INCLUDED IN THE DIRECTORY

This edition contains information on 894 titles and services produced by over 440 organisations. The entries are based largely on information from the publishers obtained between October and December 2005, supported by desk research by IRN Research. The compilers would like to thank all those publishing organisations for responding to our request for information.

Statistics of interest to business and industry, and which are produced regularly, are included. For a source to be considered as regular, it must be produced at least once every six years. Most publications and services included are continuous or annual, twice-yearly, quarterly or monthly. One-off surveys or market reports do not qualify but market reports updated regularly are included.

Only sources issued in, and concerning, the United Kingdom or Great Britain are covered. Material with international coverage has been excluded unless it has a strong element of UK coverage. Some regional sources relating to Scotland, Wales, Northern Ireland and other regions have been included as well as material covering the capital city, London. Other local statistics on very specific local areas have been excluded.

Most sources included are available generally but there are some titles and services which have a restricted circulation. These have been included as summaries or older editions may be made available to others. In some cases, publishers have asked to be excluded from the directory and we have agreed to this request.

As well as standard time series statistics, forecasts, trend surveys and opinion surveys are also included but data dealing with only one corporate body, such as company annual reports, have generally been excluded.

Finally, the sources listed cover a range of delivery formats including the standard book form, those which are produced on one or two sheets of paper such as press releases and pamphlets, through to data available on the web, or via proprietary databases, CD-ROM, disc, or magnetic tape.

STRUCTURE OF THE DIRECTORY

The directory is divided into the three parts.

Part I: The statistical sources

The entries are arranged alphabetically by publishing organisation, and numbered consecutively. Usually, if an organisation publishes more than one title, each title has a separate entry. The exceptions are regular market research surveys produced by one publisher on various topics. As most of these latter surveys follow the same format, they are included in one general entry rather than listed separately.

All of the categories below may be included in an individual entry although some entries may have no information in certain categories if these are not relevant, or if the information is not available:

- **Name** of the publishing body.
- **Title** of source.
- **Coverage,** including details of any text/analysis supporting the data, and sources of statistics.
- **Frequency** of source.
- **Website,** with details of any data free on site, paid-for access to data, online ordering facilities or general details of sources.
- **Cost,** usually refers to cost per year unless otherwise stated.
- **Comments,** about the publication, including any restrictions on availability.
- **Address** of publisher.
- **Telephone and fax** numbers.
- **Website and e-mail** URL and address.

Part II: Title index

All the specific titles and services covered in the directory are listed alphabetically here. Titles beginning with numbers are listed at the beginning of the sequence. Annual reports are listed individually under 'Annual Reports' followed by the name of the organisation publishing a particular annual report. The numbers given for each title are entry numbers not page numbers.

Part III: Subject index

A detailed subject index containing references to the relevant entry number in Part 1.

The Sources

3I PLC

Title	**Enterprise Barometer**
Coverage	Based on an opinion survey of its companies, 3I produces a regular report on likely trends in turnover, profit, investment, employment etc. A commentary supports the statistics. Includes data on France, Italy, Germany, Spain and the Nordic region as well as UK.
Frequency	Regular.
Web facilities	A free PDF version of the survey available on site.
Cost	Free.
Comments	Previously a UK report was published separately but now part of European survey.
Address	47 Marylebone Road, London W1M 6LD
Tel./e-mail	0207 535 0200
Fax/Website	0207 535 0201 www.3i.com/publications/industry.html

A and B – ARTS AND BUSINESS WORKING TOGETHER

Title	**Private Investment Benchmarking Survey**
Coverage	An annual review of business sponsorship of the arts and cultural organisations based on responses from 2000 organisations. Broken down by type of sponsorship, type of art form and regions.
Frequency	Annual.
Web facilities	Summary data from previous surveys on the site.
Cost	£40; £20 for members.
Comments	
Address	Nutmeg House, 60 Gainsford Street, Butlers Wharf, London SE1 2NY
Tel./e-mail	0207 378 8143 head.office@AandB.org.uk
Fax/Website	0207 378 7527 www.AandB.org.uk

ABACUS DATA SERVICES (UK) LTD

Title	**UK Import and Export Statistics**
Coverage	Import and export data, from 1987 onwards, for any traded product with basic data available by value, volume, month or year to date, country of origin, country of destination, port of entry or departure, flag or carrier used. Abacus is an officially appointed agent of HM Customs and Excise.
Frequency	Monthly and annual.
Web facilities	General details of statistics and ordering facilities, on website.
Cost	Depends on information required.
Comments	Data available in various machine readable formats including CD-ROM and discette.
Address	Waterloo House, 59 New Street, Chelmsford CM1 1NE
Tel./e-mail	01245 252222 info@abacusuk.co.uk
Fax/Website	01245 252244 www.abacusuk.co.uk

AC NIELSEN MMS

Title	**Digest of UK Advertising Expenditure**
Coverage	Total advertising expenditure for brands spending over £75 000 per annum; includes 550 product groups. Data cover the latest quarter, a monthly breakdown within the quarter and a moving annual total. Based on a monitoring of advertising in the press, television, satellite TV, radio, outdoors and the cinema.
Frequency	Quarterly.
Web facilities	
Cost	On request.
Comments	
Address	Madison House, High Street, Sunninghill, Ascot SL5 9NP
Tel./e-mail	01344 627583 mms@mediamonitoring.co.uk
Fax/Website	01344 621037

ADMAP

Title	**Adstats**
Coverage	Statistics on various aspects of advertising and the media including total expenditure, expenditure by media expenditure in selected product categories. Most of the data are from Advertising Association surveys.
Frequency	Monthly in a monthly journal
Web facilities	General details of recent issues on site and subscription options.
Cost	£262.
Comments	
Address	Admap, Farm Road, Henley-on-Thames RG9 1EJ
Tel./e-mail	01491 411000 enquiries@warc.com
Fax/Website	01491 418600 www.admapmagazine.com

ADVERTISING ASSOCIATION

Title	**Advertising Forecast**
Coverage	Two-year forecasts for the main media categories – TV, radio, newspapers, colour supplements, magazines, classifieds, display advertising and posters. Also forecasts of expenditure in the main product sectors, e.g. retail, industrial, financial, government, services, durables and consumables. Historical data are also included.
Frequency	Quarterly
Web facilities	Some free statistics on the site.
Cost	£895; £575 for members
Address	WARC, Farm Road, Henley-on-Thames RG9 1EJ
Tel./e-mail	01491 411000 info@warc.com
Fax/Website	01491 418600 www.adassoc.org.uk

ADVERTISING ASSOCIATION

Title	**Advertising Statistics Yearbook**
Coverage	General trends in advertising and the annual Advertising Association survey. Statistics by type of advertising, e.g. cinema, direct mail, poster, newspapers, magazines, directories, radio, TV. Also statistics on prices, expenditure by product sector, top advertisers, agencies, complaints, attitudes and international trends. Data for earlier years and based on various sources.
Frequency	Annual.
Web facilities	Some free statistics available on the site.
Cost	£170.
Comments	
Address	WARC, Farm Road, Henley-on-Thames RG9 1EJ
Tel./e-mail	01491 411000 info@warc.com
Fax/Website	01491 418600 www.adassoc.org.uk

ADVERTISING ASSOCIATION

Title	**Quarterly Survey of Advertising Expenditure**
Coverage	Summary tables on advertising trends by main media followed by specific sections on the total press, national newspapers, regional newspapers, consumer magazines, business and professional magazines and all magazines. A final section looks at trends in specific industry sectors.
Frequency	Quarterly.
Web facilities	Some free statistics available on the site.
Cost	£695; £575 for members of the Advertising Association.
Comments	
Address	WARC, Farm Road, Henley-on-Thames RG9 1EJ
Tel./e-mail	01491 411000 info@warc.com
Fax/Website	01491 418600 www.adassoc.org.uk

ADVERTISING STANDARDS AUTHORITY

Title	**ASA Annual Report**
Coverage	Gives a summary of complaints received by media and by type. Based on complaints received by the ASA.
Frequency	Annual.
Web facilities	Full free access to all statistics on site (including historical data).
Cost	Free.
Comments	Also publishes summary monthly complaints figures.
Address	Mid City Place, 71 High Holborn, London WC1V 6QT
Tel./e-mail	0207 492 2222 enquiries@asa.org.uk
Fax/Website	0207 242 3696 www.asa.org.uk

AGRICULTURAL ENGINEERS' ASSOCIATION

Title	**Trade Statistics**
Coverage	Import and export data for agricultural products and machinery based on central government trade statistics.
Frequency	Quarterly.
Web facilities	Basic industry facts and figures on site.
Cost	On request.
Comments	Also produces price guides for agricultural products and machinery.
Address	Samuelson House, Orton Centre, Peterborough PE2 5LT
Tel./e-mail	01733 362925 dg@aea.uk.com
Fax/Website	01733 370664 www.aea.uk.com

AGRICULTURAL INDUSTRIES CONFEDERATION

Title	**British Survey of Fertiliser Practice**
Coverage	Covers area of crops, consumption of inorganic fertilisers, straight fertilisers and compound fertilisers; also concentration, application rates and usage of compound fertilisers. Based mainly on the association's own research with additional data from central government. Most of the review is made up of text.
Frequency	Annual.
Web facilities	Free summary information and tables on site.
Cost	£38.
Comments	Previously published by the Fertiliser Manufacturers Association but now merged with the confederation.
Address	Confederation House, East of England Showground, Peterborough PE2 6XE
Tel./e-mail	01733 385230 enquiries@agindustries.org.uk
Fax/Website	01733 385270 www.agindustries.org.uk

ALAN JONES & ASSOCIATES

Title	**Salary Surveys**
Coverage	The company publishes over 50 salary surveys including general, geographical, industry, job function and specialist surveys.
Frequency	Regular.
Web facilities	General details of all publications on site.
Cost	On request.
Comments	Also produces various industry specific and geographical surveys.
Address	Apex House, Wonastow Road, Monmouth NP25 5JB
Tel./e-mail	01600 716916 surveys@alan-jones.co.uk
Fax/Website	01600 715521 www.alan-jones.co.uk

ALLEGRA STRATEGIES

Title	**Project Café**
Coverage	A report on the coffee shop market and industry with data on market sizes and trends, segments, suppliers, forecasts and results of a detailed consumer survey undertaken in various cities regarding perceptions of coffee shops and brands.
Frequency	Annual.
Web facilities	General details and key findings from research free on site.
Cost	£3000 plus VAT (hard copy), £4500 plus VAT (PDF licence).
Comments	Various other one-off reports also published.
Address	1 Northumberland Terrace, Trafalgar Square, London WC2N 5BW
Tel./e-mail	0207 691 8800 info@allegra.co.uk
Fax/Website	0207 691 8810 www.allegra.co.uk

ALLEGRA STRATEGIES

Title	**Project Home**
Coverage	A report on the homewares and furniture market with data on market sizes and trends, segments, suppliers, forecasts and results from a survey of 5776 homeware shoppers.
Frequency	Annual.
Web facilities	General details and key findings from report free on site.
Cost	£3000 plus VAT (hard copy), £4500 plus VAT (PDF licence).
Comments	Various other one-off reports also published.
Address	1 Northumberland Terrace, Trafalgar Square, London WC2N 5BW
Tel./e-mail	0207 691 8800 info@allegra.co.uk
Fax/Website	0207 691 8810 www.allegra.co.uk

ALLIANCE AGAINST COUNTERFEITING AND PIRACY

Title	**Cost of Counterfeiting Survey**
Coverage	A group of industry bodies concerned about counterfeiting produce a compilation of statistics on the issue from various sources.
Frequency	Regular.
Web facilities	Key data on site plus link to full study.
Cost	Free.
Comments	
Address	167 Great Portland Street, London W1W 5PE
Tel./e-mail	0207 436 0041 lavinia@bva.org.uk
Fax/Website	0207 436 0043 www.aacp.org.uk

ALUMINIUM FEDERATION LTD

Title	**Aluminium Federation Annual Report**
Coverage	Contains some basic statistics covering production, overseas trade etc.
Frequency	Annual.
Web facilities	Ten-year production data and price data free on site.
Cost	On request.
Comments	More detailed statistics available to members.
Address	Broadway House, Calthorpe Road, Five Ways, Birmingham B15 1TN
Tel./e-mail	0121 456 1103 alfed@alfed.org.uk
Fax/Website	0121 456 2274 www.alfed.org.uk

ALUMINIUM STOCKHOLDERS ASSOCIATION

Title	**Data on Wrought and Cast Aluminium Products**
Coverage	12-year run of data on production, despatches, exports, imports.
Frequency	Annual.
Web facilities	Free access to data on site.
Cost	Free.
Comments	
Address	Broadway House, Calthorpe Road, Five Ways, Birmingham B15 1TN
Tel./e-mail	0121 456 1103 asa@alfed.org.uk
Fax/Website	0121 456 2274 www.asauk.co.uk

AMA RESEARCH

Title	**AMA Market Reports**
Coverage	A series of 100 regularly updated reports on building, construction and home improvements.
Frequency	Regular.
Web facilities	Details and press summaries of reports on site.
Cost	£595.
Comments	
Address	Montpellier House, Cheltenham GL50 1TX
Tel./e-mail	01242 235724 sales@amaresearch.co.uk
Fax/Website	01242 262948 www.amaresearch.co.uk

ARCHITECTS' JOURNAL

Title	**Workload Survey**
Coverage	Workload trends for the latest quarter compared to the previous quarter and the corresponding quarter in the previous year. Includes data on the value of new commissions, staffing levels and sector trends. Based on a survey by the journal.
Frequency	Quarterly in a weekly journal.
Web facilities	General details and full access to site with journal subscription.
Cost	£129.
Comments	
Address	EMAP Construct, 151 Rosebery Avenue, London EC1R 4QX
Tel./e-mail	0207 505 6700 isabel.allen@construct.emap.com
Fax/Website	0207 505 6701 www.agplus.co.uk

ARCHITECTS' JOURNAL

Title	**Industry Forecast**
Coverage	Commentary and statistics on likely trends in the architecture sector in the coming 12 months.
Frequency	Annual.
Web facilities	General details and full access to site with journal subscription.
Cost	£129.
Comments	
Address	EMAP Construct, 151 Rosebery Avenue, London EC1R 4QX
Tel./e-mail	0207 505 6700 isabel.allen@construct.emap.com
Fax/Website	0207 505 6701 www.agplus.co.uk

ASPHALT INDUSTRY ALLIANCE

Title	**Annual Local Authority Road Maintenance Survey (ALARM)**
Coverage	Based on data collected from local authorities, the survey covers frequency and standards of maintenance, funding and other related issues.
Frequency	Annual.
Web facilities	Free access to full survey on site.
Cost	Free.
Comments	
Address	14a Eccleston Street, London SW1W 9LT
Tel./e-mail	0207 730 1100 asphalt@hmpr.co.uk
Fax/Website	0207 730 2213 www.asphaltindustryalliance.com

ASSOCIATION FOR PAYMENT CLEARING SERVICES

Title	**ATM Survey**
Coverage	A survey of ATM locations, transactions volumes and values.
Frequency	Annual.
Web facilities	Free facts and figures for last ten years on site plus free downloads.
Cost	£50.
Comments	
Address	Mercury House, Triton Court, 14 Finsbury Square, London EC2A 1LQ
Tel./e-mail	0207 711 6200 stats@apacs.org.uk
Fax/Website	0207 256 5527 www.apacs.org.uk

ASSOCIATION FOR PAYMENT CLEARING SERVICES

Title	**Plastic Card Review**
Coverage	A review of trends in the credit card market.
Frequency	Annual.
Web facilities	Free facts and figures for last ten years on the site plus downloads.
Cost	£150.
Comments	
Address	Mercury House, Triton Court, 14 Finsbury Square, London EC2A 1LQ
Tel./e-mail	0207 711 6200 stats@apacs.org.uk
Fax/Website	0207 256 5527 www.apacs.org.uk

ASSOCIATION FOR PAYMENT CLEARING SERVICES

Title	**Annual Review**
Coverage	A review of bank clearings and payment trends based mainly on data from members.
Frequency	Annual.
Web facilities	Free facts and figures for last 10 years on site plus free downloads.
Cost	Free.
Comments	
Address	Mercury House, Triton Court, 14 Finsbury Square, London EC2A 1LQ
Tel./e-mail	0207 711 6200 stats@apacs.org.uk
Fax/Website	0207 256 5527 www.apacs.org.uk

ASSOCIATION FOR PAYMENT CLEARING SERVICES

Title	**Yearbook of Payment Statistics**
Coverage	Statistics on the turnover of inter-bank clearings, automated clearings, inter-branch clearings, Scottish clearings and London currency dealings. Based on figures collected by APACS from its members.
Frequency	Annual.
Web facilities	Free facts and figures for last ten years on site plus free downloads.
Cost	£130.
Comments	
Address	Mercury House, Triton Court, 14 Finsbury Square, London EC2A 1LQ
Tel./e-mail	0207 711 6200 stats@apacs.org.uk
Fax/Website	0207 256 5527 www.apacs.org.uk

ASSOCIATION FOR PAYMENT CLEARING SERVICES

Title	**Clearing Statistics**
Coverage	Statistics on the turnover of inter-bank clearings through the clearing house and automated clearings. Based on figures collected by APACS from its members.
Frequency	Monthly and annual.
Web facilities	Free facts and figures for last 10 years on site plus free downloads.
Cost	Free.
Comments	
Address	Mercury House, Triton Court, 14 Finsbury Square, London EC2A 1LQ
Tel./e-mail	0207 711 6200 stats@apacs.org.uk
Fax/Website	0207 256 5527 www.apacs.org.uk

ASSOCIATION FOR PAYMENT CLEARING SERVICES

Title	**UK Payment Markets – Trends and Forecasts**
Coverage	A general review of trends in the payments market based mainly on data from members. Included are forecasts up to ten years ahead.
Frequency	Annual.
Web facilities	Free facts and figures on site plus free downloads.
Cost	Free.
Comments	
Address	Mercury House, Triton Court, 14 Finsbury Square, London EC2A 1LQ
Tel./e-mail	0207 711 6200 stats@apacs.org.uk
Fax/Website	0207 256 5527 www.apacs.org.uk

ASSOCIATION FOR THE STUDY OF OBESITY

Title	**Prevalence of Obesity in the UK**
Coverage	Data on levels and extent of obesity plus various links to related surveys and other data.
Frequency	Regular.
Web facilities	Free access to a range of data on site.
Cost	Free.
Comments	
Address	20 Brook Meadow Close, Woodford Green IG8 9NR
Tel./e-mail	0208 503 2042 chris@aso.ndo.co.uk
Fax/Website	0208 503 2042 www.aso.org.uk

ASSOCIATION OF BRITISH INDEPENDENT OIL EXPLORATION COMPANIES (BRINDEX)

Title	**Key Facts**
Coverage	Basic data on exploration and appraisal wells drilled plus investment trends.
Frequency	Regular.
Web facilities	Free access to data on site.
Cost	Free.
Comments	
Address	c/o Ray Franklin, Paladin Resources PLC, 1 Pall Mall East, London SW1Y 5PR
Tel./e-mail	0207 024 4500 jackie@brindex.co.uk
Fax/Website	www.brindex.co.uk

ASSOCIATION OF BRITISH INSURERS

Title	**Insurance Statistical Subscription Service**
Coverage	Full access to all ABI statistics on all classes of insurance and historical data. Data mainly based on the association's own surveys.
Frequency	Annual.
Web facilities	Free key facts on site plus PDF files of basic data in key areas, e.g. life insurance, general insurance etc.
Cost	£2000.
Comments	
Address	51 Gresham Street, London EC2V 7HQ
Tel./e-mail	0207 216 7390 research@abi.org.uk
Fax/Website	0207 216 7449 www.abi.org.uk

ASSOCIATION OF BRITISH INSURERS

Title	**Insurance Data Subscription Services**
Coverage	Individual subscription services giving access to data on key topics, e.g. motor insurance, general insurance, property insurance, life insurance, long-term business etc. Data mainly based on association's surveys.
Frequency	Annual.
Web facilities	Free key facts on site plus PDFs of basic data in key areas such as life insurance, general insurance.
Cost	Various prices for each data subscription.
Comments	
Address	51 Gresham Street, London EC2V 7HQ
Tel./e-mail	0207 216 7390 research@abi.org.uk
Fax/Website	0207 216 7449 www.abi.org.uk

ASSOCIATION OF BRITISH TRAVEL AGENTS LTD (ABTA)

Title	**ABTA Travel Statistics and Trends**
Coverage	A compilation of data from ABTA's own surveys and other sources on travel and tourism.
Frequency	Annual.
Web facilities	Free access to PDF on site.
Cost	Free.
Comments	
Address	68–71 Newman Street, London W1T 3AH
Tel./e-mail	0207 637 2444 information@abta.co.uk
Fax/Website	0207 637 0713 www.abta.com

ASSOCIATION OF BRITISH TRAVEL AGENTS LTD (ABTA)

Title	**ABTA/PwC Tour Operators Benchmarking Survey**
Coverage	An analysis of the financial and operating performance of tour operators.
Frequency	Every two years.
Web facilities	Access to summary data and contents on site. Also online ordering on site.
Cost	£179; £79 for members.
Comments	Next edition in 2006.
Address	68–71 Newman Street, London W1T 3AH
Tel./e-mail	0207 637 2444 information@abta.co.uk
Fax/Website	0207 637 0713 www.abta.com

ASSOCIATION OF BUSINESS RECOVERY PROFESSIONALS (R3)

Title	**Corporate Insolvency Survey**
Coverage	Based on returns from members, this report shows the trends in company insolvencies over the last 12 months. The report analyses the reasons for failure and the characteristics of failed companies. Based on almost 3000 individual cases.
Frequency	Annual.
Web facilities	Free access to report on site.
Cost	Free.
Comments	Previously known as the Society of Practitioners in Insolvency.
Address	8th Floor, 120 Aldersgate Street, London EC1A 4JP
Tel./e-mail	0207 566 4200 association@r3.org.uk
Fax/Website	0207 566 4224 www.r3.org.uk

ASSOCIATION OF BUSINESS RECOVERY PROFESSIONALS (R3)

Title	**Personal Insolvency Survey**
Coverage	An analysis of personal insolvency trends over the last year based on returns from members. The latest issue is based on over 1200 individual cases.
Frequency	Annual.
Web facilities	Free access to report on the site.
Cost	Free.
Comments	Previously known as the Society of Practitioners in Insolvency.
Address	8th Floor, 120 Aldersgate, London EC1A 4JP
Tel./e-mail	0207 566 4200 association@r3.org.uk
Fax/Website	0207 566 4224 www.r3.org.uk

ASSOCIATION OF CATERING EQUIPMENT MANUFACTURERS AND IMPORTERS (CESA)

Title	**CESA Industry Research**
Coverage	Based on returns from member companies and estimates of sales by non-members, the association produces statistics for sales, imports and exports broken down by type of catering equipment.
Frequency	Annual.
Web facilities	
Cost	Free.
Comments	Usually only available to members but requests considered.
Address	Carlyle House, 235 Vauxhall Bridge Road, London SW1V 1EJ
Tel./e-mail	0207 233 7724 enquiries@cesa.org.uk
Fax/Website	0207 828 0667 www.cesa.org.uk

ASSOCIATION OF CONTACT LENS MANUFACTURERS

Title	**Annual Statistics**
Coverage	Annual statistics relating to the sales of contact lenses and contact lens solutions. Based on a survey of members' sales by the association.
Frequency	Annual.
Web facilities	Website is currently being redeveloped.
Cost	
Comments	Published in the association's journal.
Address	PO Box 735, Devises SN10 3TQ
Tel./e-mail	01380 860418 secgen@aclm.org.uk
Fax/Website	01380 860863 www.aclm.org.uk

ASSOCIATION OF CONVENIENCE STORES

Title	**Quarterly Crime Statistics**
Coverage	Statistics on burglaries, robberies, customer thefts and till snatches with volume and value figures. Based on data supplied by members.
Frequency	Quarterly.
Web facilities	Free access to summary data on site, plus various statistics from other sources.
Cost	Free.
Comments	
Address	Federation House, 17 Farnborough Street, Farnborough GU14 8AG
Tel./e-mail	01252 515001 acs@acs.org.uk
Fax/Website	01252 515002 www.thelocalshop.com

ASSOCIATION OF FRANCHISED DISTRIBUTORS OF ELECTRONIC COMPONENTS

Title	**AFDEC Statistical Forecasts**
Coverage	Forecasts of market trends for electronic components based on research by the association.
Frequency	Monthly and quarterly.
Web facilities	
Cost	On request.
Comments	Sold to non-members as well as available to members.
Address	The Manor House, High Street, Buntingford SG9 9AB
Tel./e-mail	01763 274748 enquiries@afdec.org.uk
Fax/Website	01763 273255 www.afdec.org.uk

ASSOCIATION OF INVESTMENT TRUST COMPANIES

Title	**AITC Monthly Information Service**
Coverage	Monthly performance data on investment trusts and companies. Based on data collected by the association.
Frequency	Monthly.
Web facilities	Free access to monthly reports on site.
Cost	Free.
Comments	Other detailed statistics free on site.
Address	9th Floor, 24 Chiswell Street, London EC1Y 4YY
Tel./e-mail	0207 282 5555 enquiries@aitc.co.uk
Fax/Website	0207 282 5556 www.aitc.co.uk

ASSOCIATION OF INVESTMENT TRUST COMPANIES

Title	**AITC Monthly Information Release**
Coverage	Monthly data on assets, portfolio spread, charges etc. based on data collected by the association.
Frequency	Monthly.
Web facilities	Free access to data on site.
Cost	Free.
Comments	Other detailed statistics free on site.
Address	9th Floor, 24 Chiswell Street, London EC1Y 4YY
Tel./e-mail	0207 282 5555 enquiries@aitc.co.uk
Fax/Website	0207 282 5556 www.aitc.co.uk

ASSOCIATION OF INVESTMENT TRUST COMPANIES

Title	**Key Facts and Activity of the Investment Trust Industry**
Coverage	General statistics on the investment trust industry updated every month and mainly based on association data.
Frequency	Monthly.
Web facilities	Free access to data on site.
Cost	Free.
Comments	Other detailed statistics free on site.
Address	9th Floor, 24 Chiswell Street, London EC1Y 4YY
Tel./e-mail	0207 282 5555 enquiries@aitc.co.uk
Fax/Website	0207 282 5556 www.aitc.co.uk

ASSOCIATION OF MANUFACTURERS OF DOMESTIC ELECTRICAL APPLIANCES (AMDEA)

Title	**AMDEA Survey Yearbook**
Coverage	Deliveries by UK manufacturers and imports by country of origin for various appliances including fridges, freezers, dryers, washing machines, cookers, vacuum cleaners, heaters, electric blankets etc. Additional data on prices and employment plus reports on market trends, manufacturing news and retail developments. Based primarily on AMDEA data supported by some official statistics.
Frequency	Annual.
Web facilities	
Cost	£600, or £750 with combined subscription to *AMDEA Quarterbook* (see next entry).
Comments	Extracts from the yearbook for specific product sectors are also available with trends for the last ten years.
Address	Rapier House, 40–46 Lambs Conduit Street, London WC1N 3NW
Tel./e-mail	0207 405 0666 info@amdea.org.uk
Fax/Website	0207 405 6609 www.amdea.org.uk

ASSOCIATION OF MANUFACTURERS OF DOMESTIC ELECTRICAL APPLIANCES (AMDEA)

Title	**AMDEA Quarterbook**
Coverage	Deliveries and imports of various electrical appliances covering over 25 product headings. Similar data to that contained in the *AMDEA Survey Yearbook* (see entry above) with statistics for the latest quarter and summary data for the earlier quarter. Based primarily on AMDEA data supported by some official statistics.
Frequency	Quarterly.
Web facilities	
Cost	£750 with combined subscription to *AMDEA Survey Yearbook*, or £150 per issue.
Comments	
Address	Rapier House, 40–46 Lambs Conduit Street, London WC1N 3NW
Tel./e-mail	0207 405 0666 info@amdea.org.uk
Fax/Website	0207 405 6609 www.amdea.org.uk

ASSOCIATION OF MANUFACTURERS OF DOMESTIC ELECTRICAL APPLIANCES (AMDEA)

Title	**AMDEA Monthly Statistics**
Coverage	Monthly data in 16 separate reports each covering a specific product sector. There is also a summary volume. Based on data collected by the association.
Frequency	Monthly.
Web facilities	
Cost	Prices range from £250 to £1000 per report.
Comments	
Address	Rapier House, 40–46 Lambs Conduit Street, London WC1N 3NW
Tel./e-mail	0207 405 0666 info@amdea.org.uk
Fax/Website	0207 405 6609 www.amdea.org

ASSOCIATION OF NEWSPAPER AND MAGAZINE WHOLESALERS

Title	**Industry Data**
Coverage	Regular statistics on the performance of the industry (e.g. delivery times/speeds etc.) based on data collected by the association.
Frequency	Regular.
Web facilities	Free access to data on site.
Cost	Free.
Comments	
Address	8–14 Vine Street, London EC1R 5DX
Tel./e-mail	0207 520 0480 enquiries@anmw.co.uk
Fax/Website	0207 278 6853 www.anmw.co.uk

ASSOCIATION OF PRIVATE CLIENT INVESTMENT MANAGERS AND STOCKBROKERS

Title	**Private Client Investment in the UK**
Coverage	Statistics on the value of investments, company trends etc. based on original surveys.
Frequency	Quarterly and annual.
Web facilities	Free access to quarterly press releases with summary data on site.
Cost	On request.
Comments	Annual surveys compiled by research company ComPeer.
Address	114 Middlesex Street, London E1 7JH
Tel./e-mail	0207 247 7080 info@apcims.co.uk
Fax/Website	0207 377 0939 www.apcims.co.uk

ASSOCIATION OF PUBLISHING AGENTS (APA)

Title	**The Advantage Study**
Coverage	A regular survey of the performance of customer magazines and benchmarking across the industry and against other media.
Frequency	Twice yearly.
Web facilities	Free access to executive summaries on site.
Cost	On request.
Comments	Produced in association with Millward Brown; first survey in March 2005.
Address	Queens House, 28 Kingsway, London WC2B 6JR
Tel./e-mail	0207 404 4166 kelly.goddard@apa.co.uk
Fax/Website	0207 404 4167 www.apa.co.uk

ASSOCIATION OF THE BRITISH PHARMACEUTICAL INDUSTRY

Title	**ABPI Health Care Handbook**
Coverage	Yearbook containing information and data on the NHS and relevant health issues.
Frequency	Annual.
Web facilities	PDF version on site.
Cost	£10.
Comments	
Address	12 Whitehall, London SW1A 2DY
Tel./e-mail	0207 930 3477 info@abpi.org.uk
Fax/Website	0207 747 1414 www.abpi.org.uk

ASSOCIATION OF THE BRITISH PHARMACEUTICAL INDUSTRY

Title	**ABPI Facts and Statistics**
Coverage	Data on healthcare and drugs including NHS, medicines, R&D spending, pharmaceutical industry etc.
Frequency	Annual.
Web facilities	Free access to data on site.
Cost	Free.
Comments	
Address	12 Whitehall, London SW1A 2DY
Tel./e-mail	0207 930 3477 info@abpi.org.uk
Fax/Website	0207 747 1414 www.abpi.org.uk

AUDIT BUREAU OF CIRCULATIONS LTD (ABC)

Title	**ABC Review**
Coverage	A well-established report on audited certified net sales, circulation and distribution data for over 2000 publications. Covers journals, magazines and newspapers. Based on a survey by the company.
Frequency	Twice yearly.
Web facilities	Free access to circulation data for 3500 magazines, newspapers, directories, exhibitions on site. Also link to ABC Electronic offering data on electronic media.
Cost	£150; £15 for members.
Comments	The data are held on a computerised database and various packages and searches are available. Also publishes monthly *National Newspaper Figures* (annual subscription – £495).
Address	Black Prince Yard, 207–209 High Street, Berkhamstead HP4 1AD
Tel./e-mail	01442 870800 rayh@abc.org.uk
Fax/Website	01422 877407 www.abc.org.uk

AUTOMATIC VENDING ASSOCIATION

Title	**AVAB Census**
Coverage	In 1994, the association carried out its first detailed census of the beverage and snack foods vending sector. The survey, now produced annually, has details of machines in use, types of machines and products vended.
Frequency	Annual.
Web facilities	Some free summary data on the site.
Cost	£175.
Comments	Now AVA but previously AVAB – the Automatic Vending Association of Great Britain.
Address	1 Villiers Court, Upper Mulgrave Road, Cheam SM2 7AJ
Tel./e-mail	0208 661 1112 info@ava-vending.org
Fax/Website	0208 661 2224 www.ava-vending.org

BAA PLC

Title	**BAA Monthly Traffic Summary**
Coverage	Based on traffic counts of freight, passengers and aircraft at BAA airports, this monthly report is a traffic summary for the UK.
Frequency	Monthly.
Web facilities	Free press release with summary data on site.
Cost	Free.
Comments	
Address	Jubilee House, Furlong Way, North Terminal, Gatwick Airport RH6 0JN
Tel./e-mail	0870 000 2468 baamediacentre@baa.com
Fax/Website	www.baa.co.uk

BANK OF ENGLAND

Title	**Bank of England Monetary & Financial Statistics**
Coverage	Statistical data covering UK and international banking, money stock, official market operations, government finance, reserves and official borrowing, exchange rates, interest rates and national financial accounts. Mainly the bank's own figures.
Frequency	Monthly and quarterly.
Web facilities	The whole publication is available free on the website. Monthly data on the website and quarterly in hard copy.
Cost	£60 subscription for hard copy.
Comments	
Address	Monetary and Financial Statistics Division, Threadneedle Street, London EC2R 8AH
Tel./e-mail	0207 601 5353 webmaster@bankofengland.co.uk
Fax/Website	0207 601 3208 www.bankofengland.co.uk

BANK OF ENGLAND

Title	**Inflation Report**
Coverage	A review of current price trends in the economy and the outlook for prices in the short term.
Frequency	Monthly.
Web facilities	The whole publication is available free on the website.
Cost	£12, or £40 with a combined subscription to *Bank of England Quarterly Bulletin*.
Comments	
Address	Monetary and Financial Statistics Division, Threadneedle Street, London EC2R 8AH
Tel./e-mail	0207 601 4353 webmaster@bankofengland.co.uk
Fax/Website	0207 601 3208 www.bankofengland.co.uk

BANK OF ENGLAND

Title	**Quarterly Survey of Inflation Attitudes**
Coverage	Regular survey to ascertain perceptions of link between interest rates and inflation and awareness of who sets interest rates.
Frequency	Quarterly.
Web facilities	Reported in the Bank's quarterly bulletin and free access to articles on site.
Cost	Free.
Comments	
Address	Monetary and Financial Statistics Division, Threadneedle Street, London EC2R 8AH
Tel./e-mail	0207 601 5353 webmaster@bankofengland.co.uk
Fax/Website	0207 601 3208 www.bankofengland.co.uk

BANK OF ENGLAND

Title	**Statistical Releases**
Coverage	Regular releases covering economic, financial and monetary topics.
Frequency	Regular.
Web facilities	Free access to releases on site.
Cost	Free.
Comments	
Address	Monetary and Financial Statistics Division, Threadneedle Street, London EC2R 8AH
Tel./e-mail	0207 601 5353 webmaster@bankofengland.co.uk
Fax/Website	0207 601 3208 www.bankofengland.co.uk

BARCLAYS BANK

Title	**UK Business Customer Economic Focus**
Coverage	A general commentary on the UK and international economy and a statistical appendix with data on exchange rates, interest rates and the money market.
Frequency	Three times a year.
Web facilities	Free access to reports on site.
Cost	Free.
Comments	Also publishes various reports free on site on specific UK markets and sectors.
Address	1 Wimborne Road, Poole BH15 2BB
Tel./e-mail	0845 605 2345
Fax/Website	www.barclays.co.uk/business/

BARCLAYS BANK

Title	**Interest and Exchange Rate Monitor**
Coverage	Commentary, graphs and statistical tables covering trends in interest rates and exchange rates. Based on various official and non-official sources.
Frequency	Monthly.
Web facilities	Free access to reports on site.
Cost	Free.
Comments	Also publishes various reports free on site on specific UK markets and sectors.
Address	1 Wimborne Road, Poole BH15 2BB
Tel./e-mail	0845 605 2345
Fax/Website	www.barclays.co.uk/business/

BARCLAYS BANK

Title	**Small Business Survey**
Coverage	Analysis and data on forthcoming trends in the small business sector and developments over the previous few months.
Frequency	Twice yearly.
Web facilities	Free access to reports on site.
Cost	Free.
Comments	Also publishes various reports free on site on specific UK markets and sectors.
Address	1 Wimborne Road, Poole BH15 2BB
Tel./e-mail	0845 605 2345
Fax/Website	www.barclays.co.uk/business/

BARCLAYS BANK

Title	**Quarterly Start-Up Figures**
Coverage	A survey of new business startups in the UK by sector.
Frequency	Regular.
Web facilities	Free access to reports on site.
Cost	Free.
Comments	Also publishes various reports free on site on specific UK markets and sectors.
Address	1 Wimborne Road, Poole BH15 2BB
Tel./e-mail	0845 605 2345
Fax/Website	www.barclays.co.uk/business/

BCR PUBLISHING

Title	**Factoring in the UK**
Coverage	The annual report includes an industry analysis sector which has growth statistics and future trends, plus details of client industries, factoring environment and associations.
Frequency	Annual.
Web facilities	General details of publication on site.
Cost	£395.
Comments	
Address	3 Cobden Court, Wimpole Close, Bromley BR2 9OF
Tel./e-mail	0208 466 6987 info@bcrpub.co.uk
Fax/Website	0208 466 6654 www.bcrpub.co.uk

BEAUFORT RESEARCH LTD

Title	**Welsh Omnibus Surveys**
Coverage	Quarterly surveys of a sample of 1000 adults resident in Wales. Data on opinions, attitudes, advertising and product recall and awareness, purchase and usage, image and perception. Analysis available by sex, age, gender, social class, region, Welsh speaking.
Frequency	Quarterly.
Web facilities	
Cost	On request.
Comments	Also carries out a regular omnibus survey of Welsh speakers.
Address	2 Museum Place, Cardiff CF1 3BG
Tel./e-mail	01222 378565 enquiries@beaufortresearch.co.uk
Fax/Website	01222 382872 www.beaufortresearch.co.uk

BEECHWOOD HOUSE PUBLISHIING LTD

Title	**Binley's NHS Guide**
Coverage	Detailed data and commentary on funding, employment and trends by type of care, region, county etc.
Frequency	Annual.
Web facilities	
Cost	£18.45; or £11.45 to the NHS.
Comments	
Address	Beechwood House, 2–3 Commercial Way, Southfields, Basildon SS16 6EF
Tel./e-mail	01268 495600
Fax/Website	01268 495601 www.binleys.com

BISCUIT, CAKE, CHOCOLATE & CONFECTIONERY ALLIANCE (BCCCA)

Title	**Four-Weekly Summaries Services**
Coverage	Monthly data on the deliveries of products with individual reports on biscuits, chocolate confectionery and sugar confectionery. Detailed breakdowns in each report by type of product. Based on returns from members.
Frequency	Monthly.
Web facilities	
Cost	On request.
Comments	The BCCA no longer publishes a Statistical Yearbook following the closure of the statistics unit. The four-weekly summary is prepared by Manx Associates and details of costs are available from the company: telephone – 01494 524409; e-mail – mike.w@man-is.co.uk.
Address	37–41 Bedford Row, London WC1R 4JH
Tel./e-mail	0207 420 7200 office@bccca.org.uk
Fax/Website	www.bccca.org.uk

BOOK MARKETING LTD

Title	**Books and the Consumer**
Coverage	Based on research using a panel of 7000 households. Reports on the book market covering buying, book types purchased, reading habits, prices, retailing of books, postal buying of books, library usage. Specific reports for children's and adult's books.
Frequency	Annual.
Web facilities	A summary report from the research is available to anyone. Full survey results and tabulations are only available to survey subscribers.
Cost	On request.
Comments	
Address	7a Bedford Square, London WC1B 3RA
Tel./e-mail	0207 580 7282 bml@bookmarketing.co.uk
Fax/Website	0207 580 7236 www.bookmarketing.co.uk

BOOKSELLER

Title	**Book Prices/Publishers' Output/Libraries**
Coverage	Various surveys appear throughout the year including surveys of book prices, number of titles published, public and academic library expenditure, salary surveys.
Frequency	Regular in a weekly journal.
Web facilities	News and some data on site.
Cost	£175.
Comments	
Address	5th Floor, Endeavour House, 189 Shaftesbury Avenue, London WC2H 1TJ
Tel./e-mail	0207 420 6006
Fax/Website	0207 420 6103 www.thebookseller.com

BOOKSELLERS ASSOCIATION OF GREAT BRITAIN AND IRELAND

Title	**Book Industry Statistics**
Coverage	A total of 17 files on the website covering various aspects of the book trade; for example, books published, prices, library loans, retail prices, bookstores, sources of purchase, and top websites for sales and the book publishing industry.
Frequency	Regular.
Web facilities	Free access to data on site.
Cost	Free.
Comments	
Address	Minster House, 272 Vauxhall Bridge Road, London SW1V 1BA
Tel./e-mail	0207 802 0802 mail@booksellers.org.uk
Fax/Website	0207 802 0803 www.booksellers.org.uk

BOTTLED WATER COOLER ASSOCIATION

Title	**Industry Data**
Coverage	Data on sales of bottled water and market trends from market research sources.
Frequency	Regular.
Web facilities	Free access to summary data on site.
Cost	Free.
Comments	
Address	Hartfield House, 40–44 High Street, Northwood HA6 1UJ
Tel./e-mail	01923 825355 bwca@dial.pipex.com
Fax/Website	01923 848391 www.bwca.org.uk

BRAKE!

Title	**Brake Statistics**
Coverage	Statistics from a road safety organisation on accidents, road deaths, drinking and driving etc. Based on various sources.
Frequency	Regular.
Web facilities	Free access to data and links to other data on site.
Cost	Free.
Comments	
Address	PO Box 548, Huddersfield HD1 2XZ
Tel./e-mail	01484 559909 brake@brake.org.uk
Fax/Website	01484 559983 www.brake.org.uk

BREWING AND DISTILLING INTERNATIONAL

Title	**Crop Commentary**
Coverage	Details of the UK barley crop and hop output based on BDI's European Malting Barley Survey.
Frequency	Regular in a weekly journal.
Web facilities	General details and news on site.
Cost	On request.
Comments	UK beer production figures and surveys of specific areas of the brewing trade are also included in the journal at regular intervals.
Address	52 Glenhouse Road, Eltham, London SE9 1JQ
Tel./e-mail	0208 859 4300 editor@bdinews.com
Fax/Website	0208 859 5813 www.bdinews.com

BRITISH ADHESIVES AND SEALANTS ASSOCIATION

Title	**UK Adhesives Market/UK Sealants Market**
Coverage	Sales in value terms of various types of sealant plus value and volume sales split by chemical type. Based on a survey of members.
Frequency	Twice yearly.
Web facilities	
Cost	Free.
Comments	Available to participating members only.
Address	Alderson Road, Worksop S80 1UZ
Tel./e-mail	01909 480888 secretary@basa.online.org
Fax/Website	01909 473834 www.basa.uk.com

BRITISH AEROSOL MANUFACTURERS' ASSOCIATION

Title	**BAMA Annual Report – UK Aerosol Production**
Coverage	Gives details of aerosol filling statistics by various product categories. Based on a survey of members.
Frequency	Annual.
Web facilities	General details and free access to all statistics in PDF.
Cost	Free.
Comments	
Address	King's Building, Smith Square, London SW1P 3JJ
Tel./e-mail	0207 828 5111 enquiries@bama.co.uk
Fax/Website	0207 834 8436 www.bama.co.uk

BRITISH AGRICULTURAL AND GARDEN MACHINERY ASSOCIATION

Title	**Garden Machinery Price Guide**
Coverage	A guide to prices of various types of garden machinery based on a survey by the association.
Frequency	11 issues a year.
Web facilities	
Cost	On request.
Comments	The guide is published by Indices Publications Ltd (see their entry, page 175) and price details/subscriptions available from them at 0870 205 2934; URL www.indices.co.uk.
Address	Salamander Quay West, Park Lane, Harefield UB9 6NZ
Tel./e-mail	0870 205 2834 info@bagma.com
Fax/Website	0870 205 2835 www.bagma.com

BRITISH AGRICULTURAL AND GARDEN MACHINERY ASSOCIATION

Title	**Market Guide to Used Tractors**
Coverage	A guide to the used tractors and farm machinery market based on a survey by the association.
Frequency	11 issues a year.
Web facilities	
Cost	On request.
Comments	The guide is published by Indices Publications Ltd (see their entry, page 175) and price details/subscriptions available from them at 0870 205 2934; URL www.indices.co.uk.
Address	Salamander Quay West, Park Lane, Harefield UB9 6NZ
Tel./e-mail	0870 205 2834 info@bagma.com
Fax/Website	0870 205 2835 www.bagma.com

BRITISH APPAREL AND TEXTILE CONFEDERATION

Title	**Trendata**
Coverage	Statistics covering production, exports, imports, balance of trade, consumer expenditure, employment for the UK apparel and textile industry. Based on both official and non-official sources.
Frequency	Quarterly.
Web facilities	Website under re-development at time of compilation.
Cost	£195; £95 for members.
Comments	Available in loose-leaf format.
Address	5 Portland Place, London W1N 3AA
Tel./e-mail	0207 636 7788 batc@dial.pipex.com
Fax/Website	0207 636 7515 www.batc.co.uk

BRITISH APPAREL AND TEXTILE CONFEDERATION

Title	**Quarterly Statistical Review – Cotton & Allied Textiles**
Coverage	Statistics on production, imports, exports and apparent consumption particularly for cotton and allied fibres. Based on a mixture of official and non-official sources.
Frequency	Quarterly.
Web facilities	Website under re-development at time of compilation.
Cost	£135.
Comments	
Address	5 Portland Place, London W1N 3AA
Tel./e-mail	0207 636 7788 batc@dial.pipex.com
Fax/Website	0207 636 7515 www.batc.co.uk

BRITISH APPAREL AND TEXTILE CONFEDERATION

Title	**Industry Statistical Overview**
Coverage	Statistics covering production, consumption, overseas trade, employment etc.
Frequency	Annual.
Web facilities	Website under redevelopment at time of compilation.
Cost	£35.
Comments	
Address	5 Portland Place, London W1N 3AA
Tel./e-mail	0207 636 7788 batc@dial.pipex.com
Fax/Website	0207 636 7515 www.batc.co.uk

BRITISH APPAREL AND TEXTILE CONFEDERATION

Title	**Quarterly Production Data – Cotton and Allied Textiles**
Coverage	Production trends for cotton and textiles.
Frequency	Quarterly.
Web facilities	Website under redevelopment at time of compilation.
Cost	£70.
Comments	
Address	5 Portland Place, London W1N 3AA
Tel./e-mail	0207 636 7788 batc@dial.pipex.com
Fax/Website	0207 636 7515 www.batc.co.uk

BRITISH APPAREL AND TEXTILE CONFEDERATION

Title	**Quarterly Import Data - All Textiles and Made-up Items**
Coverage	Import statistics by product category.
Frequency	Quarterly.
Web facilities	Website under redevelopment at time of compilation.
Cost	£70.
Comments	
Address	5 Portland Place, London W1N 3AA
Tel./e-mail	0207 636 7788 batc@dial.pipex.com
Fax/Website	0207 636 7515 www.batc.co.uk

BRITISH APPAREL AND TEXTILE CONFEDERATION

Title	**Quarterly Export Data – All Textiles and Made-up Items**
Coverage	Export statistics by product category.
Frequency	Quarterly.
Web facilities	Website under redevelopment at time of compilation.
Cost	£50.
Comments	
Address	5 Portland Place, London W1N 3AA
Tel./e-mail	0207 636 7788 batc@dial.pipex.com
Fax/Website	0207 636 7515 www.batc.co.uk

BRITISH ASSOCIATION FOR ADOPTION AND FOSTERING

Title	**All UK Summary Statistics**
Coverage	Detailed statistics on placements, children in care, time from care to adoption, foster care numbers, etc.
Frequency	Annual.
Web facilities	Free access to PDFs on site.
Cost	Free.
Comments	
Address	Skyline House, 200 Union Street, London SE1 0LX
Tel./e-mail	0207 593 2000 mail@baaf.org.uk
Fax/Website	0207 593 2001 www.baaf.org.uk

BRITISH ASSOCIATION OF CONFERENCE DESTINATION VENUES

Title	**British Conference Venues Survey**
Coverage	An annual survey of venue operators offering data on types of events and venues used, income, budgets, length of events, delegate rates, etc.
Frequency	Annual.
Web facilities	General details and free summary information on site.
Cost	£125.
Comments	
Address	6th Floor, Charles House, 148/149 Great Charles Street, Birmingham BB3 3HT
Tel./e-mail	0121 212 1400 info@bacd.org.uk
Fax/Website	0121 212 3131 www.bacd.org.uk

BRITISH ASSOCIATION OF RECORD DEALERS

Title	**BARD Statistics**
Coverage	Data for music recordings retailing including consumer spending, video/CD/DVD sales, hardware sales and market shares.
Frequency	Regular.
Web facilities	Free access to data on site.
Cost	Free.
Comments	Weekly detailed sales figures are available to members only.
Address	Colonnade House, 2 Westover Road, Bournemouth BH1 2BY
Tel./e-mail	01202 292063 admin@bardltd.org
Fax/Website	01202 292067 www.bardltd.org

BRITISH BANKERS' ASSOCIATION

Title	**Annual Banking Statistics**
Coverage	Detailed statistics on the banks and banking with sections on bank groups, clearing statistics, credit card statistics, branches and financial data. Based on various sources, including data from the association. Many tables have ten-year statistical series.
Frequency	Annual.
Web facilities	Monthly statistics free on site, some other data and online ordering facilities.
Cost	£110; £85 for members.
Comments	Also known as the 'Orange Book'.
Address	10 Lombard Street, London EC3V 9AP
Tel./e-mail	0207 623 4001
Fax/Website	0207 283 7037 www.bba.org.uk

BRITISH BANKERS' ASSOCIATION

Title	**Major British Banking Groups' Mortgage and Consumer Lending**
Coverage	Trends in mortgage advances and other lending by UK banks with figures for the latest month and cumulative data. Based on returns from members.
Frequency	Monthly.
Web facilities	Monthly statistics, some other data and online ordering facilities on site.
Cost	Free.
Comments	
Address	10 Lombard Street, London EC3V 9AP
Tel./e-mail	0207 623 4001
Fax/Website	0207 283 7037 www.bba.org.uk

BRITISH BANKERS' ASSOCIATION

Title	**Monthly Statement**
Coverage	General statistics covering the activities of the major UK banks. Based largely on data from members.
Frequency	Monthly.
Web facilities	Monthly statistics, some other data and online ordering facilities on site.
Cost	Free.
Comments	
Address	10 Lombard Street, London EC3V 9AP
Tel./e-mail	0207 623 4001
Fax/Website	0207 283 7037 www.bba.org.uk

BRITISH BEER AND PUB ASSOCIATION

Title	**BBPA Statistical Handbook**
Coverage	Data on beer and other alcoholic drinks including production, consumption, brewing materials, prices, incomes, duties, licensing data, industry structure, drunkenness. Based on official data plus some data from the association.
Frequency	Annual.
Web facilities	General details of statistics.
Cost	£47.50; £27.75 for members.
Comments	Online ordering of handbook on website.
Address	42 Portman Square, London W1K 6BD
Tel./e-mail	0207 486 4831 web@beerandpub.com
Fax/Website	0207 935 3991 www.beerandpub.com

BRITISH BUSINESS AND GENERAL AVIATION ASSOCIATION

Title	**GA Trends**
Coverage	Annual data on pilot licences issued, planes, helicopters, number of companies in the sector and turnover. Historical data in many tables.
Frequency	Annual.
Web facilities	Free access to data on site.
Cost	Free.
Comments	Previously known as the General Aviation Manufacturers and Traders Association.
Address	19 Church Street, Brill, Aylesbury HP18 9RT
Tel./e-mail	01844 238020 info@bbga.aero.
Fax/Website	01844 238087 www.bbga.aero.

BRITISH CARPET MANUFACTURERS' ASSOCIATION

Title	**Annual Report**
Coverage	A statistical section concentrates on carpet imports and exports. Based mainly on central government data.
Frequency	Annual.
Web facilities	
Cost	Free.
Comments	
Address	PO Box 1155, 60 New Road, Kidderminster DY10 1WW
Tel./e-mail	01562 747351 bcma@clara.net
Fax/Website	01562 747359

BRITISH CEMENT ASSOCIATION

Title	**Industry Statistics**
Coverage	Statistics covering production, imports, exports, channels of sale, deliveries, regional deliveries and consumption.
Frequency	Annual.
Web facilities	Free access to data on site.
Cost	Free.
Comments	
Address	Riverside House, 4 Meadows Business Park, Station Approach, Blackwater, Camberley GU17 9AB
Tel./e-mail	01276 608700 info@bca.org.uk
Fax/Website	01276 608701 www.bca.org.uk

BRITISH CERAMIC CONFEDERATION

Title	**Annual Production and Trade Statistics by Sub-Sector**
Coverage	Summary of the total production and sales of the ceramic industry, plus overseas trade data. Based largely on government statistics.
Frequency	Annual.
Web facilities	Access to statistics for members on website.
Cost	Free.
Comments	Usually only available to members.
Address	Federation House, Station Road, Stoke-on-Trent ST4 2SA
Tel./e-mail	01782 744631 bcc@ceramfed.co.uk
Fax/Website	01782 744102 www.ceramfed.co.uk

BRITISH CERAMIC CONFEDERATION

Title	**Quarterly Trade Statistics**
Coverage	Details of the imports and exports of ceramic products broken down into various industry sub-sectors. Based on government statistics.
Frequency	Quarterly.
Web facilities	Access to statistics for members on website.
Cost	Free.
Comments	Usually only available to members.
Address	Federation House, Station Road, Stoke-on-Trent ST4 2SA
Tel./e-mail	01782 744631 bcc@ceramfed.co.uk
Fax/Website	01782 744102 www.ceramfed.co.uk

BRITISH CHAMBERS OF COMMERCE

Title	**Quarterly Economic Survey**
Coverage	A quarterly review of business and economic conditions based on returns from a sample of members of a selection of the major regional chambers.
Frequency	Quarterly.
Web facilities	Summary data available free on site plus online ordering facilities.
Cost	£200; £60 each.
Comments	
Address	65 Petty France, London SW1H 9EU
Tel./e-mail	0207 654 8000 info@britishchambers.org.uk
Fax/Website	0207 654 5819 www.chambersonline.org.uk

BRITISH CLOTHING INDUSTRY ASSOCIATION

Title	**Report of Activities**
Coverage	Includes a facts and figures section with data on output, trade, production, consumer expenditure, top markets and EU production.
Frequency	Annual.
Web facilities	
Cost	On request.
Comments	
Address	5 Portland Place, London W1N 3AA
Tel./e-mail	0207 636 7788 bcia@dial.pipex.com
Fax/Website	0207 636 7515

BRITISH COATINGS FEDERATION

Title	**Coatings Industry Statistics**
Coverage	Sales volumes for paint and sales values for paints and inks.
Frequency	Annual
Web facilities	Free access to data on site.
Cost	Free
Comments	
Address	James House, Bridge Street, Leatherhead KT22 7EP
Tel./e-mail	01372 360660 enquiry@bcf.co.uk
Fax/Website	01372 376069 www.coatings.org.uk

BRITISH CONTRACT FURNISHINGS ASSOCIATION

Title	**UK Contract Furnishing Market Report**
Coverage	Analysis and data on sales of furnishings by type and sector and market trends. Based on original research.
Frequency	Regular.
Web facilities	Free summary of the report on site.
Cost	On request.
Comments	
Address	Project House, 25 West Wycombe Road, High Wycombe HP11 2LQ
Tel./e-mail	01494 896790 enquiries@bcfa.org.uk
Fax/Website	01494 896799 www.thebcfa.com

BRITISH EDIBLE PULSE ASSOCIATION

Title	**BEPA Market Review**
Coverage	Monthly report on crop volumes and production from data collected by the association.
Frequency	Monthly.
Web facilities	Free summary data on site plus price information.
Cost	On request.
Comments	
Address	c/o Alan Wymer, Saxon Agriculture Ltd, The Old Forge, Church Road, Walton, Kings Lynn PE33 1PP
Tel./e-mail	01760 338338
Fax/Website	www.bepa.co.uk

BRITISH EDUCATIONAL SUPPLIERS' ASSOCIATION

Title	**UK School Survey on Budget and Resource Provision**
Coverage	Includes data for expenditure by schools on supplies and equipment.
Frequency	Annual.
Web facilities	General details and free summary statistics on site. Access to statistics for members only.
Cost	£350.
Comments	
Address	20 Beaufort Court, Admirals Way, London E14 9XL
Tel./e-mail	0207 537 4997 besa@besa.org.uk.
Fax/Website	0207 537 4846 www.besanet.org.uk

BRITISH EDUCATIONAL SUPPLIERS' ASSOCIATION

Title	**Information and Communication Technology in UK State Schools**
Coverage	A review of IT in UK state schools including expenditure data.
Frequency	Annual.
Web facilities	General details and free summary statistics on site. Access to statistics for members only.
Cost	£250.
Comments	
Address	20 Beaufort Court, Admirals Way, London E14 9XL
Tel./e-mail	0207 537 4997 besa@besa.org.uk
Fax/Website	0207 537 4846 www.besanet.org.uk

BRITISH EGG INFORMATION SERVICE

Title	**Egg Market Data**
Coverage	Basic data on sales, egg types and production from data collected by the service.
Frequency	Regular.
Web facilities	Free on website.
Cost	Free.
Comments	
Address	1 Chelsea Manor Gardens, London SW3 5PN
Tel./e-mail	0207 808 9790 info@britegg.co.uk
Fax/Website	www.britegg.co.uk

BRITISH ENERGY ASSOCIATION

Title	**British Annual Energy Review**
Coverage	A review of trends in the British energy industry, broken down by sector and based on a combination of sources.
Frequency	Annual.
Web facilities	
Cost	On request.
Comments	
Address	c/o BNFL 2nd Floor, 65 Buckingham Gate, London SW1E 6AP
Tel./e-mail	0208 767 9744 beawec@aol.com
Fax/Website	0208 767 9744

BRITISH FILM INSTITUTE

Title	**Film and TV Statistics**
Coverage	Data on films produced, box office trends, audiences, cinemas, etc. based on various sources.
Frequency	Regular.
Web facilities	Free access to data on site.
Cost	Free.
Comments	Published *The Stats* in 2004, a compilation of data covering 1990–2001.
Address	21 Stephen Street, London W1T 1LN
Tel./e-mail	0207 255 1444 feedback@bfi.org.uk
Fax/Website	www.bfi.org.uk

BRITISH FLUID POWER ASSOCIATION

Title	**BFPA Annual Hydraulic Equipment Survey**
Coverage	A survey of a sample of member companies providing information on market trends and characteristics. The survey is supplemented by some official statistics and international data.
Frequency	Annual.
Web facilities	General details on site
Cost	On request.
Comments	Various salary surveys for specific sectors also produced.
Address	Cheriton House, Cromwell Business Park, Banbury Road, Chipping Norton OX7 5SR
Tel./e-mail	01608 647900 bfpa@bfpa.demon.co.uk
Fax/Website	01608 647919 www.bfpa.co.uk

BRITISH FLUID POWER ASSOCIATION

Title	**Distributor Monthly UK Orders and Sales Index**
Coverage	Orders and sales trends based on returns from member companies.
Frequency	Monthly.
Web facilities	General details on site.
Cost	On request.
Comments	Various salary surveys for specific sectors also produced.
Address	Cheriton House, Cromwell Business Park, Banbury Road, Chipping Norton OX7 5SR
Tel./e-mail	01608 647900 bfpa@bfpa.demon.co.uk
Fax/Website	01608 647919 www.bfpa.co.uk

BRITISH FLUID POWER ASSOCIATION

Title	**Distributor Annual Survey**
Coverage	A survey of distributors providing information on sales, market trends, end users and companies. Also includes salary structure data and some official statistics.
Frequency	Annual.
Web facilities	General details on site.
Cost	On request.
Comments	Various salary surveys for specific sectors also produced.
Address	Cheriton House, Cromwell Business Park, Banbury Road, Chipping Norton OX7 5SR
Tel./e-mail	01608 647900 bfpa@bfpa.demon.co.uk
Fax/Website	01608 647919 www.bfpa.co.uk

BRITISH FLUID POWER ASSOCIATION

Title	**Hydraulic Equipment Industry Trends Survey**
Coverage	Commentary and statistics on short-term trends based on returns from member companies.
Frequency	Quarterly.
Web facilities	General details on site.
Cost	On request.
Comments	Various salary surveys for specific sectors also produced.
Address	Cheriton House, Cromwell Business Park, Banbury Road, Chipping Norton OX7 5SR
Tel./e-mail	01608 647900 bfpa@bfpa.demon.co.uk
Fax/Website	01608 647919 www.bfpa.co.uk

BRITISH FLUID POWER ASSOCIATION

Title	**Hydraulic Equipment Monthly UK Orders and Sales Index**
Coverage	Orders and sales trends based on returns from member companies.
Frequency	Monthly.
Web facilities	General details on site.
Cost	On request.
Comments	Various salary surveys for specific sectors also produced.
Address	Cheriton House, Cromwell Business Park, Banbury Road, Chipping Norton OX7 5SR
Tel./e-mail	01608 647900 bfpa@bfpa.demon.co.uk
Fax/Website	01608 647919 www.bfpa.co.uk

BRITISH FLUID POWER ASSOCIATION

Title	**Pneumatic Control Equipment Monthly UK Orders and Sales Index**
Coverage	Orders and sales trends based on returns from member companies.
Frequency	Monthly.
Web facilities	General details on site.
Cost	On request.
Comments	Various salary surveys for specific sectors also produced.
Address	Cheriton House, Cromwell Business Park, Banbury Road, Chipping Norton OX7 5SR
Tel./e-mail	01608 647900 bfpa@bfpa.demon.co.uk
Fax/Website	01608 647919 www.bfpa.co.uk

BRITISH FLUID POWER ASSOCIATION

Title	**Annual Salary Survey**
Coverage	Based on a survey of members, it includes data on remuneration, company cars, working hours, holiday entitlements.
Frequency	Annual.
Web facilities	General details on site.
Cost	On request.
Comments	
Address	Cheriton House, Cromwell Business Park, Banbury Road, Chipping Norton OX7 5SR
Tel./e-mail	01608 647900 bfpa@bfpa.demon.co.uk
Fax/Website	01608 647919 www.bfpa.co.uk

BRITISH FOOTWEAR ASSOCIATION

Title	**Footwear Facts and Figures**
Coverage	Five-year production, imports and exports and consumption data. Based mainly on central government data.
Frequency	Regular.
Web facilities	The data are available free on the website.
Cost	Free.
Comments	The association no longer publishes a range of monthly, quarterly and annual statistical titles.
Address	3 Burgstead Place, Wellingborough NN8 1AH
Tel./e-mail	01933 229005 info@britfoot.com
Fax/Website	01933 225009 www.britfoot.com

BRITISH FRANCHISE ASSOCIATION

Title	**BFA/NATWEST Survey of Franchising**
Coverage	Statistics and commentary on the number of franchisees, types, sectors, sales and people in employment with the latest year's data compared to the previous year. Based on original research by the association. Commentary supports the text.
Frequency	Annual.
Web facilities	General details and free summary statistics on the site. Online ordering of publications and e-mail alerting services.
Cost	£87.50; £20 for BFA members.
Comments	
Address	Thames View, Newtown Road, Henley-on-Thames RG9 1HG
Tel./e-mail	01491 578050 mailroom@british-franchise.org.uk
Fax/Website	01491 573517 www.british-franchise.org.uk

BRITISH FROZEN FOOD FEDERATION

Title	**Monthly Bulletin**
Coverage	Includes statistics on the UK frozen food market with data on consumption, expenditure and markets for specific frozen foods. Based on various sources.
Frequency	Regular.
Web facilities	Various frozen food statistics are freely available on the site.
Cost	£40.
Comments	
Address	3rd Floor, Springfield House, Springfield Business Park, Grantham NG31 7BG
Tel./e-mail	01476 515300
Fax/Website	01476 515309 www.bfff.co.uk

BRITISH GEAR ASSOCIATION

Title	**UK Mechanical Power Transmission Industry and Statistics**
Coverage	Production and trade statistics for the industry and product areas for the last three years based mainly on official statistics.
Frequency	Annual.
Web facilities	Free access to data on site.
Cost	Free.
Comments	
Address	Suite 43, Imex Business Park, Shobnall Road, Burton-upon-Trent DE14 2AU
Tel./e-mail	01283 515521 admin@bga.org.uk
Fax/Website	01283 515841 www.bga.org.uk

BRITISH GLASS MANUFACTURERS' CONFEDERATION

Title	**Glass Recycling Report**
Coverage	Statistics on the recycling of glass bottles and other glass products based on data collected by the confederation.
Frequency	Regular.
Web facilities	Some statistics freely available on site.
Cost	On request.
Comments	
Address	Northumberland Road, Sheffield S10 2UA
Tel./e-mail	0114 2901850 sales@britglass.co.uk
Fax/Website	0114 2901851 www.britglass.org.uk

BRITISH HARDWARE AND HOUSEWARES MANUFACTURERS' ASSOCIATION

Title	**Business Trends Survey**
Coverage	Based on a survey of members with data on sales, stocks, margins and business expectations.
Frequency	Quarterly.
Web facilities	
Cost	£50; £25 for members, £5 for participants in the Business Trends Survey.
Comments	
Address	Brooke House, 4 The Lakes, Bedford Road, Northampton NN4 7YD
Tel./e-mail	01604 622023 bhhma@brookehouse.co.uk
Fax/Website	01604 631252 www.bhhma.co.uk

BRITISH HOSPITALITY ASSOCIATION

Title	**Food and Service Management Survey**
Coverage	A detailed annual review of the UK food service management industry with commentary and statistics on the number of businesses, turnover, costs and number of meals served; summary data on the international contract catering industry; and future trends. The report is based on a survey by the association.
Frequency	Annual.
Web facilities	
Cost	£35, free for members. PDF copy available for £20.
Comments	Previously titled *UK Contract Catering Survey*.
Address	Queen's House, 55–56 Lincoln's Inn Fields, London WC2A 3BH
Tel./e-mail	0207 404 7744 bha@bha.org.uk
Fax/Website	0207 404 7799 www.bha-online.org.uk

BRITISH HOSPITALITY ASSOCIATION

Title	**BHA Trends and Statistics**
Coverage	Commentary and statistics on tourism and hospitality trends. Based on a combination of government data and other data.
Frequency	Annual.
Web facilities	
Cost	£195, free for members. PDF copy available for £146.25.
Comments	
Address	Queen's House, 55–56 Lincoln's Inn Fields, London WC2A 3BH
Tel./e-mail	0207 404 7744 bha@bha.org.uk
Fax/Website	0207 404 7799 www.bha-online.org.uk

BRITISH KNITTING AND CLOTHING EXPORT COUNCIL

Title	**Industry Statistical Overview**
Coverage	Five-year series of data covering production, imports, exports, employment and consumer expenditure based on various sources.
Frequency	Annual.
Web facilities	Free access to data on site.
Cost	Free.
Comments	
Address	5 Portland Place, London W1B 1PW
Tel./e-mail	0207 636 5577 paul.algen@ukfashionexports.com
Fax/Website	www.ukfashionexports.com

BRITISH MARINE FEDERATION

Title	**National Survey of Boating and Watersports Participation**
Coverage	A review of the percentage of the population participating, expenditure, equipment and services, training, craft ownership by type, frequency of visits to water, attitudes to watersports and consumer profiles. Based largely on original research.
Frequency	Every three or four years
Web facilities	Free access to and downloading, of some statistics on site.
Cost	£195; £100 for members.
Comments	
Address	Meadlake Place, Thorpe Lea Road, Egham TW20 8HE
Tel./e-mail	01784 473377 research@britishmarine.co.uk
Fax/Website	01784 439678 www.britishmarine.co.uk

BRITISH MARINE FEDERATION

Title	**UK Leisure Marine Industry Bulletin**
Coverage	Trends in the boating industry and market based on original research.
Frequency	Annual.
Web facilities	Free access to and downloading of, some statistics on site.
Cost	Free.
Comments	
Address	Meadlake Place, Thorpe Lea Road, Egham TW20 8HE
Tel./e-mail	01784 473377 research@britishmarine.co.uk
Fax/Website	01784 439678 www.britishmarine.co.uk

BRITISH MARINE FEDERATION

Title	**Industry Trends Survey**
Coverage	An opinion survey of member companies producing analysis and data on industry sentiment and confidence.
Frequency	Twice yearly.
Web facilities	Free access to and downloading of, some statistics on site.
Cost	Free.
Comments	
Address	Meadlake Place, Thorpe Lea Road, Egham TW20 8HE
Tel./e-mail	01784 473377 research@britishmarine.co.uk
Fax/Website	01784 439678 www.britishmarine.co.uk

BRITISH MARKET RESEARCH ASSOCIATION (BMRA)

Title	**BMRA Annual Statistics**
Coverage	The BMRA publishes a league table of its member companies by turnover, plus industry-wide data on turnover by type of client (i.e., sector), turnover by research method and turnover by survey type. Based on a survey of members.
Frequency	Annual.
Web facilities	Summary statistics on the industry available free on the site. PDF copy of summary annual data.
Cost	On request.
Comments	The BMRA was formed in 1998 through a merger of the Association of Market Survey Organisations (AMSO) and the Association of British Market Research Companies (ABMRC).
Address	Devonshire House, 60 Goswell Road, London EC1M 7AD
Tel./e-mail	0207 566 3636 admin@bmra.org.uk
Fax/Website	0207 689 6220 www.bmra.org.uk

BRITISH MARKET RESEARCH BUREAU (BMRB) INTERNATIONAL

Title	**Target Group Index (TGI)**
Coverage	A national product and media survey based on information from 25 000 adults. The results are published in various reports: general demographic information is followed by individual consumer product areas. Detailed consumer profiles and penetration data are given for each product.
Frequency	Quarterly.
Web facilities	Summary data from TGI and other surveys free on site.
Cost	On request.
Comments	Specific prices available for reports on individual brands or specific consumer fields. Also available online.
Address	26–30 Uxbridge Road, Ealing W5 2BP
Tel./e-mail	0208 566 4288 web@bmrb.co.uk
Fax/Website	0208 579 4003 www.brmb-tgi.co.uk

BRITISH MARKET RESEARCH BUREAU (BMRB) INTERNATIONAL

Title	**Premier TGI**
Coverage	TGI data specifically for consumers in the AB social grades with data covering holidays, leisure, sports, travel, clothing, personal possessions, cosmetics, gifts, household goods, home and car, drinks and food.
Frequency	Annual.
Web facilities	Summary data from TGI and other surveys free on site.
Cost	Varies according to the range and nature of the information required. Standard results published in eight volumes.
Comments	Also available online.
Address	26–30 Uxbridge Road, Ealing W5 2BP
Tel./e-mail	0208 566 4288 web@bmrb.co.uk
Fax/Website	0208 579 4003 www.bmrb-tgi.co.uk

BRITISH MARKET RESEARCH BUREAU (BMRB) INTERNATIONAL

Title	**Youth TGI**
Coverage	TGI data specifically for children and youths aged between 7 and 19. Includes data on purchases and consumption of key products.
Frequency	Annual.
Web facilities	Summary data from TGI and other surveys free on site.
Cost	Varies according to the range and nature of the information required. Standard results published in two volumes.
Comments	Also available online.
Address	26–30 Uxbridge Road, Ealing W5 2BP
Tel./e-mail	0208 566 4288 web@bmrb.co.uk
Fax/Website	0208 579 4003 www.brmb-tgi.co.uk

BRITISH MARKET RESEARCH BUREAU (BMRB) INTERNATIONAL

Title	**Access Omnibus Survey**
Coverage	Includes a weekly omnibus survey of 2000 adults above the age of 14 with face-to-face interviews carried out in the home. A telephone survey is carried out every weekend and uses a sample of 1000 adults. Also web-based surveys.
Frequency	Weekly.
Web facilities	Summary data from TGI and other surveys free on site.
Cost	On request.
Comments	
Address	26–30 Uxbridge Road, Ealing W5 2BP
Tel./e-mail	0208 566 4288 access.omnibus@bmrb.co.uk
Fax/Website	0208 579 4003 www.bmrb.co.uk

BRITISH MARKET RESEARCH BUREAU (BMRB) INTERNATIONAL

Title	**TGI Wavelength**
Coverage	A TGI survey investigating demographics and purchases of listeners to local radio.
Frequency	Weekly and quarterly.
Web facilities	General details on site.
Cost	On request.
Comments	Also available online.
Address	26–30 Uxbridge Road, Ealing W5 2BP
Tel./e-mail	0208 566 4288 web@bmrb.co.uk
Fax/Website	0208 579 4003 www.brmb-tgi.co.uk

BRITISH METALS RECYCLING ASSOCIATION

Title	**BMRA Yearbook and Members Directory**
Coverage	Yearbook includes a section reviewing trends in the foundry industry, plus data on steel production, stainless steel and alloys.
Frequency	Annual.
Web facilities	
Cost	On request.
Comments	
Address	16 High Street, Brampton, Huntingdon PE28 4TU
Tel./e-mail	01480 465249 admin@recyclemetals.org
Fax/Website	01480 463680 www.recyclemetals.org

BRITISH OFFICE SYSTEMS AND STATIONERY FEDERATION (BOSS)

Title	**BOSS Market Tracking Service**
Coverage	The BOSS Federation survey of manufacturers' turnover gives quarterly data, and comparable data for previous quarters, for three sectors: furniture, machines, office products. The survey is based on returns from companies representing approximately one third of the total market.
Frequency	Quarterly.
Web facilities	Facts and figures from survey free on the site.
Cost	
Comments	Only available to participating companies.
Address	12 Corporation Street, High Wycombe HP13 6TQ
Tel./e-mail	0845 450 1565 info@bossfederation.co.uk
Fax/Website	0870 770 6789 www.bossfederation.co.uk

BRITISH PHONOGRAPHIC INDUSTRY (BPI)

Title	**BPI Statistical Handbook**
Coverage	Includes statistics on the production of CDs, tapes and records plus imports and exports, deliveries, sales, prices, advertising expenditure, hardware ownership, video trends, piracy and leisure market trends.
Frequency	Annual.
Web facilities	General details and free summary statistics.
Cost	£50.
Comments	
Address	Riverside Building, County Hall, Westminster Bridge Road, London SE1 7JA
Tel./e-mail	0207 803 1300
Fax/Website	0207 803 1310 www.bpi.co.uk

BRITISH PLASTICS FEDERATION

Title	**BPF Business Trends Survey**
Coverage	A survey of companies in three areas: materials supplies, processing and machinery manufacturers. Data on sales, orders, stocks, exports, investment, profits, prices and capacity utilisation. Includes an opinion survey outlining likely future trends and a commentary supports the text.
Frequency	Twice yearly.
Web facilities	Basic data on the site.
Cost	£96; free for members.
Comments	
Address	6 Bath Place, Rivington Street, London EC2A 3JE
Tel./e-mail	0207 457 5000 dgreenaway@bpf.co.uk
Fax/Website	0207 235 5045 www.bpf.co.uk

BRITISH PLASTICS FEDERATION

Title	**BPF Statistics Handbook**
Coverage	Statistics on the UK consumption of plastic materials, material consumption by major end use, imports, exports and plastics in packaging, building and the automotive sectors. Based on BPF and other data with some supporting text. Published in two volumes: 1 – *The Bulk Polymers*; 2 – *The Semi-Commodity Engineering Plastics*.
Frequency	Annual.
Web facilities	Basic data on the site.
Cost	£280 per volume.
Comments	
Address	6 Bath Place, Rivington Street, London EC2A 3JE
Tel./e-mail	0207 457 5000 dgreenaway@bpf.co.uk
Fax/Website	0207 235 5045 www.bpf.co.uk

BRITISH PLASTICS FEDERATION

Title	**BPF Economic Survey**
Coverage	A review of the economy and business trends and specific trends in the plastics sector.
Frequency	Annual.
Web facilities	Basic data on the site.
Cost	£80; free for members.
Comments	
Address	6 Bath Place, Rivington Street, London EC2A 3JE
Tel./e-mail	0207 457 5000 dgreenaway@bpf.co.uk
Fax/Website	0207 235 5045 www.bpf.co.uk

BRITISH POTATO COUNCIL

Title	**Potato Weekly**
Coverage	Weekly prices for potatoes in UK and international markets.
Frequency	Weekly.
Web facilities	Free access to data on site, plus weekly news.
Cost	Free.
Comments	Also publishes *Potato Weekly* news service.
Address	4300 Nash Court, John Smith Drive, Oxford Business Park, Oxford OX4 2RT
Tel./e-mail	01865 714455
Fax/Website	01865 782231 www.potato.org.uk

BRITISH POULTRY COUNCIL

Title	**Annual Statistics**
Coverage	Farm production data for broilers and turkeys plus import and export data. Statistics cover the last five years.
Frequency	Annual.
Web facilities	Free access to data on site.
Cost	Free.
Comments	
Address	Europoint House, 5 Lavington Street, London SE1 0NZ
Tel./e-mail	0207 202 4760 bpc@poultry.uk.com
Fax/Website	0207 928 6366 www.poultry.uk.com

BRITISH PRINTING INDUSTRIES' FEDERATION

Title	**BPIF Salary Survey**
Coverage	Salary trends in printing and graphics industry by sector, occupation etc. Based on returns from participating organisations.
Frequency	Annual.
Web facilities	Free facts and figures pages on the site
Cost	£500; £250 to non-member participating companies.
Comments	
Address	Farringdon Point, 29–35 Farringdon Road, London EC1M 3JF
Tel./e-mail	0870 240 4085 info@bpif.org.uk
Fax/Website	0207 405 7784 www.britishprint.com

BRITISH PRINTING INDUSTRIES' FEDERATION

Title	**Directions**
Coverage	A report on the economic state of the printing industry with statistics covering the last 30 months.
Frequency	Quarterly.
Web facilities	Free facts and figures pages on site.
Cost	£25 per issue.
Comments	
Address	Farringdon Point, 29–35 Farringdon Road, London EC1M 3JF
Tel./e-mail	0870 240 4085 info@bpif.org.uk
Fax/Website	0207 405 7784 www.britishprint.com

BRITISH RADIO AND ELECTRONIC EQUIPMENT MANUFACTURERS' ASSOCIATION (BREEMA)

Title	**Annual Report**
Coverage	The annual report contains some statistics on deliveries of consumer electronic products and a report on the statistical activities of the association.
Frequency	Annual.
Web facilities	Annual report can be viewed on the site and downloaded for free.
Cost	Free.
Comments	In summer 2001, the association announced a merger with the Federation of the Electronics Industry (FEI).
Address	Russell Square House, 10–12 Russell Square, London WC1B 5EE
Tel./e-mail	0207 331 2000 information@brema.org.uk
Fax/Website	0207 331 2040 www.brema.org.uk

BRITISH RETAIL CONSORTIUM

Title	**BRC-KPMG Retail Sales Monitor**
Coverage	Volume and value of UK retail sales based mainly on government statistics supported by data from some non-official sources.
Frequency	Monthly.
Web facilities	Free summary data in press release on site.
Cost	On request.
Comments	
Address	21 Dartmouth Street, London SW1H 9BP
Tel./e-mail	0207 854 8986 info@brc.org.uk
Fax/Website	0207 647 1599 www.brc.org.uk

BRITISH RETAIL CONSORTIUM

Title	**Retail Crime Survey**
Coverage	Based on a survey of approximately 53 000 outlets, the report analyses retail crime and includes data on the total cost, crime by retailers, type of crime.
Frequency	Annual.
Web facilities	Free summary data in press release on site.
Cost	£100; £90 for members.
Comments	
Address	21 Dartmouth Street, London SW1H 9BP
Tel./e-mail	0207 854 8986 info@brc.org.uk
Fax/Website	0207 647 1599 www.brc.org.uk

BRITISH RETAIL CONSORTIUM

Title	**Shop Price Index**
Coverage	Information on monthly price movements for 200 goods purchased regularly with general comparisons with the retail price index.
Frequency	Monthly.
Web facilities	Free summary data in press release on site.
Cost	On request.
Comments	
Address	21 Dartmouth Street, London SW1H 9BP
Tel./e-mail	0207 854 8986 info@brc.org.uk
Fax/Website	0207 647 1599 www.brc.org.uk

BRITISH ROBOT AND AUTOMATION ASSOCIATION

Title	**Industrial Robot Facts**
Coverage	Annual report on UK robot installations within a given year plus historical trends. Data by industry.
Frequency	Annual.
Web facilities	Free access to PDF of survey on the site.
Cost	Free.
Comments	Also publishes a yearbook.
Address	c/o Dr Ken Young, International Manufacturing Centre, University of Warwick, Coventry CV5 7AL
Tel./e-mail	02476 573742 info@bara.org.uk
Fax/Website	02476 573743 www.bara.org.uk

BRITISH SECURITY INDUSTRY ASSOCIATION

Title	**Industry Statistics**
Coverage	Data covering sales, employment, number of companies in the industry etc. Based mainly on the association's own surveys.
Frequency	Annual.
Web facilities	Free access to data on site.
Cost	Free.
Comments	
Address	Security House, Barbourne Road, Worcester WR1 1RS
Tel./e-mail	01905 21464
Fax/Website	01905 613625 www.bsia.co.uk

BRITISH SOFT DRINKS ASSOCIATION LTD

Title	**BSDA Annual Report**
Coverage	Contains some statistics on various aspects of the industry.
Frequency	Annual.
Web facilities	Summary information on the industry on site.
Cost	Free.
Comments	
Address	20–22 Stukely Street, London WC2B 5LR
Tel./e-mail	0207 430 0356
Fax/Website	0207 831 6014 www.britishsoftdrinks.com

BRITISH TOURIST AUTHORITY

Title	**BTA Annual Report**
Coverage	Includes summary statistics on tourism in the UK with a general review of the short-term outlook for tourism.
Frequency	Annual.
Web facilities	Available free on the site.
Cost	Free.
Comments	
Address	Research Department, Thames Tower, Black's Road, Hammersmith, London W6 9EL
Tel./e-mail	0208 846 9000 blvcinfo@visitbritain.org
Fax/Website	0208 563 0302 www.bta.org.uk

BRITISH TOURIST AUTHORITY

Title	**Key Tourism Facts**
Coverage	Regularly updated statistics on inbound and domestic tourism levels, employment trends and tourist expenditure.
Frequency	Annual.
Web facilities	Free access to statistics on site.
Cost	Free.
Comments	
Address	Research Department, Thames Tower, Black's Road, Hammersmith, London W6 9EL
Tel./e-mail	0208 846 9000 blvcinfo@visitbritain.org
Fax/Website	0208 563 0302 www.bta.org.uk

BRITISH VEHICLE RENTAL AND LEASING ASSOCIATION

Title	**BVRLA Statistics**
Coverage	Data for the last 15 years on the size of the chauffeur drive/private hire, rental and leasing fleets operated by members of the BVRLA.
Frequency	Annual.
Web facilities	Free access to data on site.
Cost	Free.
Comments	Previously published the *BVRLA Industry Review* but latest issue is 2002.
Address	River Lodge, Badminton Court, Amersham HP7 0DD
Tel./e-mail	01494 434747 info@bvrla.co.uk
Fax/Website	01494 434499 www.bvrla.co.uk

BRITISH VENTURE CAPITAL ASSOCIATION

Title	**Report on Investment Activity**
Coverage	Investment trends and activities of member companies over the previous year. Commentary and statistics based on the association's own survey.
Frequency	Annual.
Web facilities	Free 'Key Facts' summary information free on site.
Cost	£50; £40 + VAT for a PDF version
Comments	
Address	3 Clements Inn, London WC2R 2AZ
Tel./e-mail	0207 025 2950 bvca@bvca.co.uk
Fax/Website	0207 025 2951 www.bvca.co.uk

BRITISH VENTURE CAPITAL ASSOCIATION

Title	**Performance Measurement Survey**
Coverage	An annual survey offering data on the aggregate net returns to investors from independent venture capitalists and private equity funds. Data by year and by type of fund.
Frequency	Annual.
Web facilities	Free Key Facts summary data on site.
Cost	£50; £40 + VAT for a PDF version.
Comments	
Address	3 Clements Inn, London WC2R 2AZ
Tel./e-mail	0207 025 2950 bvca@bvca.co.uk
Fax/Website	0207 025 2951 www.bvca.co.uk

BRITISH VENTURE CAPITAL ASSOCIATION

Title	**BVCA Confidence and Attitudes Survey**
Coverage	A quarterly survey by YouGov soliciting opinions on the private equity market.
Frequency	Quarterly.
Web facilities	Free 'Key Facts' summary data on site.
Cost	On request.
Comments	
Address	3 Clements Inn, London WC2R 2AZ
Tel./e-mail	0207 025 2950 bvca@bvca.co.uk
Fax/Website	0207 025 2951 www.bvca.co.uk

BRITISH VIDEO ASSOCIATION

Title	**British Video Association Yearbook**
Coverage	Commentary, statistical tables and charts covering sales and rental of videotapes. The sales section includes data on distribution channels, sales by video type, sales by month, region, price group, retailer shares, number of tapes bought, bestsellers and a demographic breakdown. The rental section has data on the market value, seasonality, rentals by video type, source of rentals, frequency of rentals and viewing and a demographic breakdown. A final section gives statistics on hardware, cinema admissions and employment, and lists BVA members. Many tables give historical data.
Frequency	Annual.
Web facilities	Summary data and top ten rankings on site.
Cost	£65.
Comments	Published in April each year.
Address	167 Great Portland Street, London W1N 5FD
Tel./e-mail	0207 436 0041 general@bva.org.uk
Fax/Website	0207 436 0043 www.bva.org.uk

BRITISH WIND ENERGY ASSOCIATION

Title	**Statistical Overview of Wind Farms Today**
Coverage	General data on numbers, locations, output, operating data etc. based on survey by the association.
Frequency	Annual.
Web facilities	Free access to data on the site.
Cost	Free.
Comments	
Address	Renewable Energy House, 1 Aztec Row, Berners Road, London N1 0PW
Tel./e-mail	0207 689 1960 info@bwea.com
Fax/Website	0207 689 1969 www.bwea.com

BRITISH WIND ENERGY ASSOCIATION

Title	**BWEA Quarterly Statistical Report**
Coverage	Regular operating data on UK wind farms and wind energy.
Frequency	Quarterly.
Web facilities	Free access to data on the site.
Cost	Free.
Comments	
Address	Renewable Energy House, 1 Aztec Row, Berners Road, London N1 0PW
Tel./e-mail	0207 689 1960 info@bwea.com
Fax/Website	0207 689 1969 www.bwea.com

BRITISH WOODPULP ASSOCIATION

Title	**Annual Report**
Coverage	Includes a statistical section with data on imports of pulp by grade and country of origin, production and consumption of paper and board.
Frequency	Annual.
Web facilities	
Cost	Free for members; a small charge to others.
Comments	
Address	9 Glenair Avenue, Lower Parkstone, Poole BH14 5AD
Tel./e-mail	01202 738732
Fax/Website	01202 738747 www.woodpulp.org.uk

BRITISH WOODPULP ASSOCIATION

Title	**Digest of Woodpulp Import Statistics**
Coverage	Tonnage imports of wood pulp for paper making and other purposes based on data supplied by HM Customs and Excise.
Frequency	Monthly.
Web facilities	
Cost	Free for members, annual subscription to others.
Comments	
Address	9 Glenair Avenue, Lower Parkstone, Poole BH14 5AD
Tel./e-mail	01202 738732
Fax/Website	01202 738747 www.woodpulp.org.uk

BRITISH WOODWORKING FEDERATION

Title	**Fire Door and Doorset Scheme Quarterly Trends Report**
Coverage	An opinion survey of member companies to assess sales trends for doors, plus likely future trends.
Frequency	Quarterly.
Web facilities	Free access to survey PDFs on site.
Cost	Free.
Comments	
Address	55 Tutton Street, London SW1P 3QL
Tel./e-mail	08704 586939 bwf@bwf.org.uk
Fax/Website	08704 586949 www.bwf.org.uk

BRITISH WOOL MARKETING BOARD

Title	**Annual Report and Accounts**
Coverage	Mainly details of the board and its finances, but also contains statistics on wool production by type of wool produced. Based on the board's own figures.
Frequency	Annual.
Web facilities	Some free general data on site.
Cost	Free.
Comments	
Address	Wool House, Euroway Trading Estate, Bradford BD4 6SE
Tel./e-mail	01274 688666 mail@britishwool.org.uk
Fax/Website	01274 652233 www.britishwool.org.uk

BRITISH WOOL MARKETING BOARD

Title	**Basic Data**
Coverage	Summary information on the sheep population, wool production, prices, registered producers and the production of mutton and lamb. Based on a board survey.
Frequency	Annual.
Web facilities	Some free general data on site.
Cost	Free.
Comments	
Address	Wool House, Euroway Trading Estate, Bradford BD4 6SE
Tel./e-mail	01274 688666 mail@britishwool.org.uk
Fax/Website	01274 652233 www.britishwool.org.uk

BRITISH WOOL MARKETING BOARD

Title	**Price Indicators**
Coverage	Data on prices sent automatically to producers.
Frequency	Annual.
Web facilities	Some free general data on site.
Cost	Free.
Comments	
Address	Wool House, Euroway Trading Estate, Bradford BD4 6SE
Tel./e-mail	01274 688666 mail@britishwool.org.uk
Fax/Website	01274 652233 www.britishwool.org.uk

BROADCASTERS AUDIENCE RESEARCH BOARD (BARB)

Title	**BARB Weekly and Monthly Audience Reports**
Coverage	Television viewing figures produced from a sample survey of 11 000 respondents using electronic TV meters.
Frequency	Weekly and monthly.
Web facilities	Summary data from weekly and monthly reports plus 'TV Facts' pages on site.
Cost	£3000 annual registration.
Comments	Detailed figures for clients but also general data published in a weekly press release. Other types of analysis available on request.
Address	18 Dering Street, London W1R 9AF
Tel./e-mail	0208 741 9110 enquiries@barb.co.uk
Fax/Website	0208 741 1943 www.barb.co.uk

BUILDERS MERCHANTS' FEDERATION

Title	**BMF Profits and Costs Report**
Coverage	Based on returns from members with benchmarking data on return on capital employed, net margins, sales per employee, overhead costs, etc.
Frequency	Annual.
Web facilities	
Cost	£95; £50 for members.
Comments	
Address	15 Soho Square, London W1D 3HL
Tel./e-mail	0870 901 3380 info@bmf.org.uk
Fax/Website	0207 734 2766 www.bmf.org.uk

BUILDING

Title	**Share Watch**
Coverage	General changes in share prices for the building sector plus specific details of the week's main gainers and losers.
Frequency	Weekly in a weekly journal.
Web facilities	
Cost	£118.
Comments	
Address	CMP Information, Anchorage House, 2 Close Crescent, London E14 2DE
Tel./e-mail	0207 560 4140 abarricl@cmpinformation.com
Fax/Website	0207 560 4404 www.building.co.uk

BUILDING

Title	**Cost Update**
Coverage	Details of unit rates, material prices and labour costs.
Frequency	Quarterly in a weekly journal.
Web facilities	
Cost	£118.
Comments	
Address	CMP Information, Anchorage House, 2 Close Crescent, London E14 2DE
Tel./e-mail	0207 560 4140 abarrick@cmpinformation.com
Fax/Website	0207 560 4404 www.building.co.uk

BUILDING

Title	**Datafile**
Coverage	Graphs and commentary on general trends in the building industry, based largely on central government data.
Frequency	Monthly in a weekly journal.
Web facilities	
Cost	£118.
Comments	
Address	CMP Information, Anchorage House, 2 Close Crescent, London E14 2DE
Tel./e-mail	0207 560 4140 abarrick@cmpinformation.com
Fax/Website	0207 560 4404 www.building.co.uk

BUILDING

Title	**Tender Cost Forecast**
Coverage	Tender prices for various types of work, broken down by region. Tender prices are compared with general price trends and forecasts are given for the coming year.
Frequency	Quarterly.
Web facilities	
Cost	£118.
Comments	
Address	CMP Information, Anchorage House, 2 Close Crescent, London E14 2DE
Tel./e-mail	0207 560 4140 abarrick@cmpinformation.com
Fax/Website	0207 560 4404 www.building.co.uk

BUILDING

Title	**Building Procurement**
Coverage	Average procurement lead times for specific types of work and for specialist contractors.
Frequency	Six times a year in a weekly journal.
Web facilities	
Cost	£118.
Comments	
Address	CMP Information, Anchorage House, 2 Close Crescent, London E14 2DE
Tel./e-mail	0207 560 4140 abarrick@cmpinformation.com
Fax/Website	0207 560 4404 www.building.co.uk

BUILDING

Title	**Employment Survey**
Coverage	A survey caried out by Gallup examining trends in temporary and permanent employment broken down into two sectors: consultants and contractors.
Frequency	Regular in a weekly journal.
Web facilities	
Cost	£118.
Comments	
Address	CMP information, Anchorage House, 2 Close Crescent, London E14 2DE
Tel./e-mail	0207 560 4140 abarrick@cmpinformation.com
Fax/Website	0207 560 4404 www.building.co.uk

BUILDING COST INFORMATION SERVICE

Title	**BMI Quarterly Cost Briefing**
Coverage	Cost information on occupancy and running costs of buildings.
Frequency	Ten issues a year.
Web facilities	General details, online ordering and paid-for access to statistics on site.
Cost	£230 to £280.
Comments	Now available online via BMI Occupancy and Maintenance Costs Survey Online.
Address	3 Cadogan Gate, London SW1X 0AS
Tel./e-mail	0207 695 1500 bcis@bcis.co.uk
Fax/Website	0207 695 1501 www.bcis.co.uk

BUILDING COST INFORMATION SERVICE

Title	**BCIS Quarterly Review of Building Prices**
Coverage	Prices by type of building and by region based on a survey of subscribers to BCIS.
Frequency	Quarterly.
Web facilities	General details, online ordering and paid-for access to statistics on site.
Cost	£150 to £350.
Comments	Now available online via *BCIS Review of Building Prices Online*.
Address	3 Cadogan Gate, London SW1X 0AS
Tel./e-mail	0207 695 1500 bcis@bcis.co.uk
Fax/Website	0207 695 1501 www.bcis.co.uk

BUILDING COST INFORMATION SERVICE

Title	**Building Cost Information Service**
Coverage	An annual subscription service covering tenders, labour and materials and based on information supplied by members of BCIS. Also includes forecasts.
Frequency	Monthly.
Web facilities	General details, online ordering and paid-for access to statistics on site.
Cost	£670; web access – £900.
Comments	
Address	3 Cadogan Gate, London SW1X 0AS
Tel./e-mail	0207 695 1500 bcis@bcis.co.uk
Fax/Website	0207 695 1501 www.bcis.co.uk

BUILDING SOCIETIES ASSOCIATION

Title	**Building Society Yearbook**
Coverage	Key statistics on housing finance and building societies with data on loans, assets, mortgages, commitments, etc. Based largely on data collected by the association.
Frequency	Annual.
Web facilities	Press release data and summary statistics free on site.
Cost	£60.
Comments	The annual report is available on the website. Also publishes some titles jointly with the Council of Mortgage Lenders based at the same address (see separate entry).
Address	3 Savile Row, London W1S 3PB
Tel./e-mail	0207 437 0655 rachel.blakmore@bsa.org.uk
Fax/Website	0207 734 6416 www.bsa.org.uk

BUILDING SOCIETIES ASSOCIATION

Title	**Building Society Statistics**
Coverage	Monthly data on advances, lending and receipts produced as a press release with supporting data.
Frequency	Monthly.
Web facilities	Press release data and summary statistics available free on site.
Cost	Free.
Comments	The annual report is available on the website. Also publishes some titles jointly with the Council of Mortgage Lenders based at the same address (see separate entry).
Address	3 Savile Row, London W15 3PB
Tel./e-mail	0207 437 0655 rachel.blakmore@bsa.org.uk
Fax/Website	0207 734 6416 www.bsa.org.uk

BUSINESS AND TRADE STATISTICS LTD

Title	**External Trade Statistics**
Coverage	Detailed statistics, from 1979 onwards, on product imports and exports, analysed by trading partners, port of entry and exit. Business and Trade Statistics is an official agent of HM Customs and Excise.
Frequency	Monthly.
Web facilities	General details on site.
Cost	Depends on the amount and type of data required.
Comments	
Address	Lancaster House, More Lane, Esher KT10 8AP
Tel./e-mail	01372 463121 sales@worldtradestats.com
Fax/Website	01372 469847 www.worldtradestats.com

BUSINESS IN SPORT AND LEISURE

Title	**BISL Handbook**
Coverage	Includes statistics on sports and fitness, health, pubs, restaurants, hotels, cinema, arts, nightclubs and discos. Based on various sources.
Frequency	Annual.
Web facilities	General details on site.
Cost	On request.
Comments	
Address	46 Fieldsend Road, Cheam SM3 8NR
Tel./e-mail	0208 255 3782 amandafry@btconnect.com
Fax/Website	0208 644 8528 www.bisl.org

C CZARNIKOW SUGAR LTD

Title	**The UK Sugar Market**
Coverage	A brief review of the UK sugar market with commentary and statistics covering production, imports, consumption and companies.
Frequency	Regular.
Web facilities	General details of all publications and services on site and some basic data.
Cost	Free.
Comments	
Address	24 Chiswell Street, London EC1Y 4SG
Tel./e-mail	0207 972 6600
Fax/Website	0207 972 6699 www.czarnikow.com

CACI INFORMATION SOLUTIONS

Title	**Wealth of the Nation Report**
Coverage	Data on levels of disposable incomes by area and postcodes and details of best and worst areas.
Frequency	Annual.
Web facilities	Abridged version of the report available free on site.
Cost	On request.
Comments	
Address	CACI House, Kensington Village, Avonmore Road, London W14 8TS
Tel./e-mail	0207 602 6000 info@caci.co.uk
Fax/Website	0207 603 5862 www.caci.co.uk

CACI INFORMATION SOLUTIONS

Title	**Acorn Profiles/Area Reports**
Coverage	Various demographic and area profiles based on an analysis of census data plus postcode address files and electoral roll data. Also uses Target Group Index (TGI) and Financial Research Survey (FRS) data as well as some other market research sources.
Frequency	Continuous.
Web facilities	The site has access to various free sets of data, area reports and survey summaries.
Cost	On request and depending on range and nature of information required.
Comments	
Address	CACI House, Kensington Village, Avonmore Road, London W14 8TS
Tel./e-mail	0207 602 6000 info@caci.co.uk
Fax/Website	0207 603 5862 www.caci.co.uk

CADBURY TREBOR BASSETT

Title	**Confectionery Market**
Coverage	Figures for recent years on the confectionery market with data on specific sectors, e.g. chocolate, sugar, seasonal sales etc. Data on key brands, trade sector performance, advertising, retailing, the consumer. Includes a supporting commentary.
Frequency	Annual.
Web facilities	Free access to recent reports on the site under the 'Information and Careers' page.
Cost	Free.
Comments	
Address	PO Box 12, Bournville, Birmingham B30 2LU
Tel./e-mail	0121 451 4444
Fax/Website	www.cadbury.co.uk

CAMBRIDGE ECONOMETRICS

Title	**Industry and the British Economy**
Coverage	A detailed forecast of the British economy and industry with forecasts up to ten years ahead. Detailed analysis of 41 industrial sectors and 19 service sectors.
Frequency	Twice yearly.
Web facilities	General details and free summary statistics, on the site. Paid-for access to all data.
Cost	£2000.
Comments	Published in January and June.
Address	Covent Garden, Cambridge CB1 2HS
Tel./e-mail	01223 460760 info@camecon.com
Fax/Website	01223 464378 www.camecon.co.uk

CAMBRIDGE ECONOMETRICS

Title	**Regional Economic Prospects**
Coverage	Detailed analysis and forecasts on economic trends in the UK regions. Long-term forecasts and commentary.
Frequency	Twice yearly.
Web facilities	General details and free summary statistics, on the site. Paid-for access to all data.
Cost	£2000.
Comments	Published in February and July.
Address	Covent Garden, Cambridge CB1 2HS
Tel./e-mail	01223 460760 info@camecon.com
Fax/Website	01223 464378 www.camecon.co.uk

CAN MAKERS

Title	**Can Makers UK Market Report**
Coverage	Details of the beverage can industry and market, broken down by soft drinks and beer. Market data covers the latest four years in some tables and there are also some data on European trends. Based mainly on a mixture of non-official sources including trade association, market research and Gallup data. Detailed commentary supports the tables.
Frequency	Annual.
Web facilities	Free access to data on site and facilities to obtain reports electronically.
Cost	Free.
Comments	Also publishes regular press releases and bulletins with statistics and a European report.
Address	New Bridge Street House, 30–34 Westminster Bridge Street, London EC4V 6BJ
Tel./e-mail	0207 072 4083 canmakers@gciuk.com
Fax/Website	0207 072 4020 www.canmakers.co.uk

CAPITAL ECONOMICS

Title	**UK Macro Service**
Coverage	Various reports and bulletins are part of the service including weekly, monthly and quarterly economic data and trends reports plus quarterly forecasts up to two years ahead.
Frequency	Regular.
Web facilities	General details on site and sample copies.
Cost	£3000 plus VAT (compact service); £6000 plus VAT (full service).
Comments	
Address	150 Buckingham Palace Road, London SW1W 9TR
Tel./e-mail	0207 823 5000 business@capitaleconomics.com
Fax/Website	0207 823 6666 www.capitaleconomics.com

CAPITAL ECONOMICS

Title	**UK Consumer Service**
Coverage	Various reports and bulletins are part of the service including weekly, monthly and quarterly economic and consumer data and trends reports plus quarterly forecasts up to two years ahead.
Frequency	Regular.
Web facilities	General details on site and sample copies.
Cost	£3000 plus VAT (compact service); £6000 plus VAT (full service).
Comments	
Address	150 Buckingham Palace Road, London SW1W 9TR
Tel./e-mail	0207 823 5000 business@capitaleconomics.com
Fax/Website	0207 823 6666 www.capitaleconomics.com

CAPITAL ECONOMICS

Title	**UK Commercial Property**
Coverage	Various reports and bulletins are part of the service including weekly, monthly and quarterly economic and property data and trends reports plus property forecasts up to five years ahead.
Frequency	Regular.
Web facilities	General details on site and sample copies.
Cost	£3000 plus VAT (compact service); £6000 plus VAT (full service).
Comments	
Address	150 Buckingham Palace Road, London SW1W 9TR
Tel./e-mail	0207 823 5000 business@capitaleconomics.com
Fax/Website	0207 823 6666 www.capitaleconomics.com

CAPITAL ECONOMICS

Title	**UK Housing Market**
Coverage	Various reports and bulletins are part of the service including weekly, monthly and quarterly economic and housing market data and trends reports plus property forecasts up to five years ahead.
Frequency	Regular.
Web facilities	General details on site and sample copies.
Cost	£3000 plus VAT (compact service); £6000 plus VAT (full service).
Comments	
Address	150 Buckingham Palace Road, London SW1W 9TR
Tel./e-mail	0207 823 5000 business@capitaleconomics.com
Fax/Website	0207 823 6666 www.capitaleconomics.com

CARRICK JAMES MARKET RESEARCH

Title	**Child Omnibus**
Coverage	Continuous survey of children from the age of five upwards and teenagers up to the age of 19. Various questions relating to spending, behaviour, opinions, awareness, etc.
Frequency	Monthly.
Web facilities	General details of services on site.
Cost	Varies according to the range of questions/information required
Comments	Also carries out a regular *European Child Omnibus*.
Address	6 Homer Street, London W1H 1HN
Tel./e-mail	0207 724 3836
Fax/Website	0207 224 8257 www.cjmr.co.uk

CARRICK JAMES MARKET RESEARCH

Title	**Youth Omnibus**
Coverage	Based on a sample of 1200 young people aged between 11 and 24. Questions cover behaviour, spending, product and advertising awareness, etc.
Frequency	Six times per year.
Web facilities	General details of services on site.
Cost	Varies according to the range of questions/information required.
Comments	
Address	6 Homer Street, London W1H 1HN
Tel./e-mail	0207 724 3836
Fax/Website	0207 224 8257 www.cjmr.co.uk

CARRICK JAMES MARKET RESEARCH

Title	**Child Tracker**
Coverage	Regular survey based on 350 questions covering 280 topics about children.
Frequency	Regular.
Web facilities	General details of services on site.
Cost	Varies according to the range of questions/information required.
Comments	
Address	6 Homer Street, London W1H 1HN
Tel./e-mail	0207 724 3836
Fax/Website	0207 224 8257 www.cjmr.co.uk

CARRICK JAMES MARKET RESEARCH

Title	**Baby Tracker**
Coverage	Regular survey covering topics related to children aged six and under and their parents.
Frequency	Regular.
Web facilities	General details of services on site.
Cost	Varies according to the range of questions/information required.
Comments	
Address	6 Homer Street, London W1H 1HN
Tel./e-mail	0207 724 3836
Fax/Website	0207 224 8257 www.cjmr.co.uk

CARRICK JAMES MARKET RESEARCH

Title	**Mobile Phone Tracker**
Coverage	Regular survey of mobile phone users covering use, purchasing, ownership, networks, etc.
Frequency	Regular.
Web facilities	General details of services on site.
Cost	Varies according to the range of questions/information required.
Comments	
Address	6 Homer Street, London W1H 1HN
Tel./e-mail	0207 724 3836
Fax/Website	0207 224 8257 www.cjmr.co.uk

CATERER & HOTELKEEPER

Title	**The Bench**
Coverage	Daily online update of hotel revenues per room taken from various industry sources.
Frequency	Daily.
Web facilities	Access to update on site plus free access to trends data for key catering sectors.
Cost	£80.
Comments	The journal also has occasional features on catering and hotel sectors.
Address	Reed Business Publishing Ltd, Windsor Court, East Grinstead House, East Grinstead RH19 1XA
Tel./e-mail	01342 326972
Fax/Website	01342 335612 www.caterersearch.com

CATERER & HOTELKEEPER

Title	**Trends and Data**
Coverage	Various statistics on the catering and hotel trades available on the website. Arranged by segment – hotels, pubs, restaurants, foodservice etc. – and taken from various sources.
Frequency	Regular.
Web facilities	Free access to data on site.
Cost	£80.
Comments	The journal also has occasional features on hotel and catering sectors.
Address	Reed Business Publishing Ltd, Windsor Court, East Grinstead House, East Grinstead RH19 1XA
Tel./e-mail	01342 326972
Fax/Website	01342 335612 www.caterersearch.com

CB RICHARD ELLIS

Title	**UK Monthly Index**
Coverage	General commentary and statistics on property values and yields with a monthly index covering the latest 12 months. Based on data collected by the company.
Frequency	Monthly.
Web facilities	Free access to all reports (except the *Monthly Index*) on site.
Cost	On request.
Comments	Occasional reports on property trends and issues.
Address	Kingsley House, Wimpole Street, London W1G 0RE
Tel./e-mail	0207 182 2000 rosalind.pontifex@cbre.com
Fax/Website	0207 182 2001 www.cbre.com

CB RICHARD ELLIS

Title	**Central London Office Market**
Coverage	Rents, values and property availability in various areas of London, e.g. Docklands, West End, City, Mid-Town etc. Based on data collected by the company.
Frequency	Quarterly.
Web facilities	Free access to all reports (except the *Monthly Index*) on site.
Cost	Free.
Comments	Occasional reports on property trends and issues.
Address	Kingsley House, Wimpole Street, London W1G 0RE
Tel./e-mail	0207 182 2000 rosalind.pontifex@cbre.com
Fax/Website	0207 182 2001 www.cbre.com

CB RICHARD ELLIS

Title	**Retail Market Monitor**
Coverage	Data on retails revenues and investments based on data collected by the company.
Frequency	Quarterly.
Web facilities	Free access to all reports on site.
Cost	Free.
Comments	
Address	Kingsley House, Wimpole Street, London W1G 0RE
Tel./e-mail	0207 182 2000 rosalind.pontifex@cbre.com
Fax/Website	0207 182 2001 www.cbre.com

CB RICHARD ELLIS

Title	**London Retail Markets**
Coverage	Data on retail revenues and investments in London based on data collected by the company.
Frequency	Quarterly.
Web facilities	Free access to reports on site.
Cost	Free.
Comments	
Address	Kingsley House, Wimpole Street, London W1G 0RE
Tel./e-mail	0207 182 2000 rosalind.pontifex@cbre.com
Fax/Website	0207 182 2001 www.cbre.com

CB RICHARD ELLIS

Title	**Scottish Quarterly Index**
Coverage	General commentary and statistics on property values and yields based on data collected by the company.
Frequency	Quarterly.
Web facilities	Free access to report on the site.
Cost	Free.
Comments	
Address	Kingsley House, Wimpole Street, London W1G 0RE
Tel./e-mail	0207 182 2000 rosalind.pontifex@cbre.com
Fax/Website	0207 182 2001 www.cbre.com

CB RICHARD ELLIS

Title	**Northern Ireland Property Market Review**
Coverage	General commentary and statistics on property trends in Northern Ireland based largely on data collected by the company.
Frequency	Quarterly.
Web facilities	Free access to report on the site.
Cost	Free.
Comments	
Address	Kingsley House, Wimpole Street, London W1G 0RE
Tel./e-mail	0207 182 2000 rosalind.pontifex@cbre.com
Fax/Website	0207 182 2001 www.cbre.com

CB RICHARD ELLIS

Title	**Regional Office Markets Annual Review**
Coverage	General commentary and statistics on office markets in key regions across the UK. Based on data collected by the company.
Frequency	Annual.
Web facilities	Free access to the report on the site.
Cost	Free.
Comments	
Address	Kingsley House, Wimpole Street, London W1G 0RE
Tel./e-mail	0207 182 2000 rosalind.pontifex@cbre.com
Fax/Website	0207 182 2001 www.cbre.com

CEMENT ADMIXTURES ASSOCIATION

Title	**Statistical Return**
Coverage	Sales by weight and value for a variety of admixtures based on a survey of members.
Frequency	Regular.
Web facilities	
Cost	Free.
Comments	
Address	36a Tilehouse Green Lane, Knowle B93 9EY
Tel./e-mail	01564 776362
Fax/Website	01564 776362 www.admixtures.org.uk

CENTRE FOR SOCIOLOGY OF SPORT

Title	**National Fan Surveys**
Coverage	Regular surveys of a sample of UK football supporters.
Frequency	Regular.
Web facilities	Free summary data on site.
Cost	Free.
Comments	Previously the Norman Chester Centre for Football Research.
Address	University of Leicester, University Road, Leicester LE1 7RH
Tel./e-mail	0116 252 2745 jxw@le.ac.uk
Fax/Website	www.le.ac.uk/so/css/

CENTRE FOR THE SOCIOLOGY OF SPORT

Title	**Factsheets**
Coverage	Details of football attendances, match receipts, other financial data, miscellaneous data. Based mainly on non-official sources.
Frequency	Regular.
Web facilities	Free *Factsheet* data on site.
Cost	Free.
Comments	Previously the Norman Chester Centre for Football Research.
Address	University of Leicester, University Road, Leicester LE1 7RH
Tel./e-mail	0116 252 2745 jxw@le.ac.uk
Fax/Website	www.le.ac.uk/so/css/

CENTRE FOR THE STUDY OF REGULATED INDUSTRIES

Title	**UK Airports Industry: Airport Statistics**
Coverage	Operating and financial statistics on UK airports with aggregate data and statistics on specific airports. Based on data collected by CIPFA and the centre.
Frequency	Annual.
Web facilities	General details of all publications and online ordering facilities on site.
Cost	£40.
Comments	All other annual statistical titles previously published have been stopped.
Address	School of Management, University of Bath, Bath BA2 7AY
Tel./e-mail	01225 323197 mnsjsm@management.bath.ac.uk
Fax/Website	01225 323221 www.bath.ac.uk/cri/

CHAMBER OF SHIPPING

Title	**Annual Review**
Coverage	Some statistics on fleet, trade and other market trends.
Frequency	Annual.
Web facilities	General details of statistics and some free summary data, on the website.
Cost	Free.
Comments	Usually published at the end of March. Also publishes quarterly journal – *Making Waves*.
Address	12 Carthusian Street, London EC1M 6EZ
Tel./e-mail	0207 417 2800 postmaster@british-shipping.org
Fax/Website	0207 417 2080 www.british-shipping.org

CHARITIES AID FOUNDATION

Title	**Charity Trends**
Coverage	Data and analysis on charity giving and receiving, top charities. Based on CAF research.
Frequency	Annual.
Web facilities	General details of all reports and online ordering facilities on site.
Cost	On request.
Comments	Marketed and distributed by Caritas Data Ltd at Pavilion House, 8 Shepherdess Walk, London N1 7LB; tel 0207 566 8210.
Address	24 Stevenson Way, London NW1 2DP
Tel./e-mail	0207 209 5151　　　info@cafonline.org
Fax/Website	0207 209 5049　　　www.cafonline.org

CHARTERED INSTITUTE OF LIBRARY AND INFORMATION PROFESSIONALS (CILIP)

Title	**CILIP Pay and Salary Survey**
Coverage	Pay and salary trends by job types based on data collected from the members.
Frequency	Annual.
Web facilities	Access for members to detailed salary surveys and guides on site.
Cost	On request.
Comments	Summary results published in monthly *Library and Information Update* (usually in June).
Address	7 Ridgmount Street, London WC1E 7AT
Tel./e-mail	0207 255 0500　　　info@cilip.org.uk
Fax/Website	0207 355 0505　　　www.cilip.org.uk

CHARTERED INSTITUTE OF MARKETING

Title	**Marketing Trends Survey**
Coverage	A review of economic and business trends, trends in the marketing sector.
Frequency	Quarterly.
Web facilities	Available free on the website along with details of other surveys, including some ad hoc research.
Cost	Free.
Comments	
Address	Moor Hall, Cookham, Maidenhead SL6 9QH
Tel./e-mail	01628 427500　　　marketing@cim.co.uk
Fax/Website	01628 427499　　　www.cim.co.uk

CHARTERED INSTITUTE OF PERSONNEL AND DEVELOPMENT

Title	**Absence Management Survey**
Coverage	Analysis and data on rate of sickness absence, costs, causes, targets and workplace stress.
Frequency	Annual.
Web facilities	Free downloads of reports on site.
Cost	
Comments	
Address	151 The Broadway, London SW19 1JQ
Tel./e-mail	0208 612 6400 press@cipd.co.uk
Fax/Website	0208 263 3333 www.cipd.co.uk

CHARTERED INSTITUTE OF PERSONNEL AND DEVELOPMENT

Title	**Reward Management Survey**
Coverage	Information and benchmarking data on current practices and policies in reward management. Includes data on benefits, incentives, pensions, etc.
Frequency	Annual.
Web facilities	Free downloads of reports on site.
Cost	
Comments	
Address	151 The Broadway, London SW19 1JQ
Tel./e-mail	0208 612 6400 press@cipd.co.uk
Fax/Website	0208 263 3333 www.cipd.co.uk

CHARTERED INSTITUTE OF PERSONNEL AND DEVELOPMENT

Title	**Personal Rewards Survey**
Coverage	Data and analysis on pay and benefits by grade, sector, HR specialisms, organisation size and region.
Frequency	Annual.
Web facilities	Free PDF of key findings and summary data on site.
Cost	Published in association with Croner Reward.
Comments	
Address	151 The Broadway, London SW19 1JQ
Tel./e-mail	0208 612 6400 press@cipd.co.uk
Fax/Website	0208 263 3333 www.cipd.co.uk

CHARTERED INSTITUTE OF PERSONNEL AND DEVELOPMENT

Title	**Training and Development**
Coverage	Data and analysis on training spending, training activities, skill requirements, etc.
Frequency	Annual.
Web facilities	Free downloads of reports on site.
Cost	
Comments	
Address	151 The Broadway, London SW19 1JQ
Tel./e-mail	0208 612 6400 press@cipd.co.uk
Fax/Website	0208 263 3333 www.cipd.co.uk

CHARTERED INSTITUTE OF PERSONNEL AND DEVELOPMENT

Title	**Labour Market Outlook**
Coverage	A survey of recruitment, pay, redundancies and topical issues such as migrant workers with analysis by type of job, sectors, etc. Based on a survey by CIPD.
Frequency	Quarterly.
Web facilities	Free downloads of reports on site.
Cost	Free.
Comments	
Address	151 The Broadway, London SW19 1JQ
Tel./e-mail	0208 612 6400 press@cipd.co.uk
Fax/Website	0208 263 3333 www.cipd.co.uk

CHARTERED INSTITUTE OF PUBLIC FINANCE AND ACCOUNTANCT (CIPFA)

Title	**Health Information Services**
Coverage	Data for spending, resources and services for NHS Trusts, Primary Care Trusts and Strategic Health Authorities.
Frequency	Continuous.
Web facilities	
Cost	£750 (plus VAT).
Comments	An online service available via the website.
Address	NLA Tower, 12–16 Addiscombe Road, Croydon CR0 0XT
Tel./e-mail	0208 667 1144 sisinfo@ipf.co.uk
Fax/Website	0208 681 6741 www.cipfastats.net

CHARTERED INSTITUTE OF PUBLIC FINANCE AND ACCOUNTANCY (CIPFA)

Title	**External Funding Statistics**
Coverage	Data on fund operations, bids submitted and successful, service areas, etc. Based on data supplied by local authorities.
Frequency	Annual.
Web facilities	
Cost	£110.
Comments	Detailed data also available online for £200.
Address	NLA Tower, 12–16 Addiscombe Road, Croydon CR0 0XT
Tel./e-mail	0208 667 1144 sisinfo@ipf.co.uk
Fax/Website	0208 681 6741 www.cipfastats.net

CHARTERED INSTITUTE OF PUBLIC FINANCE AND ACCOUNTANCY (CIPFA)

Title	**Prudential Indicators**
Coverage	Financial and other statistics based around CIPFA's Prudential Code.
Frequency	Quarterly.
Web facilities	
Cost	Free.
Comments	Available free on the website.
Address	NLA Tower, 12–16 Addiscombe Road, Croydon CR0 0XT
Tel./e-mail	0208 667 1144 sisinfo@ipf.co.uk
Fax/Website	0208 681 6741 www.cipfastats.net

CHARTERED INSTITUTE OF PUBLIC FINANCE AND ACCOUNTANCY (CIPFA)

Title	**Cultural Statistics in Scotland**
Coverage	Expenditure data for local authorities in Scotland on cultural activities. Based on data supplied by local authorities.
Frequency	Annual.
Web facilities	
Cost	£110.
Comments	Detailed data also available online for £300.
Address	NLA Tower, 12–16 Addiscombe Road, Croydon CR0 0XT
Tel./e-mail	0208 667 1144 sisinfo@ipf.co.uk
Fax/Website	0208 681 6741 www.cipfastats.net

CHARTERED INSTITUTE OF PUBLIC FINANCE AND ACCOUNTANCY (CIPFA)

Title	**Administration of Justice Statistics**
Coverage	Expenditure and income figures for both magistrates' and coroners' courts per thousand population. Based on returns received by CIPFA.
Frequency	Annual.
Web facilities	General details and paid-for access to all data via the SIS Internet Subscription.
Cost	£60.
Comments	Detailed data also available online for £150.
Address	NLA Tower, 12–16 Addiscombe Road, Croydon CR0 0XT
Tel./e-mail	0208 667 1144 sisinfo@ipf.co.uk
Fax/Website	0208 681 6741 www.cipfastats.net

CHARTERED INSTITUTE OF PUBLIC FINANCE AND ACCOUNTANCY (CIPFA)

Title	**Archive Services Statistics**
Coverage	Statistics on the organisation and financing of archives based on returns from local authorities collected by CIPFA.
Frequency	Annual.
Web facilities	General details and paid-for access to all data via the SIS Internet Subscription.
Cost	£60.
Comments	Detailed data also available online for £150.
Address	NLA Tower, 12–16 Addiscombe Road, Croydon CR0 OXT
Tel./e-mail	0208 667 1144 sisinfo@ipf.co.uk
Fax/Website	0208 681 6741 www.cipfastats.net

CHARTERED INSTITUTE OF PUBLIC FINANCE AND ACCOUNTANCY (CIPFA)

Title	**Capital Expenditure and Treasury Management Statistics**
Coverage	An analysis of capital payments and debt statistics for individual local authorities in England, Wales, Scotland and Northern Ireland. Based on data collected by CIPFA.
Frequency	Annual.
Web facilities	General details and paid-for access to all data via the SIS Internet Subscription.
Cost	£110.
Comments	Detailed data also available online for £300.
Address	NLA Tower, 12–16 Addiscombe Road, Croydon CR0 0XT
Tel./e-mail	0208 667 1144 sisinfo@ipf.co.uk
Fax/Website	0208 681 6741 www.cipfastats.net

CHARTERED INSTITUTE OF PUBLIC FINANCE AND ACCOUNTANCY (CIPFA)

Title	**Cemeteries Statistics**
Coverage	Expenditure, income, fees and non-financial data on cemeteries in local authority areas. Based on data collected by CIPFA.
Frequency	Annual.
Web facilities	General details and paid-for access to all data via the SIS Internet Subscription.
Cost	£60.
Comments	Detailed data also available online for £150.
Address	NLA Tower, 12–16 Addiscombe Road, Croydon CR0 0XT
Tel./e-mail	0208 667 1144 sisinfo@ipf.co.uk
Fax/Website	0208 681 6741 www.cipfastats.net

CHARTERED INSTITUTE OF PUBLIC FINANCE AND ACCOUNTANCY (CIPFA)

Title	**Council Tax Demands and Precepts Statistics**
Coverage	Statistics on the level of demands and revenues from council tax based on returns from local authorities collected by CIPFA.
Frequency	Annual.
Web facilities	General details and paid-for access to all data via the SIS Internet Subscription.
Cost	£85.
Comments	Detailed data also available online for £200.
Address	NLA Tower, 12–16 Addiscombe Road, Croydon CR0 0XT
Tel./e-mail	0208 667 1144 sisinfo@ipf.co.uk
Fax/Website	0208 681 6741 www.cipfastats.net

CHARTERED INSTITUTE OF PUBLIC FINANCE AND ACCOUNTANCY (CIPFA)

Title	**County Farms and Rural Estates Statistics**
Coverage	Financial and other data on county farms and rural estates by local authority area. Based on data collected by CIPFA.
Frequency	Annual.
Web facilities	General details and paid-for access to all data via the SIS Internet Subscription.
Cost	£60.
Comments	Detailed data also available online for £150.
Address	NLA Tower, 12–16 Addiscombe Road, Croydon CR0 0XT
Tel./e-mail	0208 667 1144 sisinfo@ipf.co.uk
Fax/Website	0208 681 6741 www.cipfastats.net

CHARTERED INSTITUTE OF PUBLIC FINANCE AND ACCOUNTANCY (CIPFA)

Title	**Crematoria – Actuals**
Coverage	Expenditure, income, fees and non-financial data on crematoria by local authority area. Based on data collected by CIPFA.
Frequency	Annual.
Web facilities	General details and paid-for access to all data via the SIS Internet Subscription.
Cost	£60.
Comments	Detailed data also available online for £150.
Address	NLA Tower, 12–16 Addiscombe Road, Croydon CR0 0XT
Tel./e-mail	0208 667 1144 sisinfo@ipf.co.uk
Fax/Website	0208 681 6741 www.cipfastats.net

CHARTERED INSTITUTE OF PUBLIC FINANCE AND ACCOUNTANCY (CIPFA)

Title	**Direct Service Organisations Statistics**
Coverage	Financial, organisational and related data on direct service organisations in local authorities. Based on returns to CIPFA from local authorities.
Frequency	Annual.
Web facilities	General details and paid-for access to all data via the SIS Internet Subscription.
Cost	£110.
Comments	Detailed data also available online for £200.
Address	NLA Tower, 12-16 Addiscombe Road, Croydon CR0 0XT
Tel./e-mail	0208 667 1144 sisinfo@ipf.co.uk
Fax/Website	0208 681 6741 www.cipfastats.net

CHARTERED INSTITUTE OF PUBLIC FINANCE AND ACCOUNTANCY (CIPFA)

Title	**Education – Actuals**
Coverage	Non-financial data on pupil, school and teacher numbers and financial data split by types of school and local authority area. The publication now also includes education unit costs, previously published in a separate volume. These costs cover institutional costs, pupil and student support costs, capital costs, salary costs, recurrent expenditure and university costs. Based largely on central government data.
Frequency	Annual.
Web facilities	General details and paid-for access to all data via the SIS Internet Subscription.
Cost	£85.
Comments	Detailed data also available online for £200.
Address	NLA Tower, 12–16 Addiscombe Road, Croydon CR0 0XT
Tel./e-mail	0208 667 1144 sisinfo@ipf.co.uk
Fax/Website	0208 681 6741 www.cipfastats.net

CHARTERED INSTITUTE OF PUBLIC FINANCE AND ACCOUNTANCY (CIPFA)

Title	**Environmental Health Statistics**
Coverage	Financial and other data relating to environmental health in specific local authorities. Based on data collected by CIPFA.
Frequency	Annual.
Web facilities	General details and paid-for access to all data via the SIS Internet Subscription.
Cost	£85.
Comments	Detailed data also available online for £200.
Address	NLA Tower, 12–16 Addiscombe Road, Croydon CR0 0XT
Tel./e-mail	0208 667 1144 sisinfo@ipf.co.uk
Fax/Website	0208 681 6741 www.cipfastats.net

CHARTERED INSTITUTE OF PUBLIC FINANCE AND ACCOUNTANCY (CIPFA)

Title	**Finance and General Statistics**
Coverage	Summary information on local authority income and expenditure with data for each local authority in England and Wales. Based on estimates collected by CIPFA with additional data on estimated income and expenditure per head of the population.
Frequency	Annual.
Web facilities	General details and paid-for access to all data via the SIS Internet Subscription.
Cost	£110.
Comments	Detailed data also available online for £500.
Address	NLA Tower, 12–16 Addiscombe Road, Croydon CR0 0XT
Tel./e-mail	0208 667 1144 sisinfo@ipf.co.uk
Fax/Website	0208 681 6741 www.cipfastats.net

CHARTERED INSTITUTE OF PUBLIC FINANCE AND ACCOUNTANCY (CIPFA)

Title	**Fire and Rescue Services Statistics**
Coverage	Summary data on fire service income and expenditure and similar figures for each local authority and per thousand population. Also statistics on fire stations, training, manpower, applications, return of calls and inspections. Based on returns from local authorities received by CIPFA.
Frequency	Annual.
Web facilities	General details and paid-for access to all data via the SIS Internet Subscription.
Cost	£85.
Comments	Detailed data also available online for £200.
Address	NLA Tower, 12–16 Addiscombe Road, Croydon CR0 0XT
Tel./e-mail	0208 667 1144 sisinfo@ipf.co.uk
Fax/Website	0208 681 6741 www.cipfastats.net

CHARTERED INSTITUTE OF PUBLIC FINANCE AND ACCOUNTANCY (CIPFA)

Title	**Personal Social Services – Estimates**
Coverage	Data on revenue, income and expenditure plus some non-financial data.
Frequency	Annual.
Web facilities	General details and paid-for access to all data via the SIS Internet Subscription.
Cost	£85.
Comments	Detailed data also available online for £300.
Address	NLA Tower, 12–16 Addiscombe Road, Croydon CR0 0XT
Tel./e-mail	0208 667 1144 sisinfo@ipf.co.uk
Fax/Website	0208 681 6741 www.cipfastats.net

CHARTERED INSTITUTE OF PUBLIC FINANCE AND ACCOUNTANCY (CIPFA)

Title	**Highways and Transportation Statistics**
Coverage	Data on highways and transportation expenditure by county councils in England and Wales. Based on returns received by CIPFA.
Frequency	Annual.
Web facilities	General details and paid-for access to all data via the SIS Internet Subscription.
Cost	£85.
Comments	Detailed data also available online for £200.
Address	NLA Tower, 12–16 Addiscombe Road, Croydon CR0 0XT
Tel./e-mail	0208 667 1144 sisinfo@ipf.co.uk
Fax/Website	0208 681 6741 www.cipfastats.net

CHARTERED INSTITUTE OF PUBLIC FINANCE AND ACCOUNTANCY (CIPFA)

Title	**Homelessness Statistics**
Coverage	A financial survey of the operations of the Housing (Homeless Persons) Act with data for individual local authorities. Based on data collected by CIPFA.
Frequency	Annual.
Web facilities	General details and paid-for access to all data via the SIS Internet Subscription.
Cost	£60.
Comments	Detailed data also available online for £150.
Address	NLA Tower, 12–16 Addiscombe Road, Croydon CR0 0XT
Tel./e-mail	0208 667 1144 sisinfo@ipf.co.uk
Fax/Website	0208 681 6741 www.cipfastats.net

CHARTERED INSTITUTE OF PUBLIC FINANCE AND ACCOUNTANCY (CIPFA)

Title	**Housing Rent Arrears and Benefits Statistics**
Coverage	An analysis of rent arrears and benefits by local authority area. Based on returns to CIPFA from local authorities.
Frequency	Annual.
Web facilities	General details and paid-for access to all data via the SIS Internet Subscription.
Cost	£85.
Comments	Detailed data also available online for £150.
Address	NLA Tower, 12–16 Addiscombe Road, Croydon CR0 0XT
Tel./e-mail	0208 667 1144 sisinfo@ipf.co.uk
Fax/Website	0208 681 6741 www.cipfastats.net

CHARTERED INSTITUTE OF PUBLIC FINANCE AND ACCOUNTANCY (CIPFA)

Title	**Housing Rents and Service Charges Statistics**
Coverage	An analysis of the housing stock by age and type, average weekly rents and rebates and allowances. Data for individual local authorities and summary tables for individual planning regions. Based on returns to CIPFA from local authorities.
Frequency	Annual.
Web facilities	General details and paid-for access to all data via the SIS Internet Subscription.
Cost	£85.
Comments	Detailed data also available online for £200.
Address	NLA Tower, 12–16 Addiscombe Road, Croydon CR0 0XT
Tel./e-mail	0208 667 1144 sisinfo@ipf.co.uk
Fax/Website	0208 681 6741 www.cipfastats.net

CHARTERED INSTITUTE OF PUBLIC FINANCE AND ACCOUNTANCY (CIPFA)

Title	**Housing Revenue Account Statistics**
Coverage	Figures for Housing Revenue Account income in total and for each housing authority in England and Wales. Based on a combination of central government statistics and CIPFA data.
Frequency	Annual.
Web facilities	General details and paid-for access to all data via the SIS Internet Subscription.
Cost	£85.
Comments	Detailed data also available online for £200.
Address	NLA Tower, 12–16 Addiscombe Road, Croydon CR0 0XT
Tel./e-mail	0208 667 1144 sisinfo@ipf.co.uk
Fax/Website	0208 681 6741 www.cipfastats.net

CHARTERED INSTITUTE OF PUBLIC FINANCE AND ACCOUNTANCY (CIPFA)

Title	**Leisure and Recreation Statistics**
Coverage	Estimated expenditure and income on sports and recreation, cultural and other related facilities by local authory area. Based on data collected by CIPFA from local authorities.
Frequency	Annual.
Web facilities	General details and paid-for access to all data via the SIS Internet Subscription.
Cost	£85.
Comments	Detailed data also available online for £200.
Address	NLA Tower, 12–16 Addiscombe Road, Croydon CR0 0XT
Tel./e-mail	0208 667 1144 sisinfo@ipf.co.uk
Fax/Website	0208 681 6741 www.cipfastats.net

CHARTERED INSTITUTE OF PUBLIC FINANCE AND ACCOUNTANCY (CIPFA)

Title	**Charges for Leisure Services Statistics**
Coverage	Sample survey of charges for leisure centre facilities, swimming pools and outdoor sports. Based on a sample of 150 local authorities.
Frequency	Annual.
Web facilities	General details and paid-for access to all data via the SIS Internet Subscription.
Cost	£60.
Comments	Detailed data also available online for £200.
Address	NLA Tower, 12–16 Addiscombe Road, Croydon CR0 0XT
Tel./e-mail	0208 667 1144 sisinfo@ipf.co.uk
Fax/Website	0208 681 6741 www.cipfastats.net

CHARTERED INSTITUTE OF PUBLIC FINANCE AND ACCOUNTANCY (CIPFA)

Title	**Local Authority Pension Fund Investment Statistics**
Coverage	A ten-year historical record of superannuation statistics with the first issue, published in 1995, covering the years 1985 to 1995. Based on data supplied by local authorities.
Frequency	Annual.
Web facilities	General details and paid-for access to all data via the SIS Internet Subscription.
Cost	£180.
Comments	
Address	NLA Tower, 12–16 Addiscombe Road, Croydon CR0 0XT
Tel./e-mail	0208 667 1144 sisinfo@ipf.co.uk
Fax/Website	0208 681 6741 www.cipfastats.net

CHARTERED INSTITUTE OF PUBLIC FINANCE AND ACCOUNTANCY (CIPFA)

Title	**Local Government Comparative Statistics**
Coverage	Summary statistical indicators covering the range of local authority services. Based on a combination of data collected by CIPFA and other non-official sources.
Frequency	Annual.
Web facilities	General details and paid-for access to all data via the SIS Internet Subscription.
Cost	£110.
Comments	Detailed data also available online for £300.
Address	NLA Tower, 12–16 Addiscombe Road, Croydon CR0 0XT
Tel./e-mail	0208 667 1144 sisinfo@ipf.co.uk
Fax/Website	0208 681 6741 www.cipfastats.net

CHARTERED INSTITUTE OF PUBLIC FINANCE AND ACCOUNTANCY (CIPFA)

Title	**Personal Social Services – Actuals**
Coverage	An analysis of residential, day and community care provision giving gross and net expenditure and the number of clients by local authority area. Based on data collected by CIPFA.
Frequency	Annual.
Web facilities	General details and paid-for access to all data via the SIS Internet Subscription.
Cost	£85.
Comments	Detailed data also available online for £300.
Address	NLA Tower, 12–16 Addiscombe Road, Croydon CR0 0XT
Tel./e-mail	0208 667 1144 sisinfo@ipf.co.uk
Fax/Website	0208 681 6741 www.cipfastats.net

CHARTERED INSTITUTE OF PUBLIC FINANCE AND ACCOUNTANCY (CIPFA)

Title	**Planning and Development Statistics**
Coverage	Capital and revenue expenditure on the planning and development functions in summary and by individual local authority. Based on data collected by CIPFA.
Frequency	Annual.
Web facilities	General details and paid-for access to all data via the SIS Internet Subscription.
Cost	£85.
Comments	Detailed data also available online for £200.
Address	NLA Tower, 12–16 Addiscombe Road, Croydon CR0 0XT
Tel./e-mail	0208 667 1144 sisinfo@ipf.co.uk
Fax/Website	0208 681 6741 www.cipfastats.net

CHARTERED INSTITUTE OF PUBLIC FINANCE AND ACCOUNTANCY (CIPFA)

Title	**Police Actuals Statistics**
Coverage	Figures are given for income, expenditure and manpower in total and by individual police force and regional crime squad. Based on data collected by CIPFA.
Frequency	Annual.
Web facilities	General details and paid-for access to all data via the SIS Internet Subscription.
Cost	£85.
Comments	Detailed data also available online for £200.
Address	NLA Tower, 12–16 Addiscombe Road, Croydon CR0 0XT
Tel./e-mail	0208 667 1144 sisinfo@ipf.co.uk
Fax/Website	0208 681 6741 www.cipfastats.net

CHARTERED INSTITUTE OF PUBLIC FINANCE AND ACCOUNTANCY (CIPFA)

Title	**Probation Service Statistics**
Coverage	Expenditure and income in the probation service per thousand population aged 15–29 and manpower for the service in England and Wales. Based on data collected by CIPFA.
Frequency	Annual.
Web facilities	General details and paid-for access to all data via the SIS Internet Subscription.
Cost	£60.
Comments	Detailed data also available online for £150.
Address	NLA Tower, 12–16 Addiscombe Road, Croydon CR0 0XT
Tel./e-mail	0208 667 1144 sisinfo@ipf.co.uk
Fax/Website	0208 681 6741 www.cipfastats.net

CHARTERED INSTITUTE OF PUBLIC FINANCE AND ACCOUNTANCY (CIPFA)

Title	**Public Libraries Actuals Statistics**
Coverage	Final out-turn figures for income and expenditure, manpower, agency services, books and other stocks and service points are given in total and for each library service in Great Britain and Northern Ireland.
Frequency	Annual.
Web facilities	General details and paid-for access to all data via the SIS Internet Subscription.
Cost	£85.
Comments	Detailed data also available online for £300.
Address	NLA Tower, 12–16 Addiscombe Road, Croydon CR0 0XT
Tel./e-mail	0208 667 1144 sisinfo@ipf.co.uk
Fax/Website	0208 681 6741 www.cipfastats.net

CHARTERED INSTITUTE OF PUBLIC FINANCE AND ACCOUNTANCY (CIPFA)

Title	**Revenue Collection Statistics**
Coverage	Revenue collection statistics broken down by local authority area and based on returns to CIPFA from local authorities.
Frequency	Annual.
Web facilities	General details and paid-for access to all data via the SIS Internet Subscription.
Cost	£85.
Comments	Detailed data also available online for £200.
Address	NLA Tower, 12–16 Addiscombe Road, Croydon CR0 0XT
Tel./e-mail	0208 667 1144 sisinfo@ipf.co.uk
Fax/Website	0208 681 6741 www.cipfastats.net

CHARTERED INSTITUTE OF PUBLIC FINANCE AND ACCOUNTANCY (CIPFA)

Title	**Trading Standards Statistics**
Coverage	Financial and non-financial data on trading standards departments with data for individual local authorities. Based on data collected by CIPFA.
Frequency	Annual.
Web facilities	General details and paid-for access to all data via the SIS Internet Subscription.
Cost	£85.
Comments	Detailed data also available online for £150.
Address	NLA Tower, 12–16 Addiscombe Road, Croydon CR0 0XT
Tel./e-mail	0208 667 1144 sisinfo@ipf.co.uk
Fax/Website	0208 681 6741 www.cipfastats.net

CHARTERED INSTITUTE OF PUBLIC FINANCE AND ACCOUNTANCY (CIPFA)

Title	**Highways and Transportation Estimates Statistics**
Coverage	Data on highways and transportation expenditure by county councils in England and Wales.
Frequency	Annual.
Web facilities	General details and paid-for access to all data via the SIS Internet Subscription.
Cost	£85.
Comments	Detailed data also available online for £200.
Address	NLA Tower, 12–16 Addiscombe Road, Croydon CR0 0XT
Tel./e-mail	0208 667 1144 sisinfo@ipf.co.uk
Fax/Website	0208 681 6741 www.cipfastats.net

CHARTERED INSTITUTE OF PUBLIC FINANCE AND ACCOUNTANCY (CIPFA)

Title	**Waste Collection and Disposal Statistics**
Coverage	Data on revenue income and expenditure, capital expenditure and financing, treatment methods, waste arising and reclaimed waste by tonnage, vehicle disposals, manpower and unit costs. Summary data and by local authority area. Based on data collected by CIPFA.
Frequency	Annual.
Web facilities	General details and paid-for access to all data via the SIS Internet Subscription.
Cost	£110.
Comments	Detailed data also available online for £300.
Address	NLA Tower, 12–16 Addiscombe Road, Croydon CR0 0XT
Tel./e-mail	0208 667 1144 sisinfo@ipf.co.uk
Fax/Website	0208 681 6741 www.cipfastats.net

CHARTERED INSTITUTE OF PUBLIC FINANCE AND ACCOUNTANCY (CIPFA)

Title	**Police Estimates Statistics**
Coverage	Financial and non-financial data on police service operations.
Frequency	Annual.
Web facilities	General details and paid-for access to all data via the SIS Internet Subscription.
Cost	£85.
Comments	Detailed data also available online for £200.
Address	NLA Tower, 12–16 Addiscombe Road, Croydon CR0 0XT
Tel./e-mail	0208 667 1144 sisinfo@ipf.co.uk
Fax/Website	0208 681 6741 www.cipfastats.net

CHARTERED INSTITUTE OF PUBLIC FINANCE AND ACCOUNTANCY (CIPFA)

Title	**Public Libraries Estimates Statistics**
Coverage	Financial and non-financial estimates of public library operations.
Frequency	Annual.
Web facilities	General details and paid-for access to all data via the SIS Internet Subscription.
Cost	£60.
Comments	Detailed data also available online for £150
Address	NLA Tower, 12–16 Addiscombe Road, Croydon CR0 0XT
Tel./e-mail	0208 667 1144 sisinfo@ipf.co.uk
Fax/Website	0208 681 6741 www.cipfastats.net

CHARTERED INSTITUTE OF PUBLIC FINANCE AND ACCOUNTANCY (CIPFA)

Title	**Education – Estimates**
Coverage	Financial and non-financial estimates for education authorities.
Frequency	Annual.
Web facilities	General details and paid-for access to all data via the SIS Internet Subscription.
Cost	£85.
Comments	Detailed data also available online for £200.
Address	NLA Tower, 12–16 Addiscombe Road, Croydon CR0 0XT
Tel./e-mail	0208 667 1144 sisinfo@ipf.co.uk
Fax/Website	0208 681 6741 www.cipfastats.net

CHARTERED INSTITUTE OF PUBLIC FINANCE AND ACCOUNTANCY (CIPFA)

Title	**Local Authority Assets Statistics**
Coverage	An analysis of local authority balance sheets with information on operational and non-operational assets, DSOs, other commercial services, Housing Revenue Account, long- and short-term borrowing, investments and reserves, and capital charges.
Frequency	Annual.
Web facilities	General details and paid-for access to all data via SIS Internet Subscription.
Cost	£110.
Comments	Detailed data also available online for £300.
Address	NLA Tower, 12–16 Addiscombe Road, Croydon CR0 0XT
Tel./e-mail	0208 667 1144 sisinfo@ipf.co.uk
Fax/Website	0208 681 6741 www.cipfastats.net

CHARTERED INSTITUTE OF PUBLIC FINANCE AND ACCOUNTANCY (CIPFA)

Title	**Local Government Trends**
Coverage	Provides a set of measures offering trend information by class of authority over a five-year period.
Frequency	Annual.
Web facilities	General details and paid-for access to all data via the SIS Internet Subscription.
Cost	£110.
Comments	Detailed data also available online for £300.
Address	NLA Tower, 12–16 Addiscombe Tower, Croydon CR0 0XT
Tel./e-mail	0208 667 1144 sisinfo@ipf.co.uk
Fax/Website	0208 681 6741 www.cipfastats.net

CHARTERED INSTITUTE OF PUBLIC FINANCE AND ACCOUNTANCY (CIPFA) – SCOTTISH BRANCH

Title	**Rating Review**
Coverage	Estimates of income and expenditure by Scottish local authority and service area.
Frequency	Annual.
Web facilities	
Cost	On request.
Comments	
Address	8 North West Circus Place, Edinburgh EH3 6ST
Tel./e-mail	0131 220 4316 cipfa.scotland@cipfa.org
Fax/Website	0131 220 4305 www.cipfa.org

CHEMICAL INDUSTRIES ASSOCIATION

Title	**UK Chemical Industry – Facts and Figures**
Coverage	Leaflet with basic statistics on the UK chemical industry with historical data over a ten-year period.
Frequency	Annual.
Web facilities	General details of publications on the website.
Cost	Free (single copy); £60 per pack of 100 for non-members, £30 for members.
Comments	The association also publishes international statistics.
Address	Kings Building, Smith Square, London SW1P 3JJ
Tel./e-mail	0207 834 3399 enquiries@cia.org.uk
Fax/Website	0207 834 4469 www.cia.org.uk

CHEMIST AND DRUGGIST

Title	**Chemist & Druggist Price List**
Coverage	Trade and retail prices for various products sold by chemists. Based on the journal's own survey with prices usually one month old.
Frequency	Monthly in a weekly journal.
Web facilities	Available on the web as as well as hard copy.
Cost	£173.
Comments	The journal also has regular features on specific markets and specific products sold via chemists.
Address	CMP Information Ltd, Sovereign House, Sovereign Way, Tonbridge TN9 1RW
Tel./e-mail	01732 377487 chemdrug@cmpinformation.com
Fax/Website	01732 367065 www.dotpharmacy.com

CHEMIST AND DRUGGIST

Title	**Business Trends Survey**
Coverage	Regular survey of retail chemists and pharmacists reporting on sales, prescription activity, margins and opinions on key issues.
Frequency	Quarterly in a weekly journal.
Web facilities	Some basic data from survey on site.
Cost	£173.
Comments	The journal also has regular features on specific markets and specific products sold via chemists.
Address	CMP Information Ltd, Sovereign House, Sovereign Way, Tonbridge TN9 1RW
Tel./e-mail	01732 377487 chemdrug@cmpinformation.com
Fax/Website	01732 367065 www.dotpharmacy.com

CHEMIST AND DRUGGIST

Title	**Business Statistics**
Coverage	Compilation of statistics from various sources covering general retail sales and spending, plus consumer spending on pharmaceuticals and personal care products, drug prices and costs.
Frequency	Eight times a year in a weekly journal.
Web facilities	General details on site.
Cost	£173.
Comments	The journal also has regular features on specific markets and specific products sold via chemists.
Address	CMP Information Ltd, Sovereign House, Sovereign Way, Tonbridge TN9 1RW
Tel./e-mail	01732 377487 chemdrug@cmpinformation.com
Fax/Website	01732 367065 www.dotpharmacy.com

CHILDWISE

Title	**Childwise Monitor Trends Report**
Coverage	Trend data on use of various media by children plus details of pocket money trends and children's spending by product. Based on a regular survey undertaken by the company with the key results presented in the report.
Frequency	Annual.
Web facilities	General details on the site.
Cost	£150 plus VAT.
Comments	
Address	111 Queens Road, Norwich NR1 3PL
Tel./e-mail	01603 630054 orders@childwise.co.uk
Fax/Website	01603 664083 www.childwise.co.uk

CHILLED FOODS ASSOCIATION

Title	**Market Data**
Coverage	General data on sales by product category in the chilled foods market.
Frequency	Regular.
Web facilities	Free access to data on site on 'Media' pages.
Cost	Free.
Comments	
Address	PO Box 6434, Kettering NN1 5XT
Tel./e-mail	01536 514365 cfa@chilledfood.org
Fax/Website	01536 515395 www.chilledfood.org

CINEMA ADVERTISING ASSOCIATION

Title	**Caviar – Cinema and Video Industry Audience Research**
Coverage	Provides audience data for cinema and pre-recorded videos from the age of seven upwards by film, genre and certificate. Based on a survey of almost 3000 people in various randomly selected sampling points around the country.
Frequency	Annual.
Web facilities	
Cost	£7150.
Comments	The data are also available online and on disc.
Address	12 Golden Square, London W1R 3AF
Tel./e-mail	0207 534 6363
Fax/Website	0207 534 6464

CINEMA ADVERTISING ASSOCIATION

Title	**CAA Admissions Monitor**
Coverage	A monthly measure of the attendances at all UK cinemas accepting advertising. Based on the association's own research.
Frequency	Monthly.
Web facilities	
Cost	Free.
Comments	The data are also available online and on disc.
Address	12 Golden Square, London W1R 3AF
Tel./e-mail	0207 534 6363
Fax/Website	0207 534 6464

CIVIL AVIATION AUTHORITY

Title	**UK Airlines**
Coverage	Operating and traffic statistics for UK airlines by domestic and international services and by types of operation, based on the CAA's own data. Statistics usually cover the previous month.
Frequency	Annual.
Web facilities	General details of publications on site.
Cost	On request.
Comments	CAA statistics also available on magnetic discs in Word for Windows format or on Excel spreadsheets. Disc subscription – £118 per annum, £11.80 for individual discs.
Address	Greville House, 37 Gratton Road, Cheltenham GL50 2BN
Tel./e-mail	01242 35151
Fax/Website	01242 584139 www.caa.co.uk

CIVIL AVIATION AUTHORITY

Title	**UK Airports**
Coverage	Monthly and annual statements of movements, passengers and cargo at UK airports, based on data collected by the CAA. Statistics usually cover the previous month.
Frequency	Monthly and annual.
Web facilities	General details of publications on site.
Cost	On request.
Comments	CAA statistics also available on magnetic disc in Word for Windows format or on Excel spreadsheets. Disc subscription – £118 per annum, £11.80 for individual discs.
Address	Greville House, 37 Gratton Road, Cheltenham GL50 2BN
Tel./e-mail	01242 35151
Fax/Website	01242 584139 www.caa.co.uk

COLLIERS CRE

Title	**Industrial Rents Map**
Coverage	A review and analysis of prime rents, secondary rents and land values based on company research.
Frequency	Annual.
Web facilities	Free access to PDF report on site.
Cost	Free.
Comments	
Address	Tower 42, 25 Old Broad Street, London EC2N 1HQ
Tel./e-mail	0207 935 4499 property@collierscre.co.uk
Fax/Website	0207 487 1894 www.colliers.com

COLLIERS CRE

Title	**Healthcare**
Coverage	Regular review of the healthcare market with commentary and data on property and business sectors, revenues, costs etc. There is a special emphasis on care homes for the elderly. Based on company research.
Frequency	Regular.
Web facilities	Free access to PDF reports on site.
Cost	Free.
Comments	
Address	Tower 42, 25 Old Broad Street, London EC2N 1HQ
Tel./e-mail	0207 935 4499 property@collierscre.co.uk
Fax/Website	0207 487 1894 www.colliers.com

COLLIERS CRE

Title	**Central London Offices**
Coverage	A review and analysis of the London offices market based on research by the company.
Frequency	Quarterly.
Web facilities	Free access to PDF reports on site.
Cost	Free.
Comments	
Address	Tower 42, 25 Old Broad Street, London EC2N 1HQ
Tel./e-mail	0207 935 4499 property@collierscre.co.uk
Fax/Website	0207 487 1894 www.colliers.com

COLLIERS CRE

Title	**Hotel Market Review**
Coverage	A review and analysis of the hotel sector with data on property developments, sales, prices and occupancy levels. Based on research by the company.
Frequency	Annual.
Web facilities	Free access to PDF reports on site.
Cost	Free.
Comments	
Address	Tower 42, 25 Old Broad Street, London EC2N 1HQ
Tel./e-mail	0207 935 4499 property@collierscre.co.uk
Fax/Website	0207 487 1894 www.colliers.com

COLLIERS CRE

Title	**Real Estate Investment Forecast**
Coverage	A review of current trends and short-term forecasts for real estate sector. Based on company research.
Frequency	Quarterly.
Web facilities	Free access to PDF reports on site.
Cost	Free.
Comments	
Address	Tower 42, 25 Old Broad Street, London EC2N 1HQ
Tel./e-mail	0207 935 4499 property@collierscre.co.uk
Fax/Website	0207 487 1894 www.colliers.com

COLLIERS CRE

Title	**Housing Market Review**
Coverage	A review and data on housing market trends. Based on company research and other data.
Frequency	Monthly.
Web facilities	Free access to PDF reports on site.
Cost	Free.
Comments	
Address	Tower 42, 25 Old Broad Street, London EC2N 1HQ
Tel./e-mail	0207 935 4499 property@collierscre.co.uk
Fax/Website	0207 487 1894 www.colliers.com

COMPANY CAR

Title	**Databank**
Coverage	Prices of new cars and the standing, running and operating costs of car fleets.
Frequency	Monthly in a monthly journal.
Web facilities	General details and news on site.
Cost	On request.
Comments	The journal has a controlled circulation.
Address	DMG Business Media Ltd, Queensway House, 2 Queensway, Redhill RH1 1QS
Tel./e-mail	01737 855017 companycar@dmgbusinessmedia.com
Fax/Website	01737 855479 www.companycar.com

COMPOSTING ASSOCIATION

Title	**State of Composting in the UK**
Coverage	General data on volumes of composting, by source of composting, waste composting, etc. Based on data collected by the association.
Frequency	Annual.
Web facilities	Free PDF survey report on site.
Cost	Free.
Comments	
Address	Avon House, Tithe Barn Road, Wellingborough NN8 1DH
Tel./e-mail	0870 160 3270 membership@compost.org.uk
Fax/Website	0870 160 3280 www.compost.org.uk

COMPUTER ECONOMICS LTD & REMUNERATION ECONOMICS

Title	**Computer Staff Salary Survey**
Coverage	A survey of 50 job descriptions analysed by location, age, experience, areas of responsibility, fringe benefits, etc. Based on a survey by the company. A small commentary supports the text.
Frequency	Twice yearly.
Web facilities	General details of statistics on the website.
Cost	£750 minimum.
Comments	Only available to subscribing members.
Address	Survey House, 51 Portland Road, Kingston-upon-Thames KT1 2SH
Tel./e-mail	0208 549 8726 info@celre.co.uk
Fax/Website	0208 541 5705 www.celre.co.uk

COMPUTER ECONOMICS LTD & REMUNERATION ECONOMICS

Title	**National Management Salary Survey**
Coverage	A survey of managers to produce statistics on earnings, fringe benefits and bonuses. Produced in three volumes: a general review of the survey, a detailed statistics volume and a small business review.
Frequency	Annual.
Web facilities	General details of statistics on website.
Cost	£700, £360 for participants.
Comments	Produced in association with the Institute of Management.
Address	Survey House, 51 Portland Road, Kingston-upon-Thames KT1 2SH
Tel./e-mail	0208 549 8726 info@celre.co.uk
Fax/Website	0208 541 5705 www.celre.co.uk

COMPUTER ECONOMICS LTD & REMUNERATION ECONOMICS

Title	**Voluntary Sector Salary Survey**
Coverage	A survey of salaries and benefits for various categories of staff in the voluntary sector.
Frequency	Annual.
Web facilities	General details of statistics on website.
Cost	£330; from £45 for participants.
Comments	
Address	Survey House, 51 Portland Road, Kingston-upon-Thames KT1 2SH
Tel./e-mail	0208 549 8726 info@celre.co.uk
Fax/Website	0208 541 5705 www.celre.co.uk

COMPUTER ECONOMICS LTD & REMUNERATION ECONOMICS

Title	**Salary Survey of Financial Staff**
Coverage	A salary survey for various levels of responsibility by company size, industry group, location, age, qualifications, etc. Additional data on benefits and recruitment. Based on the company's own survey with some supporting text.
Frequency	Annual.
Web facilities	General details of statistics on website.
Cost	£500; £300 for participants.
Comments	
Address	Survey House, 51 Portland Road, Kingston-upon-Thames KT1 2SH
Tel./e-mail	0208 549 8726 info@celre.co.uk
Fax/Website	0208 541 5705 www.celre.co.uk

COMPUTER ECONOMICS LTD & REMUNERATION ECONOMICS

Title	**Survey of HR/Personnel Staff**
Coverage	A salary survey covering various levels of responsibility by size of company, industry group, location, age, qualifications, etc. Additional data on benefits and recruitment. Based on the company's own survey with some supporting text.
Frequency	Annual.
Web facilities	General details of statistics on website.
Cost	£500; £310 for participants.
Comments	
Address	Survey House, 51 Portland Road, Kingston-upon-Thames KT1 2SH
Tel./e-mail	0208 549 8726 info@celre.co.uk
Fax/Website	0208 541 5705 www.celre.co.uk

COMPUTER ECONOMICS LTD & REMUNERATION ECONOMICS

Title	**Survey of Pensions Managers, Consultants and Administrators**
Coverage	A salary survey of pensions managers and related jobs with data by company size, industry group, location, age, etc. Based on the company's own survey with some supporting text.
Frequency	Annual.
Web facilities	General details of statistics on website.
Cost	£400; £165 for £245 for participants.
Comments	
Address	Survey House, 51 Portland Road, Kingston-upon-Thames KT1 2SH
Tel./e-mail	0208 549 8726 info@celre.co.uk
Fax/Website	0208 541 5705 www.celre.co.uk

COMPUTER ECONOMICS LTD & REMUNERATION ECONOMICS

Title	**Survey of Actuaries and Actuarial Students**
Coverage	A salary survey of actuaries and students with data by levels of responsibility, company size, age, qualifications, etc.
Frequency	Annual.
Web facilities	General details of statistics on website.
Cost	£830; £490 for participants.
Comments	Produced in association with the Institute of Actuaries.
Address	Survey House, 51 Portland Road, Kingston-upon-Thames KT1 2SH
Tel./e-mail	0208 549 8726 info@celre.co.uk
Fax/Website	0208 541 5705 www.celre.co.uk

COMPUTER ECONOMICS LTD & REMUNERATION ECONOMICS

Title	**Sales and Marketing Salary Survey**
Coverage	A salary survey covering nine levels of responsibility and broken down into various sectors. Based on data collected by the company.
Frequency	Annual.
Web facilities	General details of statistics on website.
Cost	£510; £310 for participants.
Comments	
Address	Survey House, 51 Portland Road, Kingston-upon-Thames KT1 2SH
Tel./e-mail	0208 549 8726 info@celre.co.uk
Fax/Website	0208 541 5705 www.celre.co.uk

COMPUTER ECONOMICS LTD AND REMUNERATION

Title	**Survey of Fringe Benefits, Additional Payments and Contract Staff**
Coverage	Annual survey of staff benefits and other payments, plus details of the use of contract staff.
Frequency	Annual.
Web facilities	General details of statistics on website.
Cost	£500; £300–£400 for participants.
Comments	
Address	Survey House, 51 Portland Road, Kingston-upon-Thames KT1 2SH
Tel./e-mail	0208 549 8726 info@celre.co.uk
Fax/Website	0208 541 5705 www.celre.co.uk

COMPUTER ECONOMICS LTS & REMUNERATION ECONOMICS

Title	**Salary Survey of Engineers**
Coverage	A survey of engineering salaries covering nine levels of responsibility, by company size, type of work, qualifications, location, etc. Based on the company's own survey with some supporting text.
Frequency	Annual.
Web facilities	General details of statistics on website.
Cost	£500; £320 for participants.
Comments	
Address	Survey House, 51 Portland Road, Kingston-upon-Thames KT1 2SH
Tel./e-mail	0208 549 8726 info@celre.co.uk
Fax/Website	0208 541 5705 www.celre.co.uk

COMPUTING SERVICES AND SOFTWARE ASSOCIATION

Title	**CEO Trends Survey**
Coverage	A quarterly opinion survey of members assessing trends and likely trends in the sector.
Frequency	Quarterly.
Web facilities	Press releases for trends surveys and access to detailed data for members on site.
Cost	On request.
Comments	
Address	20 Red Lion Street, London WC1R 4QN
Tel./e-mail	0207 395 6700 cssa@cssa.co.uk
Fax/Website	0207 740 4119 www.cssa.co.uk

COMPUTING SERVICES AND SOFTWARE ASSOCIATION

Title	**Annual Report**
Coverage	Includes the association's annual survey based on voluntary responses from member companies. Data on business activities, total revenue, revenue by business sector, revenue per employee, employment trends, profits and future prospects. A detailed commentary supports the text.
Frequency	Annual.
Web facilities	Press releases for trend surveys and detailed data for members on site.
Cost	Free.
Comments	
Address	20 Red Lion Street, London WC1R 4QN
Tel./e-mail	0207 395 6700 cssa@cssa.co.uk
Fax/Website	0207 740 4119 www.cssa.co.uk

CONFEDERATION OF BRITISH FORGERS

Title	**End of Year Statistics**
Coverage	Annual statistics on the forging industry including market developments, prices, deliveries. Based on the association's own survey.
Frequency	Annual.
Web facilities	
Cost	£10; free for members.
Comments	
Address	245 Grove Lane, Handsworth, Birmingham B20 2HB
Tel./e-mail	0121 554 3311
Fax/Website	0121 523 0761

CONFEDERATION OF BRITISH FORGERS

Title	**BFIA Annual Report**
Coverage	Contains some statistics on the economic performance of the forging industry.
Frequency	Annual.
Web facilities	
Cost	On request.
Comments	
Address	245 Grove Lane, Handsworth, Birmingham B20 2HB
Tel./e-mail	0121 554 3311
Fax/Website	0121 523 0761

CONFEDERATION OF BRITISH INDUSTRY (CBI)

Title	**Economic and Business Outlook**
Coverage	An economic survey plus a forecast up to six months ahead. Also a general survey of industrial and regional trends and some comparative data for other European countries. Based on a combination of CBI data and official statistics.
Frequency	Quarterly.
Web facilities	General details of publications and online ordering facilities on site.
Cost	£395; £235 for members.
Comments	
Address	103 New Oxford Street, London WC1A 1DU
Tel./e-mail	0207 395 8071 bookshop@cbi.org.uk
Fax/Website	0207 497 3646 www.cbi.org.uk

CONFEDERATION OF BRITISH INDUSTRY (CBI)

Title	**CBI Distributive Trades Survey**
Coverage	A survey of trends in over 20 distributive sectors with data on sales volume, orders, stocks, employment, investment, prices, business expenditure, etc. Based on a CBI survey.
Frequency	Monthly.
Web facilities	General details of publications and online ordering facilities on site.
Cost	£460; £385 for members.
Comments	
Address	103 New Oxford Street, London WC1A 1DU
Tel./e-mail	0207 395 8071 bookshop@cbi.org.uk
Fax/Website	0207 497 3646 www.cbi.org.uk

CONFEDERATION OF BRITISH INDUSTRY (CBI)

Title	**CBI/Price Waterhouse Coopers Financial Services Survey**
Coverage	A survey of trends in various financial services sectors with data on income, employment, short-term expectations, etc. Based on a CBI survey.
Frequency	Quarterly.
Web facilities	General details of publications and online ordering facilities on site.
Cost	£360; £210 for members.
Comments	
Address	103 New Oxford Street, London WC1A 1DU
Tel./e-mail	0207 395 8071 bookshop@cbi.org.uk
Fax/Website	0207 497 3646 www.cbi.org.uk

CONFEDERATION OF BRITISH INDUSTRY (CBI)

Title	**Industrial Trends Survey**
Coverage	Trends for over 40 industry groups covering orders, stocks, output, capital expenditure, exports, costs, labour, etc. for the last four months and the next four months. Based on a CBI survey of around 1700 companies.
Frequency	Quarterly.
Web facilities	General details of publications and online ordering facilities on site.
Cost	£495; £285 for members; joint subscription with *Monthly Trends Enquiry* (see below) £695; £435 to members.
Comments	
Address	103 New Oxford Street, London WC1A 1DU
Tel./e-mail	0207 395 8071 bookshop@cbi.org.uk
Fax/Website	0207 497 3646 www.cbi.org.uk

CONFEDERATION OF BRITISH INDUSTRY (CBI)

Title	**Monthly Trends Enquiry**
Coverage	Essentially an abbreviated version of the quarterly *Industrial Trends Survey* with summary statistics on orders, stocks, output, prices, etc. A short commentary supports the statistics. Data are based on a survey of companies with responses varying from around 1300 to over 1500.
Frequency	Monthly.
Web facilities	General details of publications and online ordering facilities on site.
Cost	£665; £400 for members, a joint subscription with *Industrial Trends Survey* (see entry above).
Comments	
Address	103 New Oxford Street, London WC1A 1DU
Tel./e-mail	0207 395 8071 bookshop@cbi.org.uk
Fax/Website	0207 497 3646 www.cbi.org.uk

CONFEDERATION OF BRITISH INDUSTRY (CBI)

Title	**CBI/Experian Regional Trends Survey**
Coverage	A survey of economic and business trends in the UK regions based on a survey of a sample of companies in these regions.
Frequency	Annual.
Web facilities	General details of publications and online ordering facilities on site.
Cost	£335; £210 for members.
Comments	
Address	103 New Oxford Street, London WC1A 1DU
Tel./e-mail	0207 395 8071 bookshop@cbi.org.uk
Fax/Website	0207 497 3646 www.cbi.org.uk

CONFEDERATION OF BRITISH INDUSTRY (CBI)

Title	**CBI/Grant Thornton Service Sector Survey**
Coverage	A quarterly survey of the services sector based on results from a sample of service industry companies.
Frequency	Quarterly.
Web facilities	General details of publications and online ordering facilities on site.
Cost	£360; £210 for members.
Comments	
Address	103 New Oxford Street, London WC1A 1DU
Tel./e-mail	0207 395 8071 bookshop@cbi.org.uk
Fax/Website	0207 497 3646 www.cbi.org.uk

CONFEDERATION OF BRITISH INDUSTRY (CBI)

Title	**CBI/GVA Grimley Property Trends Survey**
Coverage	A survey of short-term and long-term property requirements of the private sector.
Frequency	Twice yearly.
Web facilities	General details of publications and online ordering facilities on site.
Cost	Free.
Comments	
Address	103 New Oxford Street, London WC1A 1DU
Tel./e-mail	0207 395 8071 bookshop@cbi.org.uk
Fax/Website	0207 497 3646 www.cbi.org.uk

CONFEDERATION OF PAPER INDUSTRIES

Title	**Market Statistics**
Coverage	Detailed tables and charts on consumption, production, sales, stocks, imports, exports of paper and board plus consumption, production, stocks and imports of raw materials. Based on a combination of sources.
Frequency	Monthly.
Web facilities	Some free statistics pages on site plus details of all publications.
Cost	£1500.
Comments	Enquiry service can deal with ad hoc enquiries.
Address	Papermakers House, Rivenhall Road, Swindon SN5 7BD
Tel./e-mail	01793 889600 cpi@paper.org.uk
Fax/Website	01793 878700 www.paper.org.uk

CONFEDERATION OF PAPER INDUSTRIES

Title	**Reference Statistics**
Coverage	Ten-year series of tables and charts with data on production, consumption, sales, stocks, imports and exports of paper and board plus consumption, production, stocks and imports of raw materials. Also data on employment, energy and finance. Based on various sources.
Frequency	Annual.
Web facilities	Some free statistics pages on site plus details of all publications.
Cost	£150.
Comments	Enquiry service can deal with ad hoc enquiries.
Address	Papermakers House, Rivenhall Road, Swindon SN5 7BD
Tel./e-mail	01793 889600 cpi@paper.org.uk
Fax/Website	01793 878700 www.paper.org.uk

CONFEDERATION OF PAPER INDUSTRIES

Title	**Capacity Report**
Coverage	Historical data for the last few years and forecasts for three or four years ahead of capacity in the industry.
Frequency	Annual.
Web facilities	Some free statistics pages on site plus details of all publications.
Cost	£750 plus VAT.
Comments	Enquiry service can deal with ad hoc enquiries.
Address	Papermakers House, Rivenhall Road, Swindon SN5 7BD
Tel./e-mail	01793 889600 cpi@paper.org.uk
Fax/Website	01793 878700 www.paper.org.uk

CONFEDERATION OF PAPER INDUSTRIES

Title	**Key Figures**
Coverage	Monthly figures on production, consumption, sales, stocks, etc. based on data collected by the confederation.
Frequency	Monthly.
Web facilities	Some free statistics pages on site plus details of all publications.
Cost	£350.
Comments	Enquiry service can deal with ad hoc enquiries.
Address	Papermakers House, Rivenhall Road, Swindon SN5 7BD
Tel./e-mail	01793 889600 cpi@paper.org.uk
Fax/Website	01793 878700 www.paper.org.uk

CONFEDERATION OF PAPER INDUSTRIES

Title	**Production of Paper and Board**
Coverage	Monthly data and analysis on production, sales and stocks of paper and board.
Frequency	Monthly.
Web facilities	Some free statistics pages on site plus details of all publications.
Cost	£350.
Comments	Enquiry service can deal with ad hoc enquiries.
Address	Papermakers House, Rivenhall Road, Swindon SN5 7BD
Tel./e-mail	01793 889600 cpi@paper.org.uk
Fax/Website	01793 878700 www.paper.org.uk

CONFEDERATION OF PAPER INDUSTRIES

Title	**Consumption of Paper and Board**
Coverage	Monthly statistics and commentary on paper and board consumption in the UK.
Frequency	Monthly.
Web facilities	Some free statistics pages on site plus details of all publications.
Cost	£350.
Comments	Enquiry service can deal with ad hoc enquiries.
Address	Papermakers House, Rivenhall Road, Swindon SN5 7BD
Tel./e-mail	01793 889600 cpi@paper.org.uk
Fax/Website	01793 878700 www.paper.org.uk

CONFEDERATION OF PAPER INDUSTRIES

Title	**Imports of Paper and Board**
Coverage	Detailed monthly import statistics for paper and board based on central government data.
Frequency	Monthly.
Web facilities	Some free statistics pages on site plus details of all publications.
Cost	£350.
Comments	Enquiry service can deal with ad hoc enquiries.
Address	Papermakers House, Rivenhall Road, Swindon SN5 7BD
Tel./e-mail	01793 889600 cpi@paper.org.uk
Fax/Website	01793 878700 www.paper.org.uk

CONFEDERATION OF PAPER INDUSTRIES

Title	**Pulp Consumption Stocks and Trade**
Coverage	Monthly statistics covering pulp demand, stocks and trade based on various sources.
Frequency	Monthly.
Web facilities	Some free statistics on site plus details of all publications.
Cost	£350.
Comments	Enquiry service can deal with ad hoc enquiries.
Address	Papermakers House, Rivenhall Road, Swindon SN5 7BD
Tel./e-mail	01793 889600 cpi@paper.org.uk
Fax/Website	01793 878700 www.paper.org.uk

CONFEDERATION OF PAPER INDUSTRIES

Title	**Recovered Fibre Consumption, Stocks and Trade**
Coverage	Monthly statistics on waste paper demand, stocks and overseas trade based on various sources.
Frequency	Monthly.
Web facilities	Some free statistics on site plus details of all publications.
Cost	£350.
Comments	Enquiry service can deal with ad hoc enquiries.
Address	Papermakers House, Rivenhall Road, Swindon SN5 7BD
Tel./e-mail	01793 889600 cpi@paper.org.uk
Fax/Website	01793 878700 www.paper.org.uk

CONFEDERATION OF PAPER INDUSTRIES

Title	**Industry Facts**
Coverage	Key figures on industry, production and consumption plus a commentary on trends. Also has ten years' worth of data.
Frequency	Annual.
Web facilities	Some free statistics pages on site plus details of all publications.
Cost	£25.
Comments	Enquiry service can deal with ad hoc enquiries.
Address	Papermakers House, Rivenhall Road, Swindon SN5 7BD
Tel./e-mail	01793 889600 cpi@paper.org.uk
Fax/Website	01793 878700 www.paper.org.uk

CONFEDERATION OF PASSENGER TRANSPORT UK

Title	**Facts 2---**
Coverage	Annual compilation of data on passenger transport including expenditure, investment, transport trends by sector, prices, employment, use of transport, journeys, etc.
Frequency	Annual.
Web facilities	Free PDF on site.
Cost	Free.
Comments	
Address	Imperial House, 15–19 Kingsway, London WC2B 6UN
Tel./e-mail	0207 240 3131 lingt@cpt-uk.org
Fax/Website	0207 240 6565 www.cpt-uk.org

CONSENSUS RESEARCH INTERNATIONAL

Title	**Unit Trust Survey**
Coverage	A survey of the awareness of and attitudes towards, unit trusts amongst unit holders and intermediaries. Based on a company survey. A commentary supports the data.
Frequency	Quarterly.
Web facilities	
Cost	On request.
Comments	Also produces an annual *Stockbroker Survey*, based on the ratings of brokers' analysts by company executives.
Address	1–2 Castle Lane, London SW1E 6DR
Tel./e-mail	0207 592 1700 mail@consensus-research.co.uk
Fax/Website	0207 738 1271

CONSTRUCTION CONFEDERATION

Title	**Construction Industry Tracking Survey**
Coverage	Prospects for the building workload, capacity of operations, tender prices and the availability of labour and materials. Based on survey of members; the confederation states that members account for 75% of all building work. Some commentary supports the survey results.
Frequency	Quarterly.
Web facilities	Press release with basic data on website.
Cost	On request.
Comments	Published in association with the Construction Products Association (see other entry, page 108).
Address	56–64 Leonard Street, London EC2A 4JX
Tel./e-mail	0207 608 5000
Fax/Website	0207 608 5001

CONSTRUCTION NEWS

Title	**Annual Contracts Review**
Coverage	An annual review of contracts awarded by type of construction, e.g. residential, commercial, industrial and by region; also statistics on work out to tender.
Frequency	Annual in a weekly journal.
Web facilities	News and general details on site.
Cost	On request.
Comments	
Address	EMAP Construct, 151 Roseberry Avenue, London EC1R 4GB
Tel./e-mail	0207 505 6868 cneditorial@emap.com
Fax/Website	0207 505 6867 www.cnplus.co.uk

CONSTRUCTION NEWS

Title	**Workload Trends**
Coverage	Statistics covering new contracts awarded by construction type updating the data in the annual survey noted in the previous entry.
Frequency	Monthly in a weekly journal.
Web facilities	News and general details on site.
Cost	On request.
Comments	
Address	EMAP Construct, 151 Rosebery Avenue, London EC1R 4GB
Tel./e-mail	0207 505 6868 cneditorial@emap.com
Fax/Website	0207 505 6867 www.cnplus.co.uk

CONSTRUCTION PLANT HIRE ASSOCIATION

Title	**CPA Machine Cost Studies**
Coverage	Details of the costs to plant hire companies of running typical machines and cost movement indices. Based on data collected by the association.
Frequency	Twice yearly.
Web facilities	
Cost	Free to members but there may be a small charge to others.
Comments	
Address	27–28 Newbury Street, London EC1A 7HU
Tel./e-mail	0207 796 3366 enquiries@cpa.uk.net
Fax/Website	0207 796 3399 www.cpa.uk.net

CONSTRUCTION PLANT HIRE ASSOCIATION

Title	**CPA Driver Cost Studies**
Coverage	Details of the costs attached to the employment of drivers under civil engineering or plant hire working rule agreements. Based on a survey by the association.
Frequency	Annual.
Web facilities	
Cost	Free to members but there may be a small charge to others.
Comments	
Address	27–28 Newbury Street, London EC1A 7HU
Tel./e-mail	0207 796 3366 enquiries@cpa.uk.net
Fax/Website	0207 796 3399 www.cpa.uk.net

CONSTRUCTION PLANT HIRE ASSOCIATION

Title	**CPA Activity and Hire Rate Studies**
Coverage	Activity percentages and average hire rates for typical machines. Based on a survey of members.
Frequency	Quarterly.
Web facilities	
Cost	Free but only available to members.
Comments	
Address	27–28 Newbury Street, London EC1A 7HU
Tel./e-mail	0207 796 3366 enquiries@cpa.uk.net
Fax/Website	0207 796 3399 www.cpa.uk.net

CONSTRUCTION PRODUCTS ASSOCIATION

Title	**Construction Industry Forecast**
Coverage	Forecasts three years ahead for housing starts and completions, other new work and repair, maintenance and improvement. Based on BMP's own forecasts with a large amount of supporting commentary.
Frequency	Twice yearly.
Web facilities	Member access to statistics and online ordering facilities on site.
Cost	£300; £200 per issue.
Comments	Published in January and July.
Address	26 Store Street, London WC1E 7BT
Tel./e-mail	0207 323 3770 enquiries@constprod.org.uk
Fax/Website	0207 323 0307 www.constprod.org.uk

CONSTRUCTION PRODUCTS ASSOCIATION

Title	**Construction Market Trends**
Coverage	Covers housebuilding starts and completions, renovations, prices, mortgages, value of new orders and output, capital expenditure, trade and building materials. Based on a combination of central government data and non-official sources.
Frequency	Monthly.
Web facilities	Member access to statistics and online ordering facilities on site.
Cost	£175; £20 per issue.
Comments	
Address	26 Store Street, London WC1E 7BT
Tel./e-mail	0207 323 3770 enquiries@constprod.org.uk
Fax/Website	0207 323 0307 www.constprod.org.uk

CONSTRUCTION PRODUCTS ASSOCIATION

Title	**Construction Industry Trade Survey**
Coverage	A survey of the UK building materials industry based on an opinion survey of members.
Frequency	Quarterly.
Web facilities	Member access to statistics and online ordering facilities on site.
Cost	£150; £50 per issue.
Comments	Published in February, May, August, November.
Address	26 Store Street, London WC1E 7BT
Tel./e-mail	0207 323 3770 enquiries@constprod.org.uk
Fax/Website	0207 323 0307 www.constprod.org.uk

CONSUMER CREDIT TRADE ASSOCIATION

Title	**Consumer Credit**
Coverage	Commentary and statistics on consumer credit trends with comparisons trends in the previous year.
Frequency	Six issues per year.
Web facilities	
Cost	£5.50; £3.50 for members.
Comments	
Address	Suite 8, The Wool Exchange, 10 Hustlergate, Bradford BD1 1RE
Tel./e-mail	01274 390380
Fax/Website	01274 729002 www.ccta.co.uk

CONSUMER PROFILE RESEARCH LTD

Title	**Decisions**
Coverage	A regular omnibus survey aimed at researching issues relating to advertising, packaging, new product development, etc. and targeted at women with children under 16.
Frequency	Regular.
Web facilities	
Cost	On request.
Comments	
Address	5 St Andrews Court, Wellington Street, Oxford OX9 3WT
Tel./e-mail	01844 215672 mail@profile-group.com
Fax/Website	01844 261324 www.profile-group.com

CONTINENTAL RESEARCH

Title	**Mobile Phone Report**
Coverage	Quarterly review with statistics on phone use, penetration.
Frequency	Quarterly.
Web facilities	Detailed executive summaries with data free on site.
Cost	£175.
Comments	
Address	132–140 Goswell Road, London EC1V 7DP
Tel./e-mail	0207 490 5944 mail@continentalresearch.com
Fax/Website	0207 490 1174 www.continentalresearch.com

CONTINENTAL RESEARCH

Title	**Internet Report**
Coverage	Quarterly review with statistics on Internet penetration and use.
Frequency	Quarterly.
Web facilities	Detailed executive summaries with data free on site.
Cost	£175.
Comments	
Address	132–140 Goswell Road, London EC1V 7DP
Tel./e-mail	0207 490 5944 mail@continentalresearch.com
Fax/Website	0207 490 1174 www.continentalresearch.com

CONTINENTAL RESEARCH

Title	**Digital TV Report**
Coverage	Quarterly review with statistics on the number of satellite dishes, SMATV and cable installations in the UK. Also figures on intentions to purchase and viewing levels. Based on original research by the company.
Frequency	Quarterly.
Web facilities	Detailed executive summaries with data free on site.
Cost	£175.
Comments	
Address	132–140 Goswell Road, London EC1V 7OP
Tel./e-mail	0207 490 5944 mail@continentalresearch.com
Fax/Website	0207 490 1174 www.continentalresearch.com

CONTINENTAL RESEARCH

Title	**Small Business Omnibus**
Coverage	Monthly survey of 300 small businesses with various questions asked.
Frequency	Monthly.
Web facilities	Detailed executive summaries with data free on site.
Cost	On request.
Comments	
Address	132–140 Goswell Road, London EC1V 7OP
Tel./e-mail	0207 490 5944 mail@continentalresearch.com
Fax/Website	0207 490 1174 www.continentalresearch.com

CONTINENTAL RESEARCH

Title	**Medium and Large Businesses Omnibus**
Coverage	A monthly survey of directors and managers in 200 businesses.
Frequency	Monthly.
Web facilities	Detailed executive summaries with data free on site.
Cost	On request.
Comments	
Address	132–140 Goswell Road, London EC1V 7OP
Tel./e-mail	0207 490 5944 mail@continentalresearch.com
Fax/Website	0207 490 9129 www.continentalresarch.com

CONTROL RISKS GROUP

Title	**Risk Map 2---**
Coverage	A critical assessment of global and regional political and economic issues and risks based on surveys with senior executives. UK and US editions alongside global edition.
Frequency	Annual.
Web facilities	
Cost	£150.
Comments	
Address	Cottons Centre, Cottons Lane, London SE1 2QG
Tel./e-mail	0207 970 2100 riskmap@control-risks.com
Fax/Website	0207 222 2296 www.crg.com

COOPERATIVE UNION LTD

Title	**Cooperative Statistics**
Coverage	Retail distribution by individual cooperative societies and other information on cooperative wholesaling, banking and insurance. Based almost entirely on the organisation's own research.
Frequency	Annual.
Web facilities	
Cost	On request.
Comments	
Address	Holyoake House, Hanover Street, Manchester M60 0AS
Tel./e-mail	0161 832 4300
Fax/Website	0161 831 7684

CORRUGATED PACKAGING ASSOCIATION

Title	**Annual Production Statistics**
Coverage	Production by weight and area and the sales invoice value of solid and corrugated fibreboard produced in the UK. Based on a survey of members.
Frequency	Annual.
Web facilities	Key statistics available free on website.
Cost	Free but only available to members.
Comments	
Address	1 Rivenhall Road, Swindon SN5 7BD
Tel./e-mail	01372 721237 postbox@corrugated.org.uk
Fax/Website	01372 721237 www.corrugated.org.uk

CORRUGATED PACKAGING ASSOCIATION

Title	**Accident Report and Statistics**
Coverage	Details of accidents and related incidents in the industry.
Frequency	Regular.
Web facilities	Key statistics available free on website.
Cost	Free but only available to members.
Comments	
Address	1 Rivenhall Road, Swindon SN5 7BD
Tel./e-mail	01372 721237 postbox@corrugated.org.uk
Fax/Website	01372 721237 www.corrugated.org.uk

COSMETIC TOILETRY AND PERFUMERY ASSOCIATION

Title	**GB Market Estimates Report**
Coverage	Commissioned research from agencies IRI and TNS Sofres covering sales by product.
Frequency	Annual.
Web facilities	Summary data for last two years free on site.
Cost	On request.
Comments	
Address	Josaron House, 5–7 John Princes Street, London W1G 0JN
Tel./e-mail	0207 491 8891 info@ctpa.org.uk
Fax/Website	0207 493 8061 www.ctpa.org.uk

COUNCIL OF MORTGAGE LENDERS

Title	**Housing Finance**
Coverage	Includes articles and a diary of events plus a statistical section covering trends in housing, building, mortgage lending, prices, transactions and savings. Also data on specific building societies.
Frequency	Quarterly.
Web facilities	Free press release data on site and details of publications.
Cost	£95; £40 for members.
Comments	Based at the same address as the Building Societies Association and involved in some joint publications.
Address	3 Savile Row, London W1X 1AF
Tel./e-mail	0207 437 0075 info@cml.org.uk
Fax/Website	0207 734 3791 www.cml.org.uk

COUNCIL OF MORTGAGE LENDERS

Title	**CML Press Releases**
Coverage	Monthly and other press releases on various topics including gross mortgage lending, mortgage market, payment protection insurance, arrears and repossessions, etc.
Frequency	Monthly.
Web facilities	Free press release data on site and details of publications.
Cost	Free.
Comments	Based at the same address as the Building Societies Association and involved in some joint publications.
Address	3 Savile Row, London W1X 1AF
Tel./e-mail	0207 437 0075 info@cml.org.uk
Fax/Website	0207 734 3791 www.cml.org.uk

COUNCIL OF MORTGAGE LENDERS

Title	**CML Statistics Online**
Coverage	A subscription based online service covering all the data produced by the council.
Frequency	Regular.
Web facilities	Free press release data on site and details of publications.
Cost	£235.
Comments	Based at the same address as the Building Societies Association and involved in some joint publications.
Address	3 Savile Row, London W1X 1AF
Tel./e-mail	0207 437 0075 info@cml.org.uk
Fax/Website	0207 734 3791 www.cml.org.uk

COUNCIL OF MORTGAGE LENDERS

Title	**Market Briefing**
Coverage	A monthly review of economic and consumer trends and specific property and housing trends. Based on various sources.
Frequency	Monthly.
Web facilities	Free press release data on site and details of publications.
Cost	£170; £95 for members.
Comments	Based at the same address as the Building Societies Association and involved in some joint publications.
Address	3 Savile Row, London W1X 1AF
Tel./e-mail	0207 437 0075 info@cml.org.uk
Fax/Website	0207 734 3791 www.cml.org.uk

COUNCIL OF MORTGAGE LENDERS

Title	**UK Housing Review**
Coverage	Various data and analysis on the housing sector and market in the UK including housing stock, condition, prices, construction, housing investment, rents, subsidies, homelesssness, etc.
Frequency	Annual.
Web facilities	Free press release data on site and details of publications.
Cost	£40.
Comments	Based at the same address as the Building Societies Association and involved in some joint publications.
Address	3 Savile Row, London W1X 1AF
Tel./e-mail	0207 437 0075 info@cml.org.uk
Fax/Website	0207 734 3791 www.cml.org.uk

CRANFIELD SCHOOL OF MANAGEMENT

Title	**Recruitment Confidence Index**
Coverage	A regular survey of expectations of future recruitment activity with results for all staff and separately for management/professional staff.
Frequency	Quarterly.
Web facilities	Press release summaries of surveys on site.
Cost	£50 minimum per report.
Comments	Produced in association with the *Daily Telegraph* and coverage of surveys in the paper as well as *Personnel Today*.
Address	Cranfield University, Cranfield MK43 0AL
Tel./e-mail	01234 754808 emma.parry@cranfield.ac.uk
Fax/Website	01234 754806 www.rcisurvey.co.uk

CREDIT MANAGEMENT RESEARCH CENTRE

Title	**Credit Management Quarterly Review**
Coverage	A review of credit management and debt management activity based on responses from a panel of 2000 companies.
Frequency	Quarterly.
Web facilities	General details and ordering facilities on site.
Cost	£245.
Comments	Also publishes the *Debt Management Collection and Recovery Survey* with the Credit Services Association (see other entry, page 116) and various other surveys and reports.
Address	Leeds University Business School, Maurice Keyworth Building, Clarendon Road, Leeds LS2 9JT
Tel./e-mail	0113 384 5750 info@creditscorer.com
Fax/Website	0113 384 5846 www.cmrc.co.uk

CREDIT SERVICES ASSOCIATION

Title	**Debt Management Collection and Recovery: A Survey of Trends and Current Practice**
Coverage	Regular survey of debt management and collection trends and industry based on original research.
Frequency	Regular.
Web facilities	General details on site.
Cost	£300; £100 to members.
Comments	Published in association with the Credit Management Research Centre, University of Leeds (see entry under this name, page 115).
Address	Wingrove House, Ponteland Road, Newcastle-upon-Tyne NE5 3AJ
Tel./e-mail	0191 286 5656 mail@csa-uk.com
Fax/Website	0191 286 0900 www.csa-uk.com

CREMATION SOCIETY OF GREAT BRITAIN

Title	**Directory of Crematoria**
Coverage	Progress of cremation over the last 100 years. Facts and figures section includes number of crematoria, cremations carried out, fees, etc. Based on the society's own survey.
Frequency	Annual.
Web facilities	Free statistics on the website.
Cost	£25.
Comments	
Address	Brecon House (2nd Floor), 16/16a Albion Place, Maidstone ME14 5DZ
Tel./e-mail	01622 688292 info@cremation.org.uk
Fax/Website	01622 686698 www.cremation.org.uk

CREMATION SOCIETY OF GREAT BRITAIN

Title	**Cremation Statistics**
Coverage	Historical data covering number of cremations and latest year data by region.
Frequency	Annual.
Web facilities	Free on the website.
Cost	Free.
Comments	
Address	Brecon House (2nd Floor), 16/16a Albion Place, Maidstone ME14 5DZ
Tel./e-mail	01622 688292 info@cremation.org.uk
Fax/Website	01622 686698 www.cremation.org.uk

CRONER REWARD

Title	**Regional Surveys**
Coverage	Salaries and benefits in regions of the UK. Based on Reward's own survey in key centres.
Frequency	Twice yearly.
Web facilities	General details of surveys, online ordering and paid-for access to data on site.
Cost	On request.
Comments	Each regional survey is published twice a year. Specific enquiries answered from Croner Reward's data bank.
Address	145 London Road, Kingston upon Thames KT2 6SR
Tel./e-mail	0208 547 3333 info@croner.co.uk
Fax/Website	0208 547 2637 www.croner.co.uk

CRONER REWARD

Title	**Civil Service Rewards**
Coverage	An annual review of salaries and benefits based on data collected from civil service departments around the UK and relevant jobs selected from the company's database. Over 33 000 employees covered.
Frequency	Twice yearly.
Web facilities	General details of surveys, online ordering and paid-for access to data on site.
Cost	£740.
Comments	Published in February and June. Specific enquiries answered by Croner Reward's data bank.
Address	145 London Road, Kingston upon Thames KT2 6SR
Tel./e-mail	0208 547 3333 info@croner.co.uk
Fax/Website	0208 547 2637 www.croner.co.uk

CRONER REWARD

Title	**Food Industry Rewards**
Coverage	A salary report covering various jobs in the food and drink industry and based on the company's own research.
Frequency	Annual.
Web facilities	General details of surveys, online ordering and paid-for access to data on site.
Cost	£350.
Comments	Published in association with *The Grocer*. Specific enquiries answered from Croner Reward's data bank.
Address	145 London Road, Kingston upon Thames KT2 6SR
Tel./e-mail	0208 547 3333 info@croner.co.uk
Fax/Website	0208 547 2637 www.croner.co.uk

CRONER REWARD

Title	**Purchasing and Supply Rewards**
Coverage	Detailed information of salaries and benefits for 3500 jobs in the purchasing and supply sectors. Based on the company's own research.
Frequency	Annual.
Web facilities	General details of surveys, online ordering and paid-for access to data on site.
Cost	£400.
Comments	Produced in association with the Chartered Institute of Purchasing and Supply. Specific enquiries answered from Croner Reward's data bank.
Address	145 London Road, Kingston upon Thames KT2 6SR
Tel./e-mail	0208 547 3333 info@croner.co.uk
Fax/Website	0208 547 2637 www.croner.co.uk

CRONER REWARD

Title	**Sales Rewards**
Coverage	An annual review of salaries, bonuses, commission, company cars and other benefits. Based on research by the company.
Frequency	Annual.
Web facilities	General details of surveys, online ordering and paid-for access to data on site.
Cost	£280.
Comments	Specific enquiries answered from Croner Reward's data bank.
Address	145 London Road, Kingston upon Thames KT2 6SR
Tel./e-mail	0208 547 3333 info@croner.co.uk
Fax/Website	0208 547 2637 www.croner.co.uk

CRONER REWARD

Title	**Personnel Rewards**
Coverage	An annual report with details of basic and total pay, company cars and other benefits. Based on research by the company covering 10 000 jobs and 1800 organisations.
Frequency	Annual.
Web facilities	General details of surveys, online ordering and paid-for access to data on site.
Cost	£400.
Comments	Produced in association with the Chartered Institute of Personnel and Development (IPD) and discounts for members. Published in February. Specific enquiries answered from Croner Reward's data bank.
Address	145 London Road, Kingston upon Thames KT2 6SR
Tel./e-mail	0208 547 3333 info@croner.co.uk
Fax/Website	0208 547 2637 www.croner.co.uk

CRONER REWARD

Title	**Research and Development Rewards**
Coverage	An annual report covering basic salaries, total remuneration and benefits in the R&D field. Based on research by the company.
Frequency	Annual.
Web facilities	General details of surveys, online ordering and paid-for access to data on site.
Cost	£325.
Comments	Published in May. Specific enquiries answered from Croner Reward's data bank.
Address	145 London Road, Kingston upon Thames KT2 6SR
Tel./e-mail	0208 547 3333 info@croner.co.uk
Fax/Website	0208 547 2637 www.croner.co.uk

CRONER REWARD

Title	**Charity Rewards**
Coverage	A survey of salaries in the charity sector with analysis by job and level of charity income for full-time employees. Based on research by the company.
Frequency	Annual.
Web facilities	General details of surveys, online ordering and paid-for access to data on site.
Cost	£325.
Comments	Published in association with Charity & Fund Raising Appointments. Specific enquiries answered from Croner Reward's data bank.
Address	145 London Road, Kingston upon Thames KT2 6SR
Tel./e-mail	0208 547 3333 info@croner.co.uk
Fax/Website	0208 547 2637 www.croner.co.uk

CRONER REWARD

Title	**Travel Industry Rewards**
Coverage	Salaries and benefits for a range of job functions in the travel industry. A new survey in 2000.
Frequency	Twice yearly.
Web facilities	General details of surveys, online ordering and paid-for access to data on site.
Cost	£380.
Comments	Published in association with ABTA and discounts for members. Published in November. Specific enquiries answered from Croner Reward's data bank.
Address	145 London Road, Kingston upon Thames KT2 6SR
Tel./e-mail	0208 547 3333 info@croner.co.uk
Fax/Website	0208 547 2637 www.croner.co.uk

CRONER REWARD

Title	**London Secretarial and Clerical Rewards**
Coverage	A salary survey of six types of secretarial jobs in the capital. Based on research by the company.
Frequency	Twice yearly.
Web facilities	General details of surveys, online ordering and paid-for access to data on site.
Cost	£325.
Comments	Published in February and August. Specific enquiries answered from Croner Reward's data bank.
Address	145 London Road, Kingston upon Thames KT2 6SR
Tel./e-mail	0208 547 3333 info@croner.co.uk
Fax/Website	0208 547 2637 www.croner.co.uk

CRONER REWARD

Title	**Marketing Rewards**
Coverage	Salary and benefits information for all levels of marketing staff and based on a survey of around 1200 members of the Chartered Institute of Marketing (CIM).
Frequency	Annual.
Web facilities	General details of surveys, online ordering and paid-for access to data on site.
Cost	£280.
Comments	Produced in association with the Chartered Institute of Marketing (CIM) and discounts for members. Published in September. Specific enquiries answered from Croner Reward's data bank.
Address	145 London Road, Kingston upon Thames KT2 6SR
Tel./e-mail	0208 547 3333 info@croner.co.uk
Fax/Website	0208 547 2637 www.croner.co.uk

CRONER REWARD

Title	**Engineering Rewards**
Coverage	Salary and benefits information for both salaried and hourly paid staff. Based on research by the company across 315 companies.
Frequency	Twice yearly.
Web facilities	General details of surveys, online ordering and paid-for access to data on site.
Cost	£250.
Comments	Published in April and October. Produced for the first time on 2000. Specific enquiries answered from Croner Reward's data bank.
Address	145 London Road, Kingston upon Thames KT2 6SR
Tel./e-mail	0208 547 3333 info@croner.co.uk
Fax/Website	0208 547 2637 www.croner.co.uk

CRONER REWARD

Title	**Electronics Industry Rewards**
Coverage	Salary information on management, professional, technical and commercial jobs in the software and electronics sector. Based on research by the company.
Frequency	Twice yearly.
Web facilities	General details of surveys, online ordering and paid-for access to data on site.
Cost	£560.
Comments	Published in March and September. Specific enquiries answered from Croner Reward's data bank.
Address	145 London Road, Kingston upon Thames KT2 6SR
Tel./e-mail	0208 547 3333 info@croner.co.uk
Fax/Website	0208 547 2637 www.croner.co.uk

CRONER REWARD

Title	**Distribution and Transport Rewards**
Coverage	Salary information on management, professional, technical and commercial jobs in the distribution sector. Based on research by the company.
Frequency	Twice yearly.
Web facilities	General details of surveys, online ordering and paid-for access to data on site.
Cost	£560.
Comments	Produced in association with the Institute of Logistics and Transport and discounts for members. Specific enquiries answered by Croner Reward's data bank.
Address	145 London Road, Kingston upon Thames KT2 6SR
Tel./e-mail	0208 547 3333 info@croner.co.uk
Fax/Website	0208 547 2637 www.croner.co.uk

CRONER REWARD

Title	**IT Rewards**
Coverage	Pay market data for all IT and computing job functions ranging from computing directors to trainee computer operators. Based on research by the company.
Frequency	Twice yearly.
Web facilities	General details of surveys, online ordering and paid-for access to data on site.
Cost	£250.
Comments	Published in March and September. Specific enquiries answered from Croner Reward's data bank.
Address	145 London Road, Kingston upon Thames KT2 6SR
Tel./e-mail	0208 547 3333 info@croner.co.uk
Fax/Website	0208 547 2637 www.croner.co.uk

CRONER REWARD

Title	**Finance Industry Rewards**
Coverage	Salaries and benefits for financial positions across the UK. Based on research by the company across 2000 organisations.
Frequency	Annual.
Web facilities	General details of surveys, online ordering and paid-for access to data on site.
Cost	£400.
Comments	Specific enquiries answered from Croner Reward's data bank.
Address	145 London Road, Kingston upon Thames ST15 0SD
Tel./e-mail	01785 813566 info@croner.co.uk
Fax/Website	01785 817007 www.croner.co.uk

CROP PROTECTION ASSOCIATION

Title	**CPA Crop Protection Sales**
Coverage	Industry sales and pesticide usage in the UK plus data on the world agrochemicals market. Sales data are based on a survey of members with a time series covering the last seven years. Sales data are broken down into herbicides, insecticides, fungicides and others.
Frequency	Annual.
Web facilities	Free access to some statistics on the website, plus online ordering facilities for publications.
Cost	On request.
Comments	Changed name from British Agrochemicals Association.
Address	4 Lincoln Court, Lincoln Road, Peterborough PE1 2RP
Tel./e-mail	01733 349225 info@cropprotection.org.uk
Fax/Website	01733 562523 www.cropprotection.org.uk

CUSHMAN & WAKEFIELD HEALEY & BAKER

Title	**European Cities Monitor**
Coverage	Commentary and statistics on the trends in major cities across Europe, including a number in the UK. Figures for the standard regions and a table of summary data covering a ten-year period. Based on the company's own research with supporting text.
Frequency	Annual.
Web facilities	Free access to reports on site.
Cost	Free.
Comments	
Address	43–45 Portman Square, London W1A 3BG
Tel./e-mail	0207 935 5000
Fax/Website	0207 514 2366 www.healey-baker.com

CUSHMAN & WAKEFIELD HEALEY & BAKER

Title	**Quarterly Market Report**
Coverage	Data on investment trends in the retail, office and industrial property sectors across Europe with UK now included. Commentary supported by various tables.
Frequency	Quarterly.
Web facilities	Free access to reports on site.
Cost	Free.
Comments	
Address	43–45 Portman Square, London W1A 3BG
Tel./e-mail	0207 935 5000
Fax/Website	0207 514 2366 www.healey-baker.com

DELOITTE

Title	**Profitability Monitor**
Coverage	A quarterly review, with data, of the profitability of UK business and the economic factors likely to affect this profitability.
Frequency	Quarterly.
Web facilities	Free reports on site.
Cost	Free.
Comments	
Address	1 Stonecutter Court, Stonecutter Street, London EC4A 4TR
Tel./e-mail	0207 936 3000 info@deloitte.com
Fax/Website	0207 583 1198 www.deloitte.com

DELOITTE

Title	**Annual Review of Football Finances**
Coverage	Review, with data, of the overall finances of football and individual data on specific clubs.
Frequency	Annual.
Web facilities	General details and summary on site.
Cost	£400; £30 to students.
Comments	
Address	1 Stonecutter Court, Stonecutter Street, London EC4A 4TR
Tel./e-mail	0207 936 3000 info@deloitte.com
Fax/Website	0207 583 1198 www.deloitte.com

DELOITTE

Title	**Budget Hotel Survey**
Coverage	Annual review with data of the UK budget hotel sector including hotel numbers, growth trends, number of rooms, revenues, etc.
Frequency	Annual.
Web facilities	Free access to PDF reports for last few years on site.
Cost	Free.
Comments	Also produces regular reports on the international hotel sector. See www.hotelbenchmarking.com.
Address	1 Stonecutter Court, Stonecutter Street, London EC4R 4TR
Tel./e-mail	0207 936 3000 info@deloitte.com
Fax/Website	0207 583 1198 www.deloitte.com

DHL INTERNATIONAL (UK) LTD

Title	**Quarterly Export Indicator**
Coverage	This publication surveys the level of business confidence amongst the UK's manufacturing export industries and it is based on telephone interviews with approximately 500 directors and managers responsible for exports in British manufacturing. The survey results include export expectations over the next 3 and 12 months, trends in the main factors affecting exports, opinions on the role of the EU and the single European currency, and trends in raw material costs.
Frequency	Quarterly.
Web facilities	
Cost	Free.
Comments	The opinion survey is carried out by Gallup on behalf of DHL.
Address	Orbital Park, 178–188 Great South West Road, Hounslow, Middlesex TW4 6JS
Tel./e-mail	0208 818 8049
Fax/Website	0208 818 8581 www.dhl.co.uk

DIALOG

Title	**Tradstat**
Coverage	An online database of UK import and export statistics with data on specific products. Based on data supplied by HM Customs and Excise and part of an international database of foreign trade statistics.
Frequency	Regular.
Web facilities	General details of services and paid-for access to service on site.
Cost	On request.
Comments	
Address	3rd Floor, Palace House, 3 Cathedral Street, London SE1 6EE
Tel./e-mail	0207 940 6900 dialogcustomer@thomson.com
Fax/Website	0207 940 6800 www.dialog.com

DIGITAL & SCREEN PRINTING ASSOCIATION

Title	**Survey of Trends**
Coverage	A survey of trends in the previous three months and likely trends in the coming three months based on returns from members. Includes data on costs, sales, orders, margins on sales, capital expenditure, employment and prices.
Frequency	Quarterly.
Web facilities	
Cost	Free to participating members.
Comments	
Address	7A West Street, Reigate RH2 9BL
Tel./e-mail	01737 240792 info@dspa.co.uk
Fax/Website	01737 240770 www.dspa.co.uk

DIRECT MAIL INFORMATION SERVICE

Title	**DMIS In Brief**
Coverage	Compilation of key statistics covering the direct mail sector.
Frequency	Annual.
Web facilities	Free access to statistics on the website, plus online ordering facilities for other data.
Cost	Free.
Comments	
Address	5 Carlisle Street, London W1D 3JX
Tel./e-mail	0207 494 0483 jo@dmis.co.uk
Fax/Website	0207 494 0455 www.dmis.co.uk

DIRECT MAIL INFORMATION SERVICE

Title	**Consumer Direct Mail Trends**
Coverage	Commentary and graphs on the volume of direct mail, mail opened, responses, purchases, awareness. Based on interviews with over 600 interviewees.
Frequency	Every two years.
Web facilities	Free access to statistics on the website, plus online ordering facilities for other data.
Cost	Free.
Comments	Published every two years since 1985.
Address	5 Carlisle Street, London W1V 6JX
Tel./e-mail	0207 494 0483 jo@dmis.co.uk
Fax/Website	0207 494 0455 www.dmis.co.uk

DIRECT MAIL INFORMATION SERVICE

Title	**The Letterbox Factfile 2---**
Coverage	Top line summary of information on the direct mail industry. Data on the consumer letterbox, levels of receipt, business-to-business direct mail, direct mail in Europe.
Frequency	Annual.
Web facilities	Free access on the website, plus online ordering facilities for other data.
Cost	Free.
Comments	
Address	5 Carlisle Street, London W1D 3JX
Tel./e-mail	0207 494 0483 jo@dmis.co.uk
Fax/Website	0207 494 0455 www.dmis.co.uk

DIRECT MAIL INFORMATION SERVICE

Title	**Business to Business Direct Mail Trends 2---**
Coverage	A survey of business peoples' attitudes to direct mail. Includes the numbers of managers whose mail is 'filtered', the quality of mail 'filtered', the quality of addressing and the amount of mail read and responded to.
Frequency	Annual.
Web facilities	Free access to statistics on the website, plus online ordering facilities for other data.
Cost	Free.
Comments	
Address	5 Carlisle Street, London W1V 6JX
Tel./e-mail	0207 494 0483 jo@dmis.co.uk
Fax/Website	0207 494 0455 www.dmis.co.uk

DIRECT MAIL INFORMATION SERVICE

Title	**DMIS Factbook**
Coverage	Over 250 pages of data and information on the direct mail industry including historical data from the last 11 years.
Frequency	Regular.
Web facilities	General details on the website and online ordering facilities.
Cost	£250.
Comments	
Address	5 Carlisle Street, London W1V 6JX
Tel./e-mail	0207 494 0483 jo@dmis.co.uk
Fax/Website	0207 494 0455 www.dmis.co.uk

DIRECT MARKETING ASSOCIATION

Title	**Direct Marketing Expenditure Trends**
Coverage	A compilation of statistics on direct marketing budgets, expenditure by category and by media, from a variety of non-official sources.
Frequency	Annual.
Web facilities	Executive summary free on site.
Cost	£295 plus VAT.
Comments	
Address	70 Margaret Street, London W1W 8SS
Tel./e-mail	0207 291 3300 info@dma.org.uk
Fax/Website	0207 323 4426 www.dma.org.uk

DIRECT MARKETING ASSOCIATION

Title	**DMA Census of the UK Direct Marketing Industry**
Coverage	A detailed survey of the industry covering structure, sales, postings etc. based largely on original research.
Frequency	Annual.
Web facilities	Executive summary free on site.
Cost	£395; free for members.
Comments	Online access to the census also available.
Address	70 Margaret Stree, London W1W 8SS
Tel./e-mail	0207 291 3300 info@dma.org.uk
Fax/Website	0207 323 4426 www.dma.org.uk

DIRECT MARKETING ASSOCIATION

Title	**National E-mail Benchmarking Survey**
Coverage	Regular statistics on the level of e-mail marketing, categories, trends, etc.
Frequency	Quarterly.
Web facilities	Executive summary free on site.
Cost	£395 plus VAT; £195 plus VAT per quarter.
Comments	
Address	70 Margaret Street, London W1W 8SS
Tel./e-mail	0207 291 3300 info@dma.org.uk
Fax/Website	0207 323 4426 www.dma.org.uk

DODONA

Title	**Cinemagoing**
Coverage	An annual review of cinema going trends in the UK and Ireland based on research by the company. Includes data on audiences, audience demographics, films, distributors, cinemas, etc.
Frequency	Annual.
Web facilities	Free access to detailed summaries from the research and other research, on site.
Cost	£600 for UK and Ireland. Also site licences available.
Comments	Publishes various other European and international reports.
Address	PO Box 450, Leicester LE2 2TE
Tel./e-mail	0116 285 4550 customer.service@dodona.co.uk
Fax/Website	0116 285 4575 www.dodona.co.uk

DONOVAN DATA SYSTEMS

Title	**Donovan Database Services**
Coverage	Donovan has access to a number of media, TV and radio, consumer, advertising and audience/readership surveys.
Frequency	Continuous.
Web facilities	General details of services on site.
Cost	On request, depending on the nature and range of information required.
Comments	
Address	7 Farm Street, London W1X 7RB
Tel./e-mail	0207 255 7000 henry.lawson@dds.co.uk
Fax/Website	0207 255 7171 www.dds.co.uk

DTZ DEBENHAM THORPE

Title	**Retail Warehousing**
Coverage	An economic overview is followed by data on retail demographics, investment trends and performance, planning policies. Based on surveys carried out by the company.
Frequency	Annual.
Web facilities	General access to latest reports on site.
Cost	Free.
Comments	Publishes various other reports on key European cities and one-off reports on property issues, e.g. business parks, retailing, overseas investment in commercial property.
Address	1 Curzon Street, London W1A 5PZ
Tel./e-mail	0207 408 1161
Fax/Website	0207 643 6000 www.dtz.com

DTZ DEBENHAM THORPE

Title	**UK Property Market Overview**
Coverage	A review of trends in all sectors of the property market including retail, industrial and office. Data and commentary based largely on research undertaken by the company.
Frequency	Quarterly.
Web facilities	General access to latest reports on site.
Cost	Free.
Comments	Publishes various other reports on key European cities and one-off reports on property issues, e.g. business parks, retailing, overseas investment in commercial property.
Address	1 Curzon Street, London W1A 5PZ
Tel./e-mail	0207 408 1161
Fax/Website	0207 643 6000 www.dtz.com

DTZ DEBENHAM THORPE

Title	**Overseas Acquisitions in UK Commercial Property**
Coverage	Analysis and data relating to overseas investment trends in UK property. Based on company research.
Frequency	Annual.
Web facilities	General access to the latest reports on site.
Cost	Free.
Comments	
Address	1 Curzon Street, London W1A 5PZ
Tel./e-mail	0207 408 1161
Fax/Website	0207 643 6000 www.dtz.com

DTZ DEBENHAM THORPE

Title	**PMI – Property Market Indicators**
Coverage	Chartbook of data on the supply of and demand for property plus additional data on rentals performance, investment.
Frequency	Quarterly.
Web facilities	General access to latest publications on site.
Cost	Free.
Comments	
Address	1 Curzon Street, London W1A 5PZ
Tel./e-mail	0207 408 1161
Fax/Website	0207 643 6000 www.dtz.com

DTZ DEBENHAM THORPE

Title	**Money into Property**
Coverage	An annual review of investment and capital flows into the UK property sector based on the company's own research.
Frequency	Annual.
Web facilities	General access to the latest publications on the site.
Cost	Free.
Comments	
Address	1 Curzon Street, London W1A 5PZ
Tel./e-mail	0207 408 1161
Fax/Website	0207 643 6000 www.dtz.com

DTZ DEBENHAM THORPE

Title	**UK Industrial Market Report**
Coverage	A review of the industrial property market including data on enquiries, industrial space, returns and investment. Based on company's own research.
Frequency	Annual.
Web facilities	General access to the latest publications on site.
Cost	Free.
Comments	
Address	1 Curzon Street, London W1A 5PZ
Tel./e-mail	0207 408 1161
Fax/Website	0207 643 6000 www.dtz.com

DTZ DEBENHAM THORPE

Title	**UK Economic Overview**
Coverage	A review of economic trends based on official and non-official sources.
Frequency	Quarterly.
Web facilities	General access to the latest publications on site.
Cost	Free.
Comments	
Address	1 Curzon Street, London W1A 5PZ
Tel./e-mail	0207 408 1161
Fax/Website	0207 643 6000 www.dtz.com

DTZ DEBENHAM THORPE

Title	**UK Regional Office Markets**
Coverage	A review of office market trends in key urban areas around the UK. Based on company's own research.
Frequency	Regular.
Web facilities	General access to the latest publications on site.
Cost	Free.
Comments	
Address	1 Curzon Street, London W1A 5PZ
Tel./e-mail	0207 408 1161
Fax/Website	0207 643 6000 www.dtz.com

DUN AND BRADSTREET LTD

Title	**Key Business Ratios**
Coverage	Twenty key ratios arranged by SIC industry group with data for the latest three years available. Based on the company's own analysis of company financial data.
Frequency	Annual.
Web facilities	General details and some free basic data on site.
Cost	
Comments	
Address	Holmers Farm Way, High Wycombe HP12 4UL
Tel./e-mail	0870 243 2344 customerhelp@dnb.com
Fax/Website	0161 455 5193 www.dnb.com

DUN AND BRADSTREET LTD

Title	**Business Failure Statistics**
Coverage	Company liquidations and bankruptcies analysed by sector and region. A commentary supports the data which comes from records maintained by the company.
Frequency	Quarterly.
Web facilities	General details and some free basic data on site.
Cost	Free.
Comments	
Address	Holmers Farm Way, High Wycombe HP12 4UL
Tel./e-mail	0870 243 2344 customerhelp@dnb.com
Fax/Website	0161 455 5193 www.dnb.com

ECONOMIST PUBLICATIONS LTD

Title	**UK Country Report**
Coverage	A quarterly review of economic, political and business trends in the UK. Plus five-year forecasts and a financial outlook.
Frequency	Quarterly.
Web facilities	General details and some free basic data on site.
Cost	On request.
Comments	
Address	15 Regent Street, London SW1Y 4LR
Tel./e-mail	0207 830 1007 london@eiu.com
Fax/Website	0207 499 1023 www.eiu.com

ECONOMIST PUBLICATIONS LTD

Title	**United Kingdom Quarterly Economic Review**
Coverage	Commentary and statistics on general economic trends and business conditions in the UK. Based mainly on official sources.
Frequency	Quarterly.
Web facilities	Free summary data and news, plus paid-for access to detailed data and reports on site.
Cost	On request.
Comments	Various other one-off and regular reports published on UK and international markets.
Address	15 Regent Street, London SW1Y 4LR
Tel./e-mail	0207 830 1007 london@eiu.com
Fax/Website	0207 499 1023 www.eiu.com

ELECTRIC VEHICLE ASSOCIATION OF GREAT BRITAIN

Title	**Yardstick Costs for Battery Electrics**
Coverage	Basic costs for electric vehicles used in warehouses and airports. Based on data collected by the association.
Frequency	Regular.
Web facilities	
Cost	On request.
Comments	Also produces the *EVA Manual*.
Address	Alexandra House, Harrowden Road, Wellingborough NN8 5BD
Tel./e-mail	01933 276618
Fax/Website	01933 276618 www.gwassoc.dircon.co.uk/Erahome.html

EMAP MEDIA LTD

Title	**British Rate and Data (BRAD)**
Coverage	Details of all UK media advertising rates, subscription rates, cover prices, circulation trends, etc. Also general data on advertising expenditure and number of cinemas.
Frequency	Monthly.
Web facilities	Details of services on site, including new BRADnet web-based service.
Cost	£650 hard copy; £1060 online.
Comments	
Address	33–39 Bowling Green Lane, London EC1R 0DA
Tel./e-mail	0207 505 8275 nik.palmer@emap.com
Fax/Website	0207 505 8293 www.intellagencia.com

ENERGY INSTITUTE

Title	**EI Petroleum Statistical Service**
Coverage	Data sheets providing summary information on the main indicators relating to the UK and world petroleum sector. Based largely on the institute's own data.
Frequency	Quarterly.
Web facilities	Available from the website for £80 annual subscription (also in traditional hard copy).
Cost	£80.
Comments	Also publishes the monthly *Petroleum Review* which contains some statistics.
Address	61 New Cavendish Street, London W1G 7AR
Tel./e-mail	0207 467 7100 info@energyinst.org
Fax/Website	0207 255 1472 www.energyinst.org

ENERGY INSTITUTE

Title	**UK Deliveries into Inland Consumption**
Coverage	Data on petroleum deliveries onto the UK market and consumption trends.
Frequency	Annual.
Web facilities	General details of publications on the website.
Cost	£31.25 (electronic); £37.50 (hard copy).
Comments	Also publishes the monthly *Petroleum Review* which contains some statistics.
Address	61 New Cavendish Street, London W1G 7AR
Tel./e-mail	0207 467 7100 info@energyinst.org
Fax/Website	0207 255 1472 www.energyinst.org

ENERGY INSTITUTE

Title	**Retail Marketing Survey**
Coverage	Statistics and commentary on the retail market for petrol with data on sites, sales, company performance and new developments and sites. Also data on forecourt retailing.
Frequency	Annual.
Web facilities	General details of publications on the website.
Cost	£20; free as part of subscription to *Petroleum Review*.
Comments	Orders for survey should be sent to Portland Press, Commerce Way, Whitehall Industrial Estate, Colchester, CO2 8HP; telephone 01206 796351. Also publishes the monthly *Petroleum Review* which contains some statistics.
Address	61 New Cavendish Street, London W1G 7AR
Tel./e-mail	0207 467 7100 info@energyinst.org
Fax/Website	0207 255 1472 www.energyinst.org

ENERGY INSTITUTE

Title	**Petroleum Statistics – Monthly Update Services**
Coverage	Selected statistics showing oil prices, trends etc are updated monthly.
Frequency	Monthly.
Web facilities	General details of publications on the website.
Cost	£18 per sheet electronically delivered; £25 hard copy.
Comments	Also publishes the monthly *Petroleum Review* which contains some statistics.
Address	61 New Cavendish Street, London W1G 7AR
Tel./e-mail	0207 467 7100 info@energyinsy.org
Fax/Website	0207 255 1472 www.energyinst.org

ENGINEERING EMPLOYERS' FEDERATION

Title	**Engineering Outlook**
Coverage	Graphs, tables and commentary on engineering output and sales, imports and exports. Some forecasts are included usually up to one year ahead and a commentary accompanies the data. Based on a combination of official and non-official sources.
Frequency	Quarterly.
Web facilities	First release from the survey included free on site.
Cost	£200.
Comments	
Address	Broadway House, Tothill Street, London SW1H 9NQ
Tel./e-mail	0207 222 7777 enquiries@eef.org.uk
Fax/Website	0207 222 2782 www.eef.org.uk

ENGINEERING EMPLOYERS' FEDERATION

Title	**Absence and Labour Turnover Survey**
Coverage	Survey of absenteeism trends and workforce changes based on a survey of members.
Frequency	Every two years.
Web facilities	Free copy of the report on site.
Cost	Free.
Comments	
Address	Broadway House, Tothill Street, London SW1H 9NQ
Tel./e-mail	0207 222 7777 enquiries@eef.org.uk
Fax/Website	0207 222 2782 www.eef.org.uk

ENGINEERING EMPLOYERS' FEDERATION

Title	**Management and Professional Engineers Pay Survey**
Coverage	Salaries by job functions and categories and by sector. Based on returns from members.
Frequency	Annual.
Web facilities	
Cost	Free.
Comments	Only available to members.
Address	Broadway House, Tothill Street, London SW1H 9NQ
Tel./e-mail	0207 222 7777 enquiries@eef.org.uk
Fax/Website	0207 222 2782 www.eef.org.uk

ENGINEERING EMPLOYERS' FEDERATION

Title	**Employers' Liability Insurance – Survey of Insurance Costs**
Coverage	A survey of insurance costs based on member returns.
Frequency	Annual.
Web facilities	Free download of report on site.
Cost	Free.
Comments	First edition published in 2004.
Address	Broadway House, Tothill Street, London SW1H 9NQ
Tel./e-mail	0207 222 7777 enquiries@eef.org.uk
Fax/Website	0207 222 2782 www.eef.org.uk

ENGINEERING EMPLOYERS' FEDERATION

Title	**EEF Survey of Energy Prices**
Coverage	A regular survey of energy prices relevant to the engineering sector.
Frequency	Regular.
Web facilities	Free download of report on site.
Cost	Free.
Comments	
Address	Broadway House, Tothill Street, London SW1H 9NQ
Tel./e-mail	0207 222 7777 enquiries@eef.org.uk
Fax/Website	0207 222 2782 www.eef.org.uk

ENGLISH COMMUNITY CARE ASSOCIATION

Title	**Independent Healthcare Statistics**
Coverage	Details of the size of and growth trends for, the private hospital market in the UK. Based largely on information collected by the association.
Frequency	Regular.
Web facilities	Available free on the site.
Cost	
Comments	English Community Care Association merged with Independent Healthcare Association in 2004.
Address	145 Cannon Street, London EC4N 5BQ
Tel./e-mail	0207 220 9595 info@ecca.org.uk
Fax/Website	0207 220 9596 www.ecca.org.uk

ENVIRONMENTAL TRANSPORT ASSOCIATION

Title	**Factsheets**
Coverage	Various factsheets relating to transport and the environment and based on various sources.
Frequency	Regular.
Web facilities	
Cost	Free.
Comments	The association is relatively new, having been established in 1990.
Address	68 High Street, Weybridge KT13 8RS
Tel./e-mail	0800 212 810 eta@eta.co.uk
Fax/Website	01932 829015 www.eta.co.uk

EQUIFAX

Title	**Lifestyle Advance**
Coverage	A range of demographic and consumer data based on a combination of data supplied by Equifax and Claritas Axciom data.
Frequency	Continuous.
Web facilities	General details of services on site.
Cost	On request, depending on the range and nature of the information required.
Comments	
Address	Sentinel House, 16 Harcourt Street, London W1H 2AE
Tel./e-mail	0207 724 6116
Fax/Website	0181 686 7777 www.equifax.com

ERNST & YOUNG

Title	**Analysis of Profit Warnings**
Coverage	An analysis of profit warnings issued by UK quoted companies with details of the number and percentage changes over the previous quarter. Regional analysis and focus on specific sectors in issues.
Frequency	Quarterly.
Web facilities	Free access to data and other reports on site.
Cost	Free.
Comments	
Address	Becket House, 1 Lambeth Palace Road, London SE1 7EU
Tel./e-mail	0207 951 2000
Fax/Website	0207 951 1345 www.ey.com/uk

ERNST AND YOUNG ITEM CLUB

Title	**UK Economic Prospects**
Coverage	A detailed review of economic trends and prospects with data on all the main economic indicators.
Frequency	Quarterly.
Web facilities	Free access to data on Ernst and Young site.
Cost	Free.
Comments	
Address	Becket House, 1 Lambeth Palace Road, London SE1 7EU
Tel./e-mail	0207 951 2000
Fax/Website	0207 951 1345 www.ey.com/uk/economy

ERNST AND YOUNG SCOTTISH ITEM CLUB

Title	**Scottish Item Club Forecast**
Coverage	Economic trends and forecasts of the Scottish economy.
Frequency	Quarterly.
Web facilities	Free access to data on the Ernst and Young website.
Cost	Free.
Comments	
Address	Becket House, 1 Lambeth Palace Road, London SE1 7EU
Tel./e-mail	0207 951 2000
Fax/Website	0207 951 1345 www.ey.com/uk/economy

ESTATES GAZETTE

Title	**Figures and Figures**
Coverage	General data relating to the property market including house prices, farm prices, rent index, housing starts and completions, land prices, property yields, interest rates. Based mainly on various non-official sources supported by some official statistics.
Frequency	Monthly in a weekly journal.
Web facilities	News and other information on site.
Cost	£118; £2.10 for a single issue.
Comments	
Address	Estates Gazette Ltd, 151 Wardour Street, London W1V 4BN
Tel./e-mail	0207 437 0141 info@egi.co.uk
Fax/Website	0207 437 0294 www.egi.co.uk

ESTATES GAZETTE

Title	**Estates Gazette and PSD Salary & Benefits Survey**
Coverage	Comprehensive annual guide to salaries and benefits in the property industry broken down by job.
Frequency	Annual.
Web facilities	News and other information on site.
Cost	£195.
Comments	Published in association with NSM Research.
Address	Estates Gazette Ltd, 151 Wardour Street, London W1F 8BN
Tel./e-mail	0207 437 0141 info@egi.co.uk
Fax/Website	0207 437 0294 www.egi.co.uk

ESTATES GAZETTE

Title	**Office Trends**
Coverage	Annual review of trends in the commercial property sector in the UK.
Frequency	Annual.
Web facilities	News and other information on site.
Cost	£25.
Comments	Published each year in June.
Address	Estates Gazette Ltd, 151 Wardour Street, London W1F 8BN
Tel./e-mail	0207 437 0141 info@egi.co.uk
Fax/Website	0207 437 0294 www.egi.co.uk

ESTATES GAZETTE

Title	**Shopping Centre Progress**
Coverage	Annual review of shopping centre developments including data on new openings, floorspace, etc.
Frequency	Annual.
Web facilities	News and other information on site.
Cost	£30.
Comments	Published by Estates Gazette for the British Council of Shopping Centres.
Address	Estates Gazette Ltd, 151 Wardour Street, London W1F 8BN
Tel./e-mail	0207 437 0141 info@egi.co.uk
Fax/Website	0207 437 0294 www.egi.co.uk

ESTATES GAZETTE

Title	**The Valuation Office Property Market Report**
Coverage	Based on data collected by the Valuation Office's 95 UK District Valuers. The publication contains facts, figures and commentary on UK property trends.
Frequency	Twice yearly.
Web facilities	News and other information on site.
Cost	£80; £45 per issue.
Comments	
Address	Estates Gazette Ltd, 151 Wardour Street, London W1F 8BN
Tel./e-mail	0207 437 0141 info@egi.co.uk
Fax/Website	0207 437 0294 www.egi.co.uk

ETHNIC FOCUS

Title	**Ethnibus**
Coverage	Omnibus survey undertaking monthly of 750 adults 16 and over in ethnic groups.
Frequency	Monthly.
Web facilities	General details on site.
Cost	On request.
Comments	
Address	Wembley Point, 1 Harrow Road, Wembley HH9 6DE
Tel./e-mail	07000 266 587 research@ethnicfocus.com
Fax/Website	0208 900 5601 www.ethnicfocus.com

EUREST

Title	**Eurest Lunchtime Report**
Coverage	An annual review of the eating habits of workers and other activities during lunch times. Based on commissioned research.
Frequency	Annual.
Web facilities	
Cost	On request.
Comments	
Address	Rivermead, Oxford Road, Denham, Uxbridge UB9 4BP
Tel./e-mail	01895 555554 info@compass-group.co.uk
Fax/Website	www.compass-group.co.uk

EURODIRECT DATABASE MARKETING

Title	**CAMEO UK**
Coverage	CAMEO UK is a demographic classification system based on census data with additional information from the electoral roll.
Frequency	Continuous.
Web facilities	General details of services on site.
Cost	On request and depending on the range and nature of the information required.
Comments	Additional services include CAMEO Financial, CAMEO Income, CAMEO Investment, etc.
Address	One Park Lane, Leeds LS3 1EP
Tel./e-mail	0113 388 4300 info@skiptoninformationgroup.com
Fax/Website	0113 388 4308 www.skiptoninformationgroup.com

EUROPEAN COSMETIC MARKETS

Title	**Market Reviews**
Coverage	Market reports are scheduled throughout the year and each report has a review of UK trends alongside reviews of the other major European markets. The basic annual schedule is bathroom products (January), skin care (February), men's lines (March), sun care (April), women's fragrances (May), body care (June), deodorants (July), hair care (September), hair styling (October), colour cosmetics (November), oral hygiene (December). Mainly based on original consumer research.
Frequency	Monthly in a monthly journal.
Web facilities	General details of reviews on site.
Cost	£770; £85 per issue.
Comments	
Address	Wilmington Publishing Ltd, 6–14 Underwood Street, London N1 7JQ
Tel./e-mail	0207 549 8626 ecm@wilmington.co.uk
Fax/Website	0207 549 8622 www.cosmeticsbusiness.com

EUROPEAN PLASTICS NEWS

Title	**UK Plastics Annual Review**
Coverage	A commentary on the market performance of plastics raw materials in the UK with tables on the consumption of major plastics. A general outlook for the coming year is given.
Frequency	Annual in a monthly journal.
Web facilities	General details and news on site.
Cost	£250.
Comments	General data on markets and prices in each issue.
Address	EMAP Maclaren Ltd, 19th Floor, Leon House, 233 High Street, Croydon CR0 9XT
Tel./e-mail	0208 277 5000
Fax/Website	0208 277 5531 www.plasticssearch.com

EXHIBITION VENUES ASSOCIATION

Title	**UK Exhibition Facts**
Coverage	Survey of exhibition visitors, exhibitor spending, exhibition numbers, international tourism. Data usually covers the last three years.
Frequency	Annual.
Web facilities	Summary data from annual publication available free on site.
Cost	£200 plus VAT.
Comments	Produced as a CD-ROM.
Address	15 Keeble Court, North Seaton, Northumberland NE63 9SF
Tel./e-mail	01670 818801 info@exhibitionvenues.com
Fax/Website	www.exhibitionvenues.com

EXPERIAN BUSINESS STRATEGIES

Title	**Construction Forecasts**
Coverage	Short-term construction forecasts and current trends, covering housing, industrial, commercial and infrastructure. Value and volume forecasts are included and a detailed analysis of the forecasts accompanies the tables.
Frequency	Quarterly.
Web facilities	General details of statistics and online ordering facilities, on website.
Cost	On request.
Comments	
Address	Embankment House, Electric Avenue, Nottingham NG8 0EH
Tel./e-mail	0115 968 5151 business-strategies@uk.experian.com
Fax/Website	0115 968 5003 www.business-strategies.co.uk

EXPERIAN BUSINESS STRATEGIES

Title	**Construction Industry Focus**
Coverage	Data on contractors' activity, order books, tender prices and short-term prospects for employment and tender prices. Based on a combination of official and non-official data.
Frequency	Monthly.
Web facilities	General details of statistics and online ordering facilities, on the website.
Cost	On request.
Comments	
Address	Embankment House, Electric Avenue, Nottingham NG8 0EH
Tel./e-mail	0115 968 5151 business-strategies@uk.experian.com
Fax/Website	0115 968 5003 www.business-strategies.co.uk

EXPERIAN LTD

Title	**Mosaic**
Coverage	Geodemographic classification scheme and service providing analysis of census and lifestyle data.
Frequency	Continuous.
Web facilities	General details of service on site.
Cost	On request.
Comments	
Address	Talbot House, Talbot Street, Nottingham NG1 5HF
Tel./e-mail	0115 934 4547
Fax/Website	0115 934 4535 www.experian.com

EXPERIAN LTD

Title	**Neighbourhood Statistics**
Coverage	A new information service launched in 2001 offering academics free access to a database of annually updated neighbourhood statistics.
Frequency	Regular.
Web facilities	
Cost	Free for academics.
Comments	Developed through an agreement with the Economic and Social Research Council (ESRC).
Address	Talbot House, Talbot Street, Nottingham NG1 5HF
Tel./e-mail	0115 934 4547
Fax/Website	0115 934 4535 www.experian.com

FACTORS AND DISCOUNTERS ASSOCIATION

Title	**Annual Review**
Coverage	Revenues for UK factors and discounters from both their domestic and international businesses.
Frequency	Twice yearly.
Web facilities	Free access to statistics on the site.
Cost	Free.
Comments	
Address	Boston House, The Little Green, Richmond TW9 1QE
Tel./e-mail	0208 332 9955 nicola.breeze@factors.org.uk
Fax/Website	0208 332 2585 www.factors.org.uk

FACTS INTERNATIONAL LTD

Title	**Telefacts**
Coverage	An omnibus survey of 500 or 1000 adults each month. It is a telephone survey covering the whole of the UK.
Frequency	Monthly.
Web facilities	
Cost	Varies according to questions and analysis.
Comments	
Address	Facts Centre, 3 Henwood, Ashford TN24 8FL
Tel./e-mail	01233 637000 sales@facts.uk.com
Fax/Website	01233 626950 www.facts.uk.com

FARMERS' WEEKLY

Title	**Prices and Trends**
Coverage	Prices of various crops, livestock, etc. with updates weekly, monthly and quarterly.
Frequency	Regular.
Web facilities	General market data free on site.
Cost	On request.
Comments	
Address	Quadrant House, The Quadrant, Sutton SM2 5AS
Tel./e-mail	0208 652 4911 info@fwi.co.uk
Fax/Website	0208 652 4005 www.fwi.co.uk

FARMERS' WEEKLY

Title	**CropWatch**
Coverage	Regular crop reports assessing disease trends and other issues affecting crops.
Frequency	Regular.
Web facilities	General market data free on site.
Cost	On request.
Comments	
Address	Quadrant House, The Quadrant, Sutton SM2 5AS
Tel./e-mail	0208 652 4911 info@fwi.co.uk
Fax/Website	0208 652 4005 www.fwi.co.uk

FEDERATION OF BAKERS

Title	**Annual Report**
Coverage	Includes a section with statistics on production trends in the UK bakery industry.
Frequency	Annual.
Web facilities	Free industry facts on site.
Cost	Free.
Comments	
Address	6 Catherine Street, London WC2B 5JW
Tel./e-mail	0207 420 7190 info@bakersfederation.org.uk
Fax/Website	0207 397 0542 www.bakersfederation.org.uk

FEDERATION OF BRITISH CREMATION AUTHORITIES

Title	**Annual Report**
Coverage	Includes cremation statistics for individual crematoria over a five-year period. Based on the federation's own survey. A large amount of supporting text accompanies the data.
Frequency	Annual.
Web facilities	Statistics available to members only on the site.
Cost	Free.
Comments	
Address	41 Salisbury Road, Carshalton SM5 3HA
Tel./e-mail	0208 669 4521
Fax/Website	www.fbca.org.uk

FEDERATION OF MASTER BUILDERS

Title	**FMB State of Trade Survey**
Coverage	Results of a survey of member firms in England and Wales with data on workload for the previous quarter and predictions for the coming quarter. Various topical questions are also included in each survey. Text supports the data.
Frequency	Quarterly.
Web facilities	
Cost	On request.
Comments	Also produces irregular factsheets.
Address	14 Great James Street, London WC1N 3DP
Tel./e-mail	0207 242 7583 central@fmb.org.uk
Fax/Website	0207 404 0296 www.fmb.org.uk

FEDERATION OF OPHTHALMIC & DISPENSING OPTICIANS

Title	**Optics at a Glance**
Coverage	General statistics on optics including the number of opticians and average spectacle prices. Based on a combination of the federation's own survey and central government data. Some supporting commentary.
Frequency	Annual.
Web facilities	Free access to annual data on the site.
Cost	Free.
Comments	
Address	199 Gloucester Terrace, London W2 6LD
Tel./e-mail	0207 298 5151 info@fodo.com
Fax/Website	0207 298 5111 www.fodo.com

FEDERATION OF SMALL BUSINESSES

Title	**Small Business Surveys**
Coverage	Various regular surveys of the small business sector including a crime and small business survey and payment survey. Based mainly on member surveys.
Frequency	Regular.
Web facilities	
Cost	On request.
Comments	A range of small business statistics on the website.
Address	2 Catherine Place, London SW1E 6HF
Tel./e-mail	0207 233 7900 london@fsb.org.uk
Fax/Website	0207 233 7899 www.fsb.org.uk

FINANCE AND LEASING ASSOCIATION

Title	**Monthly Motor Finance**
Coverage	Statistics for the financing of new and used cars based on data obtained by the association.
Frequency	Monthly.
Web facilities	Free statistics from the monthly survey on site.
Cost	Free.
Comments	
Address	15–19 Kingsway, London WC2B 6UN
Tel./e-mail	0207 836 6511 statistics@fla.org.uk
Fax/Website	0207 420 9600 www.fla.org.uk

FINANCE AND LEASING ASSOCIATION

Title	**FLA Monthly Statistics**
Coverage	General data on business and consumer financing of motor vehicles.
Frequency	Monthly.
Web facilities	Free statistics from monthly survey on site.
Cost	Free.
Comments	
Address	15–19 Kingsway, London WC2B 6UN
Tel./e-mail	0207 836 6511 statistics@fla.org.uk
Fax/Website	0207 420 9600 www.fla.org.uk

FINANCE AND LEASING ASSOCIATION

Title	**Annual Report**
Coverage	Contains commentary and statistics on trends in the credit and leasing market with most tables giving figures for the last two years. Based on transactions by FLA members.
Frequency	Annual.
Web facilities	Free statistics on site.
Cost	Free.
Comments	
Address	15–19 Kingsway, London WC2B 6UN
Tel./e-mail	0207 836 6511 statistics@fla.org.uk
Fax/Website	0207 420 9600 www.fla.org.uk

FIRA INTERNATIONAL LTD

Title	**Statistical Digest for the UK Furniture Industry**
Coverage	Statistics include turnover, sales, deliveries, consumption, imports, exports, prices and advertising. Mainly based on central government data, supplemented by association and non-official sources.
Frequency	Annual.
Web facilities	General details on the site.
Cost	£200.
Comments	Also produces statistics on the international market.
Address	Maxwell Road, Stevenage SG1 2EW
Tel./e-mail	01438 777700 statistics@fira.co.uk
Fax/Website	01438 777800 www.fira.co.uk

FIRST TRUST BANK

Title	**Economic Outlook and Business Review**
Coverage	Economic analysis and trends data for Northern Ireland, UK and Republic of Ireland, plus articles.
Frequency	Quarterly.
Web facilities	Free access to PDF report on site.
Cost	Free.
Comments	
Address	4 Queen's Square, Belfast BT1 3DJ
Tel./e-mail	0289 032 5599 business.site@aib.ie
Fax/Website	0289 023 5480 www.firstbanktrust.co.uk

FLOUR ADVISORY BUREAU

Title	**Flour Statistics**
Coverage	A guide to flour in the UK with some basic data.
Frequency	Regular.
Web facilities	Basic data plus national bread production, consumption statistics on site.
Cost	Free.
Comments	
Address	21 Arlington Street, London SW1A 1RN
Tel./e-mail	0207 493 2521 info@fabflour.co.uk
Fax/Website	0207 493 6785 www.fabflour.co.uk

FOOD FROM BRITAIN

Title	**Annual Report**
Coverage	Includes statistics on food exports and the key export markets for UK food companies plus general details of trends in the industry. Based primarily on official statistics.
Frequency	Annual.
Web facilities	General details of statistics, online ordering and access to statistics for members only.
Cost	Free.
Comments	
Address	4th Floor, Manning House, 22 Carlisle Place, London SW1P 1JA
Tel./e-mail	0207 233 5111 info@foodfrombritain.com
Fax/Website	0207 233 9515 www.foodfrombritain.com

FOOD FROM BRITAIN

Title	**Export Trade Review**
Coverage	A review of export trends and opportunities.
Frequency	Annual.
Web facilities	General details of statistics, online ordering and access to statistics for members only on the site.
Cost	£300; free for members.
Comments	
Address	4th Floor, Manning House, 22 Carlisle Place, London SW1P 1JA
Tel./e-mail	0207 233 5111 info@foodfrombritain.com
Fax/Website	0207 233 9515 www.foodfrombritain.com

FOODSERVICE INTELLIGENCE

Title	**Foodservice Barometer**
Coverage	A survey of meals served by caterers in each of nine sectors: hotels, restaurants, public houses, cafes, takeaways, leisure, staff catering, healthcare and education. Also includes a 'balance of confidence' indicator and a special feature in each issue.
Frequency	Monthly.
Web facilities	General details of surveys plus some basic data on website.
Cost	£1250 plus VAT.
Comments	Also publishes various one-off and occasional reports on the food service market.
Address	84 Uxbridge Road, London W13 8RA
Tel./e-mail	0208 799 3205 info@horizonsforsuccess.com
Fax/Website	0208 566 2100 www.foodserviceintelligence.co.uk

FOODSERVICE INTELLIGENCE

Title	**Foodservice Industry Population File**
Coverage	A study of the structure of the catering industry giving number of outlets, value of caterers' food purchases, outlet sizes, number of meals served, sector buying concentration and a regional analysis. Eleven catering sectors are covered in detail with historical trends over a ten-year period. Based on Marketpower research, non-official sources and some official statistics.
Frequency	Annual.
Web facilities	General details of the surveys plus some basic data on the website.
Cost	£1250 plus VAT.
Comments	Also publishes various one-off and occasional reports on the food service market.
Address	84 Uxbridge Road, London W13 8RA
Tel./e-mail	0208 799 3205 info@horizonsforsuccess.com
Fax/Website	0208 566 2100 www.foodserviceintelligence.co.uk

FOODSERVICE INTELLIGENCE

Title	**Foodservice Forecasts**
Coverage	Short-term forecasts for the UK catering industry based on research carried out amongst 700 caterers with trends given sector by sector.
Frequency	Annual.
Web facilities	General details of surveys plus some basic data on the website.
Cost	£850.
Comments	Also publishes various one-off and occasional reports on the food service market.
Address	84 Uxbridge Road, London W13 8RA
Tel./e-mail	0208 799 3205 info@horizonsfor success.com
Fax/Website	0208 566 2100 www.foodserviceintelligence.co.uk

FORUM FOR PRIVATE BUSINESS

Title	**Private Businesses and their Banks**
Coverage	A regular survey of UK banks' attitudes to borrowings with a review of general attitudes towards specific sectors. Data for the latest quarter and earlier quarters.
Frequency	Twice yearly.
Web facilities	Some press release data on the site.
Cost	On request.
Comments	
Address	Ruskin Chambers, Drury Lane, Knutsford WA16 6HA
Tel./e-mail	01565 634467 research@fpb.org
Fax/Website	0870 241 9570 www.fpbltd.co.uk

FORUM FOR PRIVATE BUSINESS

Title	**FPB Quarterly Survey**
Coverage	A survey of member companies to obtain opinions on trends in the sector and opinions on specific issues.
Frequency	Quarterly.
Web facilities	Some free press release data on the site.
Cost	On request.
Comments	
Address	Ruskin Chambers, Drury Lane, Knutsford WA16 6HA
Tel./e-mail	01565 634467 research@fpb.org
Fax/Website	0870 241 9570 www.fpbltd.co.uk

FOUNDRY TRADE JOURNAL

Title	**Metal Prices**
Coverage	Prices of ferro-alloy and other metals and non-ferrous metals by type in the UK. Based on various non-official sources.
Frequency	Twice a month in a twice-monthly journal.
Web facilities	General details on site.
Cost	£144.53.
Comments	
Address	DMG Business Media Ltd, 2 Queensway, Redhill RH1 1QS
Tel./e-mail	01737 855146 foundry@dmg.co.uk
Fax/Website	01737 855469 www.foundrytradejournal.com

FRASER OF ALLENDER INSTITUTE

Title	**Quarterly Economic Commentary**
Coverage	Trends and outlook for the Scottish economy with individual reviews of industrial performance, service sector, labour market and the regions. Also some feature articles. Based mainly on central government data and a supporting commentary.
Frequency	Quarterly.
Web facilities	
Cost	£85; £22.50 per issue.
Comments	
Address	Strathclyde University, 100 Cathedral Street, Glasgow G4 0LN
Tel./e-mail	0141 548 3958 fraser@strath.ac.uk
Fax/Website	0141 552 8347 www.fraser.strath.ac.uk

FRASER OF ALLENDER INSTITUTE

Title	**Scottish Chambers' Business Survey**
Coverage	Trends in the Scottish economy and business sectors based on returns from a sample of members of Scottish chambers of commerce.
Frequency	Quarterly.
Web facilities	
Cost	On request.
Comments	
Address	Strathclyde University, 100 Cathedral Street, Glasgow G4 0LN
Tel./e-mail	0141 548 3958 fraser@strath.ac.uk
Fax/Website	0141 552 8347 www.fraser.strath.ac.uk

FRASER OF ALLENDER INSTITUTE

Title	**Business Forecasting Service**
Coverage	Forecasts of the Scottish economy and industry.
Frequency	Twice yearly.
Web facilities	
Cost	On request.
Comments	
Address	Strathclyde University, 100 Cathedral Street, Glasgow G4 0LN
Tel./e-mail	0141 548 3958 fraser@strath.ac.uk
Fax/Website	0141 552 8347 www.fraser.strath.ac.uk

FREIGHT TRANSPORT ASSOCIATION

Title	**Manager's Guide to Distribution Costs**
Coverage	Statistics on road transport costs including wages, vehicle operating costs, haulage rates. Actual costs and indices are included. Based on the association's own survey with supporting commentary.
Frequency	Quarterly.
Web facilities	Free daily fuel prices on site at www.fta.co.uk/fuelprices.
Cost	£250; £125 for members.
Comments	Primarily for member companies.
Address	Hermes House, St John's Road, Tunbridge Wells TN4 9UZ
Tel./e-mail	01892 526171 enquiries@fta.org.uk
Fax/Website	01892 534989 www.fta.co.uk

FREIGHT TRANSPORT ASSOCIATION

Title	**Quarterly Transport Activity Survey**
Coverage	A review of freight transport by air, road, sea and rail with data on demand, markets, prices, costs, safety, accidents and forecasts. Based on census returns from members, data from the Department of Transport and other sources.
Frequency	Quarterly.
Web facilities	Free daily fuel prices on site at www.fta.co.uk/fuelprices.
Cost	On request.
Comments	Primarily for member companies.
Address	Hermes House, St John's Road, Tunbridge Wells TN4 9UZ
Tel./e-mail	01892 526171 enquiries@fta.org.uk
Fax/Website	01892 534989 www.fta.co.uk

FREIGHT TRANSPORT ASSOCIATION

Title	**Manager's Fuel Price Information Service**
Coverage	Monthly monitor of prices for derv, gas, oil and petrol. Based on the association's own survey.
Frequency	Monthly.
Web facilities	Free daily fuel prices on site at www.fta.co.uk/fuelprices.
Cost	£160.
Comments	Not available to non-members.
Address	Hermes House, St John's Road, Tunbridge Wells TN4 9UZ
Tel./e-mail	01892 526171 enquiries@fta.org.uk
Fax/Website	01892 534989 www.fta.co.uk

FRESH FRUIT AND VEGETABLE INFORMATION BUREAU

Title	**UK Fresh Fruit and Vegetable Market Review**
Coverage	Commentary and statistics on the fresh produce market with sections on specific fruits and vegetables.
Frequency	Annual.
Web facilities	
Cost	Free.
Comments	
Address	126–128 Cromwell Road, London SW7 4ET
Tel./e-mail	0207 373 7734
Fax/Website	0207 373 3926 www.ffvib.co.uk

FT BUSINESS

Title	**Unit Trust & OEICs Yearbook**
Coverage	Includes a market commentary plus a statistical section on sales, total funds, performance, income from unit trusts, etc. The official yearbook of the Association of Unit Trusts and Investment Funds and many figures are taken from this source.
Frequency	Annual.
Web facilities	
Cost	On request.
Comments	
Address	Maple House, 149 Tottenham Court Road, London W1P 9LL
Tel./e-mail	0207 896 2222
Fax/Website	0207 896 2274

FTSE INTERNATIONAL

Title	**UK Market Reports**
Coverage	Data regularly updated on indices, securities, sector weightings, etc.
Frequency	Monthly.
Web facilities	Available as free PDFs on site. Various indices, news and database records available on site.
Cost	Free.
Comments	
Address	10 Upper Bank Street, Canary Wharf, London E14 5NP
Tel./e-mail	0207 866 1800 info@ftse.com
Fax/Website	0207 866 1804 www.ftse.com

GALLUP ORGANISATION

Title	**Gallup Omnibus**
Coverage	Sample surveys of around 1000 adults form the basis of this omnibus survey. Based on face-to-face interviews with adults.
Frequency	Two or three times a week.
Web facilities	Summary data and analysis from polls free on site.
Cost	On request.
Comments	Results available in various machine-readable formats.
Address	The Adelphi, 1–11 John Adams Street, London WC2N 6HS
Tel./e-mail	0207 950 4400 marianne-yates@gallup.co.uk
Fax/Website	0207 950 4402 www.gallup.co.uk

GALLUP ORGANISATION

Title	**Gallup Political and Economic Index**
Coverage	Summary data on the various opinion polls carried out by Gallup on political, economic and social issues.
Frequency	Monthly.
Web facilities	Summary data and analysis from polls free on site.
Cost	On request.
Comments	Gallup data also available in machine-readable formats.
Address	The Adelphi, 1–11 John Adams Street, London WC2N 6HS
Tel./e-mail	0207 950 4400 marianne-yates@gallup.co.uk
Fax/Website	0207 950 4402 www.gallup.co.uk

GEOPLAN (UK) LTD

Title	**Geoplan**
Coverage	A service supplying statistical and geographical data and the provision of Geographical Information Systems. Based on census data and the postcode address file.
Frequency	Continuous.
Web facilities	General details of services on site.
Cost	On request and depending on the range and nature of the information required.
Comments	
Address	Bilton Court, Wetherby Road, Harrogate HG3 1GP
Tel./e-mail	01423 569538 sales@ymi.co.uk
Fax/Website	01423 819494 www.geoplan.com

GEORGE STREET RESEARCH

Title	**Scottish Omnibus Survey**
Coverage	Monthly telephone omnibus survey of Scottish businesses interviewing CEOs, MDs and directors.
Frequency	Monthly.
Web facilities	General details on site.
Cost	Price depends on number and nature of questions – details on site.
Comments	
Address	24 Broughton Street, Edinburgh EH1 3RH
Tel./e-mail	0131 478 7505 info@george-street-research.co.uk
Fax/Website	0131 478 7504 www.george-street-research.co.uk

GEORGE STREET RESEARCH

Title	**Omnifa**
Coverage	Monthly omnibus survey interviewing independent financial advisers.
Frequency	Monthly.
Web facilities	General details on site.
Cost	Price depends on number and nature of questions – details on site.
Comments	
Address	24 Broughton Street, Edinburgh EH1 3RH
Tel./e-mail	0131 478 7505 info@george-street-research.co.uk
Fax/Website	0131 478 7504 www.george-street-research.co.uk

Gfk NOP

Title	**GP Net**
Coverage	An online qualitative omnibus survey covering a sample of doctors. Undertaken weekly.
Frequency	Weekly.
Web facilities	General details on the site.
Cost	On request.
Comments	
Address	Ludgate House, 245 Blackfriars Road, London SE1 9UL
Tel./e-mail	0207 890 9000 ukinfo@gfk.com
Fax/Website	0207 890 9001 www.gfknop.co.uk

Gfk NOP

Title	**NOP Random Omnibus Survey**
Coverage	A weekly omnibus survey covering 2000 adults and based around face-to-face in-home interviews. Demographic and lifestyle analysis plus details of purchasing trends, consumer habits, etc.
Frequency	Weekly.
Web facilities	General details on site.
Cost	On request.
Comments	
Address	Ludgate House, 245 Blackfriars Road, London SE1 9UL
Tel./e-mail	0207 890 9000 ukinfo@gfk.com
Fax/Website	0207 890 9001 www.gfknop.co.uk

Gfk NOP

Title	**NOP Telebus**
Coverage	A weekly omnibus survey of 1000 adults based on telephone interviews. The data analysis follows the same breakdown as the Random Omnibus Survey (see previous entry).
Frequency	Weekly.
Web facilities	General details on site.
Cost	On request.
Comments	
Address	Ludgate House, 245 Blackfriars Road, London SE1 9UL
Tel./e-mail	0207 890 9000 ukinfo@gfk.com
Fax/Website	0207 890 9001 www.gfknop.co.uk

Gfk NOP

Title	**NOP Financial Research Survey (FRS)**
Coverage	An omnibus survey monitoring trends in the personal finance sector based on a regular sample of 2000 people. Analysis of customer bases, products and cross holdings.
Frequency	36 surveys per year.
Web facilities	General details on site.
Cost	On request.
Comments	
Address	Ludgate House, 245 Blackfriars Road, London SE1 9UL
Tel./e-mail	0207 890 9000 ukinfo@gfk.com
Fax/Website	0207 890 9001 www.gfknop.co.uk

Gfk NOP

Title	**SME Omnibus**
Coverage	A telephone survey of 600 small businesses asking a variety of questions on business trends, purchases, etc.
Frequency	Six times a year.
Web facilities	General details on site.
Cost	On request.
Comments	
Address	Ludgate House, 245 Blackfriars Road, London SE1 9UL
Tel./e-mail	0207 890 9000 ukinfo@gfk.com
Fax/Website	0207 890 9001 www.gfknop.co.uk

Gfk NOP

Title	**Money Business**
Coverage	A regular survey for the financial services industry covering 450 interviews per week.
Frequency	Weekly.
Web facilities	General details on site.
Cost	On request.
Comments	
Address	Ludgate House, 245 Blackfriars Road, London SE1 9UL
Tel./e-mail	0207 890 9000 ukinfo@gfk.com
Fax/Website	0207 890 9001 www.gfknop.co.uk

Gfk NOP

Title	**Motor Business**
Coverage	A regular survey for the motor industry of 500 drivers per week.
Frequency	Weekly.
Web facilities	General details on site.
Cost	On request.
Comments	
Address	Ludgate House, 245 Blackfriars Road, London SE1 9UL
Tel./e-mail	0207 890 9000 ukinfo@gfk.com
Fax/Website	0207 890 9001 www.gfknop.co.uk

Gfk NOP

Title	**Britbus**
Coverage	A consumer telephone omnibus survey which runs twice a month. Covers 1000 adults 16 and over.
Frequency	Twice a month.
Web facilities	General details on site.
Cost	On request.
Comments	
Address	Ludgate House, 245 Blackfriars Road, London SE1 9UL
Tel./e-mail	0207 890 9000 ukinfo@gfk.com
Fax/Website	0207 890 9001 www.gfknop.co.uk

GIN AND VODKA ASSOCIATION OF GREAT BRITAIN

Title	**Annual Report**
Coverage	Gives production of gin, home trade sales and export sales to EU countries and non-EU countries for the last four six-month periods. Based on returns from members.
Frequency	Annual.
Web facilities	General details and some basic statistics on production, consumption free on the site.
Cost	Free.
Comments	Available primarily to members but other requests considered.
Address	Cross Keys House, Queen Street, Salisbury SP1 1EY
Tel./e-mail	01722 415892 ginvodka@lineone.net
Fax/Website	01722 415840 www.ginvodka.org

GRAHAM GILL

Title	**Legal IT Salary Survey**
Coverage	A survey of salaries of IT staff in the legal sector based on survey responses from staff in London-based firms.
Frequency	Annual.
Web facilities	
Cost	Free.
Comments	
Address	63 Lincoln's Inn Fields, London WC2A 3JW
Tel./e-mail	0207 430 1711 wp@grahamgill.com
Fax/Website	www.grahamgill.com

GRAINFARMERS GROUP

Title	**Weekly Report**
Coverage	Weekly commentary and data on prices of various crops including wheat, oil seeds, pulses, plus fertilisers.
Frequency	Weekly.
Web facilities	Free access to latest reports on site.
Cost	Free.
Comments	
Address	Honeypot Lane, Colsterworth, Grantham NG33 5LY
Tel./e-mail	01476 860123 info@grainfarmers.co.uk
Fax/Website	01476 860717 www.grainfarmers.co.uk

HALIFAX

Title	**Halifax House Price Index**
Coverage	Commentary plus indices and average values for different types of houses. Also includes a regional analysis and additional data for first time buyers, mortgage demand, etc. Based on Halifax records.
Frequency	Monthly.
Web facilities	Free access on site plus access to historical data spreadsheet and other reports.
Cost	Free.
Comments	Part of HBOS plc.
Address	The Mound, Edinburgh EH1 1YZ
Tel./e-mail	0870 600 5000
Fax/Website	www.halifax.co.uk

HARDWARE TODAY

Title	**Today's Trading Trends**
Coverage	Performance trends in various hardware sectors based on a summary of the results of a survey of members of the British Hardware Federation.
Frequency	Quarterly in a monthly journal.
Web facilities	
Cost	On request.
Comments	
Address	Indices Publications Ltd, Salamander Quay West, Park Lane, Harefield UB9 6NZ
Tel./e-mail	0870 205 2924 kevin.toole@indices.co.uk
Fax/Website	0870 205 2934 www.indices.co.uk

HAY MANAGEMENT CONSULTANTS LTD

Title	**Benchmarking Remuneration Surveys**
Coverage	Various surveys focusing on the remuneration of management and directors and based on research by the company.
Frequency	Regular.
Web facilities	General details of services on site.
Cost	On request.
Comments	
Address	33 Grosvenor Place, London SW1X 7HG
Tel./e-mail	0207 856 7000 info@haygroup.com
Fax/Website	0207 856 7100 www.haygroup.com

HAYS ACCOUNTANCY PERSONNEL

Title	**Hays Salary Guides**
Coverage	Various guides cover salaries in sectors such as construction, engineering, financial services, accountancy, media, HR, IT, office support, purchasing, sales and marketing, and property. Information based on surveys carried out in various regional centres in England and Wales. A general commentary accompanies the data.
Frequency	Regular.
Web facilities	Free access to guides on PDF formats on site.
Cost	Free.
Comments	
Address	4th Floor, 141 Moorgate, London EC2M 6TX
Tel./e-mail	0207 628 6655 info@hays-ap.co.uk
Fax/Website	0207 628 4736 www.hays-ap.com

HESA SERVICES LTD

Title	**HE Planning Plus**
Coverage	Data on staff and student numbers plus key services, etc.
Frequency	Annual.
Web facilities	Details of publications and free access to various statistics on site.
Cost	£250; £130 academic institutions.
Comments	Published in CD-ROM format.
Address	95 Promenade, Cheltenham GL50 1HZ
Tel./e-mail	01242 255577 customerservices@hesa.ac.uk
Fax/Website	01242 211122 www.hesa.ac.uk

HESA SERVICES LTD

Title	**Students in Higher Education Institutions**
Coverage	Statistics on all aspects of students in higher education including examination results and subjects of study.
Frequency	Annual.
Web facilities	Details of publications and free access to various statistics on site.
Cost	£50.
Comments	Also available on CD-ROM (£35).
Address	95 Promenade, Cheltenham GL50 1HZ
Tel./e-mail	01242 255577 customer.services@hesa.ac.uk
Fax/Website	01242 211122 www.hesa.ac.uk

HESA SERVICES LTD

Title	**Resources of Higher Education Institutions**
Coverage	Statistics covering the financing and staffing of HEIs.
Frequency	Annual.
Web facilities	Details of publications and free access to various statistics on site.
Cost	£50.
Comments	Also available on CD-ROM (£35).
Address	95 Promenade, Cheltenham GL50 1HZ
Tel./e-mail	01242 255577 customer.services@hesa.ac.uk
Fax/Website	01242 211122 www.hesa.ac.uk

HESA SERVICES LTD

Title	**Destinations of Leavers from Higher Education Institutions**
Coverage	Statistics about the first destinations of graduates including employment rates, participation in further study and training.
Frequency	Annual.
Web facilities	Details of publications and free access to various statistics on site.
Cost	£50.
Comments	Also available on CD-ROM (£35).
Address	95 Promenade, Cheltenham GL50 1HZ
Tel./e-mail	01242 255577 customer.services@hesa.ac.uk
Fax/Website	01242 211122 www.hesa.ac.uk

HESA SERVICES LTD

Title	**Higher Education Statistics for the UK**
Coverage	Published in association with the Government Statistical Service and presenting an overview of higher education trends.
Frequency	Annual.
Web facilities	Details of publications and free access to various statistics on site.
Cost	£33.
Comments	Also available on CD-ROM (£35).
Address	95 Promenade, Cheltenham GL50 1HZ
Tel./e-mail	01242 255577 customer.services@hesa.ac.uk
Fax/Website	01242 211122 www.hesa.ac.uk

HESA SERVICES LTD

Title	**HE Finance Plus**
Coverage	Detailed data on finances in higher education including income and expenditure, balance sheets.
Frequency	Annual.
Web facilities	Details of publications and free access to various statistics on site.
Cost	£250; £130 academic institutions.
Comments	Published in CD-ROM format.
Address	95 Promenade, Cheltenham GL50 1HZ
Tel./e-mail	01242 255577 customer.services@hesa.ac.uk
Fax/Website	01242 211122 www.hesa.ac.uk

HESA SERVICES LTD

Title	**Higher Education Management Statistics – Sector Level**
Coverage	Data on applications and admissions, the student population, qualifications, first destinations, etc.
Frequency	Annual.
Web facilities	Details of publications and free access to various statistics on site.
Cost	£23.
Comments	Also available on CD-ROM (£25).
Address	95 Promenade, Cheltenham GL50 1HZ
Tel./e-mail	01242 255577 customer.services@hesa.ac.uk
Fax/Website	01242 211122 www.hesa.ac.uk

HESA SERVICES LTD

Title	**Higher Education Management Statistics – Institution Level**
Coverage	A looseleaf volume with data on finances, applications, admissions, student profiles and student outcomes.
Frequency	Regular.
Web facilities	Details of publications and free access to various statistics on site.
Cost	£65.
Comments	Published in CD-ROM format.
Address	95 Promenade, Cheltenham GL50 1HZ
Tel./e-mail	01242 255577 customer.services@hesa.ac.uk
Fax/Website	01242 211122 www.hesa.ac.uk

HEWITT ASSOCIATES

Title	**Salary Increase Survey Report – UK**
Coverage	A survey of salary increases for various categories of jobs based on a sample of around 250 companies.
Frequency	Annual.
Web facilities	General details of services on site.
Cost	On request.
Comments	The company carries out various specialist salary surveys, e.g. consumer electronics, consumer finance; also maintains a salaries database. These services are available to clients only.
Address	Prospect House, Abbeyview, St Albans AL1 2QU
Tel./e-mail	01727 888200
Fax/Website	01727 888333 www.hewitt.com

HGCA

Title	**MI Saturday**
Coverage	A two-page summary outlining key market trends and statistics in the cereals and grain markets.
Frequency	Weekly.
Web facilities	Free summary statistics and paid-for access to detailed data on site.
Cost	Annual subscription at £350 available for all data.
Comments	
Address	Caledonia House, 223 Pentonville Road, London N1 9HY
Tel./e-mail	0207 520 3972 mi@hgca.com
Fax/Website	0207 520 3958 www.hgca.com

HGCA

Title	**Cereal Quality Survey Results**
Coverage	Detailed statistics on quality of wheat and barley crops plus comparison with earlier year.
Frequency	Annual.
Web facilities	Summary details available free on site.
Cost	
Comments	
Address	Caledonia House, 223 Pentonville Road, London N1 9HY
Tel./e-mail	0207 520 3972 mi@hgca.com
Fax/Website	0207 520 3958 www.hgca.com

HGCA

Title	**Cereal Data Bulletin**
Coverage	Production and supplies of specific types of cereals plus data on prices and imports and exports. Some international comparisons are included and there is a section of historical statistics. Based mainly on central government data with additional material from the authority and other non-official sources.
Frequency	Regular.
Web facilities	Free summary statistics and paid-for access to detailed data on site.
Cost	Annual subscription at £350 available for all data.
Comments	Home Grown Cereals Authority in previous edition.
Address	Caledonia House, 223 Pentonville Road, London N1 9HY
Tel./e-mail	0207 520 3972 mi@hgca.com
Fax/Website	0207 520 3958 www.hgca.com

HGCA

Title	**MI Bulletin**
Coverage	Statistics on prices, imports, exports and the futures market for cereals. International data are also included.
Frequency	Weekly.
Web facilities	Free summary statistics and paid-for access to detailed data on site.
Cost	Annual subscription at £350 available for all data.
Comments	Home Grown Cereals Authority in previous edition.
Address	Caledonia House, 223 Pentonville Road, London N1 9HY
Tel./e-mail	0207 520 3972 mi@hgca.com
Fax/Website	0207 520 3958 www.hgca.com

HGCA

Title	**MI Prospects**
Coverage	Statistics and comments on grain market trends and policies. Based on a combination of central government statistics, data from the authority and other non-official sources.
Frequency	Weekly.
Web facilities	Free summary statistics and paid-for access to detailed data on site.
Cost	Annual subscription at £350 available for all data.
Comments	Home Grown Cereals Authority in previous edition.
Address	Caledonia House, 223 Pentonville Road, London N1 9HY
Tel./e-mail	0207 520 3972 mi@hgca.com
Fax/Website	0207 520 3958 www.hgca.com

HGCA

Title	**Annual Report**
Coverage	Mainly a general commentary on the cereals sector but includes some general statistics on production, supplies, etc.
Frequency	Annual.
Web facilities	Free copy on site plus free summary statistics and paid-for access to detailed data.
Cost	Free.
Comments	Home Grown Cereals Authority in previous edition.
Address	Caledonia House, 223 Pentonville Road, London N1 9HY
Tel./e-mail	0207 520 3972 mi@hgca.com
Fax/Website	0207 520 3958 www.hgca.com

HGCA

Title	**MI Oilseeds**
Coverage	Statistics on prices, imports, exports and prospects for oilseeds. International data are also included.
Frequency	Weekly.
Web facilities	Free summary statistics plus paid-for access to detailed data on site.
Cost	Annual subscription available for all data.
Comments	Home Grown Cereals Authority in previous edition.
Address	Caledonia House, 223 Pentonville Road, London N1 9HY
Tel./e-mail	0207 520 3972 mi@hgca.com
Fax/Website	0207 520 3958 www.hgca.com

HI EUROPE

Title	**The Harris Poll**
Coverage	An omnibus survey carried out more than once a week of between 1000 and 2000 adults 16 and over.
Frequency	Every few days.
Web facilities	General details on site.
Cost	On request.
Comments	
Address	Watermans Park, Brentford TW8 0BB
Tel./e-mail	0208 263 5382 cgerlotto@hieurope.com
Fax/Website	0208 263 5222 www.hieurope.com

HIGHER EDUCATION CAREERS SERVICES UNIT

Title	**What do Graduates Do?**
Coverage	Supply of graduates and those entering employment by employer, type of work and field of study. Comparative figures for earlier years. Based on data supplied by various institutions and some supporting text.
Frequency	Annual.
Web facilities	Free access to statistics on the site plus online ordering facilities. E-mail alerts about new statistics.
Cost	£9.95.
Comments	
Address	Booth Street East, Manchester M13 9EP
Tel./e-mail	0161 2775325 d.Johnson@csu.ac.uk
Fax/Website	0161 2775240 www.prospects.csu.ac.uk

HIGHER EDUCATION CAREERS SERVICES UNIT

Title	**Graduate Market Trends**
Coverage	An analysis of graduate vacancies and salaries arranged by work type, employer type, subject of study and location. Based on data collected by CSU. A commentary is included with the data.
Frequency	Quarterly.
Web facilities	Free access to statistics on the site, plus online ordering facilities. E-mail alerts about new statistics.
Cost	Free.
Comments	
Address	Booth Street East, Manchester M13 9EP
Tel./e-mail	0161 2775325 d.Johnson@csu.ac.uk
Fax/Website	0161 2775240 www.prospects.csu.ac.uk

HM TREASURY

Title	**Forecasts for the UK Economy**
Coverage	Although published by HM Treasury the publication actually contains a summary of forecasts from non-official bodies such as banks and economic research institutes.
Frequency	Monthly.
Web facilities	General details on site plus latest issue.
Cost	£75.
Comments	Latest issue on 'Economic Data and Tools' pages of website.
Address	1 Horse Guards Road, London SW1A 2HP
Tel./e-mail	0207 270 5404 robin.duffy@hm-treasury.x.gsi.gov.uk
Fax/Website	www.hm-treasury.gov.uk

HORTICULTURAL TRADES ASSOCIATION

Title	**Garden Industry Monitor**
Coverage	Monthly survey of sales of graden products, retail shares and consumer profiles. Plus regional analysis of data.
Frequency	Monthly.
Web facilities	General details on site.
Cost	On request.
Comments	
Address	Horticulture House, 19 High Street, Theale RG7 5AH
Tel./e-mail	0118 930 3132 info@the-hta.org.uk
Fax/Website	www.the-hta.org.uk

HOSPITALITY TRAINING FOUNDATION

Title	**Skills and Labour Market Profile Report**
Coverage	Hospitality labour market trends by market segment, skills and skills gaps analysis and labour shortages. Based on research by the Foundation.
Frequency	Regular.
Web facilities	Free access to PDF report on site.
Cost	Free.
Comments	
Address	2nd Floor, Armstrong House, 38 Market Square, Uxbridge UB8 1LH
Tel./e-mail	0870 660 2550 info@htf.org.uk
Fax/Website	www.htf.org.uk

HOSPITALITY TRAINING FOUNDATION

Title	**Industry Reports**
Coverage	A series of reports on various segments of the hospitality industry focusing on number of establishments, workforce and skills gaps.
Frequency	Regular.
Web facilities	Free access to reports on the site.
Cost	Free.
Comments	
Address	2nd Floor, Armstrong House, 38 Market Square, Uxbridge UB8 1LH
Tel./e-mail	0870 660 2550 info@htf.org.uk
Fax/Website	www.htf.org.uk

HOTEL CATERING AND INSTITUTIONAL MANAGEMENT ASSOCIATION

Title	**Hospitality Yearbook**
Coverage	Includes an 'Annual Review' section with commentary and statistics on developments over the previous 12 months.
Frequency	Annual.
Web facilities	
Cost	£48.
Comments	
Address	Trinity Court, 34 West Street, Sutton SM1 1SH
Tel./e-mail	0208 661 4913 marketing@hcima.org.uk
Fax/Website	www.hcima.org.uk

HOUSE BUILDERS FEDERATION

Title	**Housing Market Intelligence**
Coverage	Data on housing supply and demand trends, plus an outlook. Based on presentations at an annual conference.
Frequency	Annual.
Web facilities	
Cost	£295; £195 for housebuilders and housing associations.
Comments	
Address	PO Box 2, Ellesmere Port, South Wirral CH65 3AS
Tel./e-mail	0151 357 7707 info@hbf.co.uk
Fax/Website	0151 357 2813 www.hbf.co.uk

HOUSE BUILDERS FEDERATION

Title	**Housing Market Report**
Coverage	Includes a survey of housebuilding and a survey of confidence and affordability in the market. Also data on housing market activity, building, labour market trends, mortgages. News items on the housing market are also included and historical data are included in many tables.
Frequency	Monthly.
Web facilities	
Cost	£290; £249 for housebuilders and housing associations.
Comments	
Address	PO Box 2, Ellesmere Port, South Wirral CH65 3AS
Tel./e-mail	0151 357 7707 info@hbf.co.uk
Fax/Website	0151 357 2813 www.hbf.co.uk

HP FOODS LTD

Title	**HP Retail Sauce Report**
Coverage	Commentary and statistics on market trends, brands, product developments, etc. based on commissioned research.
Frequency	Annual.
Web facilities	
Cost	On request.
Comments	
Address	45 Northampton Road, Market Harborough LE16 9BQ
Tel./e-mail	01858 410144
Fax/Website	01858 410053

HSBC INVESTMENT BANK

Title	**UK Chart Pack**
Coverage	UK performance evaluation and trends.
Frequency	Monthly.
Web facilities	Research and forecasts freely available on website.
Cost	Free.
Comments	
Address	Thames Exchange, 10 Queen Street Place, London EC4R 1BL
Tel./e-mail	0207 621 0011
Fax/Website	0207 336 4231 www.hsbcmarkets.com

HSBC INVESTMENT BANK

Title	**UK Performance Pack**
Coverage	FT All Share Index performance review.
Frequency	Monthly.
Web facilities	Research and forecasts freely available on website.
Cost	Free.
Comments	
Address	Thames Exchange, 10 Queen Street Place, London EC4R 1BL
Tel./e-mail	0207 621 0011
Fax/Website	0207 336 4231 www.hsbcmarkets.com

HSBC INVESTMENT BANK

Title	**UK Economics**
Coverage	Data for the current year, quarters and forecasts. Topics covered include inflation, PSBR, trade, earnings, banking, etc.
Frequency	Quarterly.
Web facilities	Research and forecasts freely available on website.
Cost	Free.
Comments	
Address	Thames Exchange, 10 Queen Street Place, London EC4R 1BL
Tel./e-mail	0207 621 0011
Fax/Website	0207 336 4231 www.hsbcmarkets.com

HUNT MARKETING RESEARCH

Title	**The UK Paint Market**
Coverage	An analysis of trends in various sectors of the paint market including DIY paints, motor vehicle paints, industrial coatings, trade paints, high performance coatings, vehicle refinishes. Based on research by the company.
Frequency	Every two years.
Web facilities	
Cost	£275.
Comments	
Address	Old Mill, Mill Street, Wantage OX12 9AB
Tel./e-mail	01235 772001
Fax/Website	01235 772001

ICM RESEARCH

Title	**ICM Omnibus**
Coverage	An omnibus survey of 1000 adults aged 15 and over at 103 sampling points around the country.
Frequency	Weekly.
Web facilities	Free access to various poll results on site.
Cost	On request.
Comments	
Address	Knighton House, 56 Mortimer Street, London W1N 7DG
Tel./e-mail	0207 436 3114 carmen.vass@icmresearch.co.uk
Fax/Website	0207 436 3179 www.icmresearch.co.uk

INBUCON LTD

Title	**Housing Association Salaries & Benefits Survey**
Coverage	Salaries and benefits for jobs arranged in 11 ranks and four main areas of activity. Based on survey carried out by the company.
Frequency	Annual.
Web facilities	
Cost	On request.
Comments	Planning more salary surveys in 2005–2006.
Address	34 Paradise Road, Richmond TW9 1FE
Tel./e-mail	0208 332 7171 info@inbucon.co.uk
Fax/Website	0208 334 5739 www.inbucon.co.uk

INBUCON LTD

Title	**UK Survey of Executive Salaries and Benefits**
Coverage	A survey of salaries and benefits covering 56 executive job titles based in over 20 industrial groupings. Based on a survey carried out by the company.
Frequency	Annual.
Web facilities	
Cost	£550; £175 for participants.
Comments	Planning more salary surveys in 2005–2006.
Address	34 Paradise Road, Richmond TW9 1FE
Tel./e-mail	0208 334 5727 info@inbucon.co.uk
Fax/Website	0208 334 5739 www.inbucon.co.uk

INCOMES DATA SERVICES

Title	**IDS Pay Benchmarking**
Coverage	Regular survey comparing pay levels across similar jobs in different organisations.
Frequency	Regular.
Web facilities	Free general statistics on site mainly covering official data.
Cost	£185 plus VAT.
Comments	Other reports and surveys can be ordered on site.
Address	77 Bastwick Street, London EC1V 3TT
Tel./e-mail	0207 250 3434 sales@incomesdata.co.uk
Fax/Website	0207 324 2510 www.incomesdata.co.uk

INCOMES DATA SERVICES

Title	**Directors Pay Report**
Coverage	Annual data and analysis covering director's pay and benefits based on data collected by company.
Frequency	Annual.
Web facilities	Free general statistics on site mainly covering official data.
Cost	£367 plus VAT.
Comments	Other reports and surveys can be ordered on site.
Address	77 Bastwick Street, London EC1V 3TT
Tel./e-mail	0207 250 3434 sales@incomesdata.co.uk
Fax/Website	0207 324 2510 www.incomesdata.co.uk

INCOMES DATA SERVICES

Title	**Pay in the Public Sector**
Coverage	An IDS survey of public sector pay based on a survey of public sector organisations and staff.
Frequency	Annual.
Web facilities	Free general statistics on site mainly covering official data.
Cost	£190 plus VAT.
Comments	Other reports and surveys can be ordered on site.
Address	77 Bastwick Street, London EC1V 3TT
Tel./e-mail	0207 250 3434 sales@incomesdata.co.uk
Fax/Website	0207 324 2510 www.incomesdata.co.uk

INCOMES DATA SERVICES

Title	**IDS Pay Report**
Coverage	Commentary and statistics on pay and bargaining trends. Based largely on data collected by the company.
Frequency	Monthly.
Web facilities	Free general statistics on site mainly covering official data.
Cost	£425 plus VAT.
Comments	Other reports and surveys can be ordered on site.
Address	77 Bastwick Street, London EC1V 3TT
Tel./e-mail	0207 250 3434 sales@incomesdata.co.uk
Fax/Website	0207 324 2510 www.incomesdata.co.uk

INCOMES DATA SERVICES

Title	**Pay and Conditions in Call Centres**
Coverage	A survey of over 97 000 staff and various staff grades in UK call centres with details of salaries and conditions.
Frequency	Annual.
Web facilities	Free general statistics on site mainly covering official data.
Cost	£225.
Comments	Other reports and surveys can be ordered on site.
Address	77 Bastwick Street, London EC1V 3TT
Tel./e-mail	0207 250 3434 sales@incomesdata.co.uk
Fax/Website	0207 324 2510 www.incomesdata.co.uk

INCOMES DATA SERVICES

Title	**IDS Executive Compensation Review**
Coverage	A survey of salary trends and other issues for management staff. Based on data collected by the company.
Frequency	Monthly.
Web facilities	Free general statistics on site mainly covering official data.
Cost	£370 plus VAT.
Comments	Other reports and surveys can be ordered on site.
Address	77 Bastwick Street, London EC1V 3TT
Tel./e-mail	0207 250 3434 sales@incomesdata.co.uk
Fax/Website	0207 324 2510 www.incomesdata.co.uk

INCORPORATED SOCIETY OF BRITISH ADVERTISERS LTD

Title	**Advertiser Relationships with Direct Marketing Agencies**
Coverage	A review of opinions on direct marketing and a survey of services used from direct market agencies.
Frequency	Regular.
Web facilities	General details on site.
Cost	£250; £150 for members.
Comments	
Address	Langham House, 1B Portland Place, London W1B 1PN
Tel./e-mail	0207 291 9020 info@isba.org.uk
Fax/Website	0207 291 9030 www.isba.org.uk

INCORPORATED SOCIETY OF BRITISH ADVERTISERS LTD

Title	**Paying for Advertising**
Coverage	A survey of the payment systems used to pay agencies and levels of remuneration.
Frequency	Regular.
Web facilities	General details on site.
Cost	£300; £150 for members.
Comments	Second in a series of tracking studies.
Address	Langham House, 1B Portland Place, London W1B 1PN
Tel./e-mail	0207 291 9020 info@isba.org.uk
Fax/Website	0207 291 9030 www.isba.org.uk

INDEPENDENT SCHOOLS COUNCIL

Title	**200 – Snapshot – Independent Schools in the UK**
Coverage	General statistical information about the number of pupils in ISIS schools, spending, current trends in independent education, etc.
Frequency	Annual.
Web facilities	Free access to report on site.
Cost	
Comments	
Address	St Vincent House, 30 Orange Street, London WC2H 7HH
Tel./e-mail	0207 766 7070 press@isc.co.uk
Fax/Website	www.isc.co.uk

INDEPENDENT SCHOOLS COUNCIL

Title	**ISC University Survey – Offers and Rejection Rates**
Coverage	Based on a survey of over 500 schools, with data on offers of university places and rejections.
Frequency	Annual.
Web facilities	Free access to report on site.
Cost	Free.
Comments	Previously called HMC/GSA Universities Sub-Committee Survey.
Address	St Vincent House, 30 Orange Street, London WC2H 7HH
Tel./e-mail	0207 766 7070 press@isc.co.uk
Fax/Website	www.isc.co.uk

INDICES PUBLICATIONS LTD

Title	**The New Grey List**
Coverage	Market prices for over 35 000 hardware and DIY products based on a survey by Indices Publications of prices throughout the country.
Frequency	Monthly.
Web facilities	
Cost	£119; £99 for British Hardware Federation members.
Comments	
Address	1 Salamander Quay West, Park Lane, Harefield UB9 6NZ
Tel./e-mail	0870 205 2934
Fax/Website	www.indices.co.uk

INDUSTRIAL RELATIONS SERVICES (IRS)

Title	**IRS Employment Review**
Coverage	The *Employment Review* comprises five journals which have been brought together under one cover. These include *Pay* and *Benefits Bulletin*, with data on earnings, settlements, prices, etc. and *IRS Employment Trends*.
Frequency	Twice a month.
Web facilities	General details of publications and services on site.
Cost	£649.
Comments	Now part of Lexis Nexis. Free access to detailed data for subscribers at www.irsemploymentreview.com.
Address	Tolley House, 2 Addiscombe Road, Croydon CR9 5AF
Tel./e-mail	0208 662 2000
Fax/Website	www.irseclipse.co.uk

INDUSTRY COUNCIL FOR PACKAGING AND THE ENVIRONMENT

Title	**Pack Facts**
Coverage	Leaflet of key facts on the packaging and packaging recycling sectors based on various sources.
Frequency	Annual.
Web facilities	Free access to data on site.
Cost	Free.
Comments	
Address	SoanePoint, 6–8 Market Place, Reading RG1 2EG
Tel./e-mail	0118 925 5991 info@incpen.org
Fax/Website	0118 925 5993 www.incpen.org

INGLEBY TRICE KENNARD

Title	**City Floorspace Survey**
Coverage	Details of floorspace in the centre of London with a geographical breakdown into three areas: city, central city, city fringe. Based on data held by the company.
Frequency	Monthly.
Web facilities	Some free data on site.
Cost	£500; £240 to some libraries and other organisations.
Comments	
Address	11 Old Jewry, London EC2R 8DU
Tel./e-mail	0207 606 7461 v.sillitoe@inglebytk.co.uk
Fax/Website	0207 726 2578 www.inglebytk.com

INSTITUTE FOR EMPLOYMENT STUDIES

Title	**IES Graduate Review**
Coverage	Statistics on graduates and the graduate recruitment market, plus characteristics of the student population. Also examines major issues relevant to graduate recruitment. Based on data collected and analysed by the institute.
Frequency	Annual.
Web facilities	General details of all publications on site.
Cost	On request.
Comments	Various other reports on the labour market produced and a publications catalogue is available.
Address	Mantell Building, University of Sussex, Falmer, Brighton BN1 9RF
Tel./e-mail	01273 686751 enquiries@employment-studies.co.uk
Fax/Website	01273 690430 www.employment-studies.co.uk

INSTITUTE FOR EMPLOYMENT STUDIES

Title	**Graduate Salaries and Vacancies**
Coverage	A twice-yearly review of trends in graduate salaries and vacancies. Based on data collected and analysed by the institute.
Frequency	Twice yearly.
Web facilities	General details of all publications on site.
Cost	On request.
Comments	Various other reports on the labour market produced and a publications catalogue is available.
Address	Mantell Building, University of Sussex, Falmer, Brighton BN1 9RF
Tel./e-mail	01273 686751 enquiries@employment-studies.co.uk
Fax/Website	01273 690430 www.employment-studies.co.uk

INSTITUTE OF DIRECTORS (IOD)

Title	**Business Opinion Survey**
Coverage	Regular opinion survey of IOD member companies with analysis of results across industry sectors.
Frequency	Quarterly.
Web facilities	Free access to basic results on the site.
Cost	Free.
Comments	
Address	123 Pall Mall, London SW1Y 5ED
Tel./e-mail	0207 766 8866 enquiries@iod.com
Fax/Website	0207 766 8833 www.iod.com

INSTITUTE OF DIRECTORS (IOD)

Title	**Economic Outlook**
Coverage	Review of economic trends and future developments from the IOD's economist.
Frequency	Regular.
Web facilities	Free access to basic data on site.
Cost	Free.
Comments	
Address	123 Pall Mall, London SW1Y 5ED
Tel./e-mail	0207 766 8866 enquiries@iod.com
Fax/Website	0207 766 8833 www.iod.com

INSTITUTE OF GROCERY DISTRIBUTION

Title	**Grocery Retailing**
Coverage	A regularly updated report on grocery retailing in the UK with details of sales and sectors, companies, consumer trends and new developments. Based on various sources.
Frequency	Annual.
Web facilities	Free 'Fact Sheet's on site with market data on grocery trade. Paid-for online access to reports.
Cost	£850; £600 for members; £300 to academic institutions.
Comments	Various other occasional and one-off reports are produced on the grocery sector.
Address	Grange Lane, Letchmore Heath, Watford WD2 8DQ
Tel./e-mail	01923 857141 igd@igd.org.uk
Fax/Website	01923 852531 www.igd.com

INSTITUTE OF GROCERY DISTRIBUTION

Title	**Grocery Wholesaling**
Coverage	A regularly updated report on grocery wholesaling with commentary and statistics covering sales, wholesaling sectors, companies, employment and new developments. Based on various sources.
Frequency	Annual.
Web facilities	Free 'Fact Sheets' on site with market data on grocery trade. Paid-for online access to reports.
Cost	£850; £600 for members; £300 to academic institutions.
Comments	Various other occasional and one-off reports are produced on the grocery sector.
Address	Grange Lane, Letchmore Heath, Watford WD2 8DQ
Tel./e-mail	01923 857141 igd@igd.org.uk
Fax/Website	01923 852531 www.igd.com

INSTITUTE OF GROCERY DISTRIBUTION

Title	**Convenience Retailing**
Coverage	An annual report on convenience retailing trends including sales, companies, consumer spending and new developments.
Frequency	Annual.
Web facilities	Free 'Fact Sheets' on site with market data on grocery trade. Paid-for online access to reports.
Cost	£850; £600 for members; £300 for academic institutions.
Comments	Various other occasional and one-off reports are produced on the grocery sector.
Address	Grange Lane, Letchmore Heath, Watford WD2 8DQ
Tel./e-mail	01923 857141 igd@igd.org.uk
Fax/Website	01923 852531 www.igd.com

INSTITUTE OF GROCERY DISTRIBUTION

Title	**Category Management**
Coverage	A regular review of category management practices and trends.
Frequency	Every two years.
Web facilities	Free 'Fact Sheets' on site with market data on grocery trade. Paid-for online access to reports on site.
Cost	£700; £500 for members; £250 for academic institutions.
Comments	Various other occasional and one-off reports are produced on the grocery sector.
Address	Grange Lane, Letchmore Heath, Watford WD2 8DQ
Tel./e-mail	01923 857141 igd@igd.co.uk
Fax/Website	01923 852531 www.igd.com

INSTITUTE OF PHYSICS

Title	**Salary Survey**
Coverage	Analysis of salaries of members by class of membership, age, sex, type of work, etc. Based on a survey of members and supported by a brief commentary.
Frequency	Annual.
Web facilities	Access to PDF survey on site after subscription paid.
Cost	£150.
Comments	
Address	76 Portland Place, London W1B 1NT
Tel./e-mail	0207 470 4800 physics@iop.org
Fax/Website	0207 470 4848 www.physicsweb.org

INSTITUTE OF PRACTITIONERS IN ADVERTISING

Title	**Bellwether Report**
Coverage	A quarterly review of advertising and marketing activities by companies to offer an indication of business confidence and economic growth.
Frequency	Quarterly.
Web facilities	Press releases on site.
Cost	£500; 25% discount for IPA members.
Comments	Published by NTC Publications (see other entry for contact details).
Address	44 Belgrave Square, London SW1X 8QS
Tel./e-mail	0207 235 7020 info@ipa.co.uk
Fax/Website	0207 245 9904 www.ipa.co.uk

INSTITUTE OF PRACTITIONERS IN ADVERTISING

Title	**IPA Agency Census**
Coverage	Estimated number of people employed in IPA member advertising agencies categorised by location, staff category, size of agency. Based on the IPA's own survey with some supporting text. Usually published early in the year following a survey in autumn of the previous year.
Frequency	Annual.
Web facilities	Free access to PDF report on site.
Cost	Free.
Comments	Also produces surveys of agency costs, usually only available to members.
Address	44 Belgrave Square, London SW1X 8QS
Tel./e-mail	0207 235 7020 info@ipa.co.uk
Fax/Website	0207 245 9904 www.ipa.co.uk

INSTITUTION OF CHEMICAL ENGINEERS

Title	**Salary Survey**
Coverage	Remuneration and employment trends for members of the institution based on the organisation's own survey.
Frequency	Every two years.
Web facilities	
Cost	£105; free for members.
Comments	
Address	1 Portland Place, London W1B 1PN
Tel./e-mail	0207 927 8200
Fax/Website	0207 927 8181 www.icheme.org

INSTITUTION OF CIVIL ENGINEERS

Title	**ICE Salary Survey**
Coverage	An analysis by employer, age, type of work, overtime payments, location, firm size, qualifications, etc. Based on a survey of members.
Frequency	Annual.
Web facilities	
Cost	£130.
Comments	Produced in association with *New Civil Engineer*.
Address	1 Great George Street, London SW1P 3AA
Tel./e-mail	0207 232 7722
Fax/Website	0207 282 7500 www.ice.org.uk

INSTITUTION OF ELECTRICAL ENGINEERS (IEE)

Title	**IEE Salary Survey**
Coverage	A random sample of members, analysed by age, position, class, type of work, levels of responsibility, size of work, qualifications, location of employment, fringe benefits, etc. A small amount of supporting text.
Frequency	Annual.
Web facilities	
Cost	£50; £30 to members.
Comments	
Address	Savoy House, London WC2R 0BL
Tel./e-mail	0207 240 1871 postmaster@iee.org.uk
Fax/Website	0207 240 7735 www.iee.org.uk

INSTITUTION OF MECHANICAL ENGINEERS

Title	**Salary Survey**
Coverage	Salary survey of the members of the institution with data by type of work, sector, type of member and geographical location. Also includes data on fringe benefits and overtime.
Frequency	Every two years.
Web facilities	
Cost	£60.
Comments	
Address	1 Birdcage Walk, London SW1H 9JJ
Tel./e-mail	0207 222 7899 s_macdonald@imeche.org.uk
Fax/Website	0207 222 4557 www.imeche.org.uk

INSTITUTIONAL FUND MANAGERS' ASSOCIATION

Title	**Fund Management Survey**
Coverage	A survey of IFMA members with data on fund ownership, funds under management, client analysis, overseas earnings and staff.
Frequency	Regular.
Web facilities	
Cost	On request.
Comments	
Address	Roman House, Wood Street, London EC2Y 5BA
Tel./e-mail	0207 588 0588
Fax/Website	0207 588 7100

INTERACTIVE MEDIA IN RETAIL GROUP (IMRG)

Title	**IMRG Index**
Coverage	Monthly analysis of Internet retail sales with value and volume data and based on data supplied by 80 e-retailers.
Frequency	Monthly.
Web facilities	Free access to data on site.
Cost	Free.
Comments	
Address	5 Dryden Street, London WC2E 9BN
Tel./e-mail	0700 464674 marketing@imrg.org
Fax/Website	0700 394674 www.imrg.org

INTERNATIONAL FINANCIAL MARKETS

Title	**IFM in UK**
Coverage	A monthly review of interntional financial markets trends in London based on a combination of official and other data.
Frequency	Monthly.
Web facilities	Free access to data and commentary on site.
Cost	Free.
Comments	Also publishes various sector reports, e.g. accountancy, management consultancy; free access on website.
Address	29–30 Cornhill, London EC3V 3NF
Tel./e-mail	0207 213 9100 enquiries@ifsl.org.uk
Fax/Website	0207 213 9133 www.ifsl.org.uk

INTERNATIONAL FINANCIAL MARKETS

Title	**City Indicators Bulletin**
Coverage	A monthly review of employment, financial and economic trends in the City of London.
Frequency	Monthly.
Web facilities	Free access to data and commentary on site.
Cost	Free.
Comments	Also publishes various sector reports, e.g. accountancy, management consultancy; free access on website.
Address	29–30 Cornhill, London EC3V 3NF
Tel./e-mail	0207 213 9100 enquiries@ifsl.org.uk
Fax/Website	0207 213 9133 www.ifsl.org.uk

INVESTMENT MANAGEMENT ASSOCIATION

Title	**Investment Funds Statistics**
Coverage	Sales of units trusts, ISAs, OEICs and PEPs in the previous month, comparisons with earlier months and cumulative data. Based on the association's own survey and accompanied by a commentary.
Frequency	Monthly.
Web facilities	Freely available on site.
Cost	Free.
Comments	
Address	65 Kingsway, London WC2B 6TD
Tel./e-mail	0207 831 0898 ima@investmentuk.org
Fax/Website	0207 831 9975 www.investmentfunds.org.uk

INVESTMENT MANAGEMENT ASSOCIATION

Title	**Asset Management Survey**
Coverage	Annual survey of UK equity income based on returns from IMA members.
Frequency	Annual.
Web facilities	Freely available on site.
Cost	Free.
Comments	
Address	65 Kingsway, London WC2B 6TD
Tel./e-mail	0207 831 0898 ima@investmentuk.org
Fax/Website	0207 831 9975 www.investmentuk.org

INVESTMENT PROPERTY DATABANK

Title	**UK Key Centres Report**
Coverage	Rental growth, investment and returns trends in 70 towns and cities. Based on data collected by IPD.
Frequency	Monthly.
Web facilities	
Cost	£6500.
Comments	
Address	7–8 Greenland Place, London NW1 0AP
Tel./e-mail	0207 482 5149
Fax/Website	0207 267 0208 www.ipdindex.co.uk

INVESTMENT PROPERTY DATABANK

Title	**IPD Annual Index**
Coverage	Presents and interprets statistics about current trends in the commercial property market. Utilises records of over 9000 properties on the IPD and includes five years' worth of data on total returns, capital growth, income return, value growth, fund strategies, etc. A large amount of text accompanies the data.
Frequency	Annual.
Web facilities	Latest copies of reports on site and details of services.
Cost	Free.
Comments	Also offers a telephone enquiry service.
Address	7–8 Greenland Place, London NW1 0AP
Tel./e-mail	0207 482 5149
Fax/Website	0207 267 0208 www.ipdindex.co.uk

INVESTMENT PROPERTY DATABANK

Title	**Monthly Index & Market Monitor**
Coverage	A monthly index examining the trends in the value of commercial property analysed by region and sector. Based on data collected by IPD.
Frequency	Monthly.
Web facilities	Latest copies of reports on site and details of services.
Cost	£2000.
Comments	Also offers a telephone enquiry service.
Address	7–8 Greenland Place, London NW1 0AP
Tel./e-mail	0207 482 5149
Fax/Website	0207 267 0208 www.ipdindex.co.uk

INVESTMENT PROPERTY DATABANK

Title	**Quarterly Review**
Coverage	A quarterly review of the trends in the value of commercial property with an analysis by region and sector. Based on data collected by IPD.
Frequency	Quarterly.
Web facilities	Latest copies of reports on site and details of services.
Cost	£1000.
Comments	Also offers a telephone enquiry service.
Address	7–8 Greenland Place, London NW1 0AP
Tel./e-mail	0207 482 5149
Fax/Website	0207 267 0208 www.ipdindex.co.uk

INVESTMENT PROPERTY DATABANK

Title	**Residential Index**
Coverage	A regular index examining trends in the value of residential property with an analysis by region.
Frequency	Regular.
Web facilities	Latest copies of reports on site and details of services.
Cost	On request.
Comments	Also offers a telephone enquiry service.
Address	7–8 Greenland Place, London NW1 0AP
Tel./e-mail	0207 482 5149
Fax/Website	0207 267 0208 www.ipdindex.co.uk

IPSOS-RSL LTD

Title	**Capibus**
Coverage	A weekly omnibus survey of 2000 adults based on face-to-face interviews in the home.
Frequency	Weekly.
Web facilities	Details of surveys on site.
Cost	On request.
Comments	
Address	Kings House, Kymberley Road, Harrow HA1 1PT
Tel./e-mail	0208 861 8000 information@ipsos-rsl.com
Fax/Website	0208 861 5515 www.ipsos.rslmedia.com

IPSOS-RSL LTD

Title	**Signpost**
Coverage	A monthly monitor of the effectiveness of outdoor advertising posters based on a consumer survey by the company.
Frequency	Monthly.
Web facilities	Details of surveys on site.
Cost	On request.
Comments	
Address	Kings House, Kymberley Road, Harrow HA1 1PT
Tel./e-mail	0208 861 8000 information@ipsos-rsl.com
Fax/Website	0208 861 5515 www.ipsos.rslmedia.com

IRN RESEARCH

Title	**Market Research on the Web**
Coverage	Website offering links to over 4500 non-governmental sites providing statistics or market data. Mainly UK and European sites.
Frequency	Continuous.
Web facilities	General details of services on site.
Cost	£100.
Comments	
Address	Field House, 72 Oldfield Road, Hampton TW12 2HQ
Tel./e-mail	0208 481 8831 info@irn-research.com
Fax/Website	0208 783 3691 www.irn-research.com

IRN RESEARCH

Title	**Travelstat**
Coverage	Detailed statistics covering inbound and outbound tourist profiles, tourist flows by origin and destination, tourist flows by purpose of visit, expenditure breakdowns, traffic by mode of transport, market shares, etc. Based primarily on central government's International Passenger Survey plus IRN's own database of travel and tourism data.
Frequency	Continuous.
Web facilities	General details of services on site.
Cost	Varies according to the nature and range of data required.
Comments	Available in hard copy or disc formats.
Address	Field House, 72 Oldfield Road, Hampton TW12 2HQ
Tel./e-mail	0208 481 8831 info@irn-research.com
Fax/Website	0208 783 3691 www.irn-research.com

IRN RESEARCH

Title	**Cruisestat**
Coverage	A detailed statistical analysis of the UK cruise market.
Frequency	Annual.
Web facilities	General details of services on site.
Cost	£250.
Comments	Produced in association with the Passenger Shipping Association. Various other cruise and general travel reports available.
Address	Field House, 72 Oldfield Road, Hampton TW12 2HQ
Tel./e-mail	0208 481 8831 info@irn-research.com
Fax/Website	0208 783 3691 www.irn-research.com

IRN RESEARCH

Title	**Ferrystat: Monthly Digest of Ferry Statistics**
Coverage	Statistics on passenger, car and coach carrying by ferries. Based on regular survey of PSA members.
Frequency	Monthly.
Web facilities	General details of services on site.
Cost	£650 (£300 for annual report only).
Comments	Produced on behalf of the Passenger Shipping Association. Various other cruise and general travel reports available.
Address	Field House, 72 Oldfield Road, Hampton TW12 2HQ
Tel./e-mail	0208 481 8831 info@irn-research.com
Fax/Website	0208 783 3691 www.irn-research.com

IRN RESEARCH

Title	**Consumer Confidence Survey**
Coverage	Based on a survey of 1000 adults, the report provides a 12–18-month outlook for consumer spending based on the likelihood of consumers spending from borrowing or reducing savings.
Frequency	Quarterly.
Web facilities	General details of services on site.
Cost	On request.
Comments	Summary data in every Key Note report (see other entry for Key Note, page 193).
Address	Field House, 72 Oldfield Road, Hampton TW12 2HQ
Tel./e-mail	0208 481 8831 info@irn-research.com
Fax/Website	0208 783 3691 www.irn-research.com

IRN RESEARCH

Title	**Passenger Profiles**
Coverage	Data on passengers on Eurostar, Eurotunnel, air and ferries to Continental Europe from the UK based on the International Passenger Survey (IPS).
Frequency	Quarterly.
Web facilities	General details of services on site.
Cost	£950.
Comments	
Address	Field House, 72 Oldfield Road, Hampton TW12 2HQ
Tel./e-mail	0208 481 8831 info@irn-research.com
Fax/Website	0208 783 3691 www.irn-research.com

ISSB LTD

Title	**UK Iron and Steel Industry: Annual Statistics**
Coverage	Figures on production, consumption, trade of iron and steel products. Also details of raw materials consumed, cokemaking, iron foundries and manpower. Historical figures given in most tables and based almost entirely on the bureau's own data.
Frequency	Annual.
Web facilities	Selected key statistics free on the site plus publication details and online ordering facilities.
Cost	£175.
Comments	Also publishes regular statistics on steel in specific countries. Name changed from UK Iron and Steel Statistics Bureau.
Address	1 Carlton House Terrace, London SW1Y 5DB
Tel./e-mail	0207 343 3900 info@issb.co.uk
Fax/Website	0207 343 3901 www.issb.co.uk

JOINT INDUSTRY COMMITTEE FOR REGIONAL PRESS RESEARCH (JICREG)

Title	**Readership Surveys**
Coverage	Regular readership surveys relating to regional and local newspapers.
Frequency	Quarterly.
Web facilities	Free access to readership reports by location and title on site. Full access to subscribers online.
Cost	On request.
Comments	
Address	Bloomsbury House, 74–77 Great Russell Street, London WC1B 3DA
Tel./e-mail	0207 636 7014
Fax/Website	0107 436 3873 www.jicreg.co.uk

JONES LANG LASALLE

Title	**Central London Market Report**
Coverage	Review of trends in property sectors in central London based on data from the company.
Frequency	Quarterly.
Web facilities	Free access to copies of latest reports on site.
Cost	Free.
Comments	
Address	9 Queen Victoria Street, London EC4N 4YY
Tel./e-mail	0207 248 6040 info@eu.jll.com
Fax/Website	0207 248 0088 www.jll.com

JONES LANG LASALLE

Title	**50 Centres: Office Rents, Industrial Rents, Retail Rents**
Coverage	Statistics on 50 main urban centres based on Jones Lang Lasalle's centres database which records transactions at the top end of the prime property market. Some supporting text.
Frequency	Twice yearly.
Web facilities	Free access to copies of latest reports on site.
Cost	Free.
Comments	Individual reports produced for offices, industrial and retail.
Address	9 Queen Victoria Street, London EC4N 4YY
Tel./e-mail	0207 248 6040 info@eu.jll.com
Fax/Website	0207 248 0088 www.jll.com

JONES LANG LASALLE

Title	**UK Property and Style Index**
Coverage	Analysis of property returns, investments, values, etc. by types of property. Commentary supporting the data.
Frequency	Monthly.
Web facilities	Free access to copies of latest reports on site.
Cost	Free.
Comments	
Address	9 Queen Victoria Street, London EC4N 4YY
Tel./e-mail	0207 248 6040 info@eu.jll.com
Fax/Website	0207 248 0088 www.jll.com

JONES LANG LASALLE

Title	**West M25 Offices Market Report**
Coverage	Review of trends in office property along the M25 based on data from the company.
Frequency	Quarterly.
Web facilities	Free access to copies of latest reports on site.
Cost	Free.
Comments	
Address	9 Queen Victoria Street, London EC4N 4YY
Tel./e-mail	0207 248 6040 info@eu.jll.com
Fax/Website	0207 248 0088 www.jll.com

JONES LANG LASALLE

Title	**Retail, Retail Park, Office OSCAR**
Coverage	Series of reports examining service charges and trends in charges for retail, retail park and office properties. Based on data from the company.
Frequency	Regular.
Web facilities	Free access to copies of latest reports on site.
Cost	Free.
Comments	New series of reports launched in February 2005.
Address	9 Queen Victoria Street, London EC4N 4YY
Tel./e-mail	0207 248 6040 info@eu.jll.com
Fax/Website	0207 248 0088 www.jll.com

JONES LANG LASALLE

Title	**Monthly Property Monitor**
Coverage	Review of financial, economic and property trends with data and commentary.
Frequency	Monthly.
Web facilities	Free access to latest copies of reports on site.
Cost	Free.
Comments	
Address	9 Queen Victoria Street, London EC4N 4YY
Tel./e-mail	0207 248 6040 info@eu.jll.com
Fax/Website	0207 248 0088 www.jll.com

JOSEPH ROWNTREE FOUNDATION

Title	**Monitoring Poverty and Social Exclusion**
Coverage	A review of poverty trends which monitors 50 indicators of povery and social exclusion. These are grouped into six categories: income, children, young adults, adults, older people and communities.
Frequency	Annual.
Web facilities	Free access to updated statistics at www.poverty.org.uk.
Cost	£16.95.
Comments	The latest volume of the report is published by New Policy Institute (see other entry, page 238) in association with Joseph Rowntree Foundation but earlier issues available from latter body.
Address	The Homestead, 40 Water End, York YO3 6WP
Tel./e-mail	01904 629241 publications@jrf.org.uk
Fax/Website	01904 620072 www.jrf.org.uk

JOSEPH ROWNTREE FOUNDATION

Title	**Housing Finance Review**
Coverage	A compendium of data on the housing sector with 150 tables covering key housing issues. Based on data collected from various sources.
Frequency	Annual.
Web facilities	
Cost	£26.
Comments	Published in association with Chartered Institute of Housing and Council of Mortgage Lenders.
Address	The Homestead, 40 Water End, York YO3 6WP
Tel./e-mail	01904 629241 publications@jrf.org.uk
Fax/Website	01904 620072 www.jrf.org.uk

JOSEPH ROWNTREE FOUNDATION

Title	**UK Housing Review**
Coverage	A factfile of housing conditions and housing renewal policies in the UK drawing together data from the National House Condition Surveys and other evidence.
Frequency	Regular.
Web facilities	
Cost	£50.
Comments	Published in association with Chartered Institute of Housing and Council of Mortgage Lenders.
Address	The Homestead, 40 Water End, York YO30 6WP
Tel./e-mail	01904 629241 publications@jrf.org.uk
Fax/Website	01904 620072 www.jrf.org.uk

JOSLIN ROWE

Title	**Salary Review**
Coverage	Series of reports on salaries in various professional services sectors based on surveys in London and other UK cities.
Frequency	Twice yearly.
Web facilities	Free access to reports on site.
Cost	Free.
Comments	
Address	Bell Court House, 11 Blomfield Street, London EC2M 7AY
Tel./e-mail	0207 786 6900 london@joslinrowe.com
Fax/Website	www.joslinrowe.com

KABLE RESEARCH

Title	**IT and Business Process Outsourcing in the Public Sector**
Coverage	Detailed review with data and forecasts of outsourcing trends in central and local government. Includes data on annual spending on outsourcing, work areas outsourced, forecasts for the next five years.
Frequency	Annual.
Web facilities	Summary data from survey on site.
Cost	£1950 plus VAT.
Comments	Various other reports on ITC and outsourcing in public sector in UK and Europe.
Address	The Courtyard, 55 Chesterston Street, London EC1M 6HA
Tel./e-mail	0207 608 8400 damien.gorman@kablenet.com
Fax/Website	www.kablenet.com

KABLE RESEARCH

Title	**UK Local Government Market Profile**
Coverage	Annual review, data and five-year forecasts covering e-government in local authorities, general ICT developments and spending.
Frequency	Annual.
Web facilities	Summary data free on site.
Cost	£3950 plus VAT.
Comments	Various other reports on ITC and outsourcing in public sector in UK and Europe.
Address	The Courtyard, 55 Chesterton Street, London EC1M 6HA
Tel./e-mail	0207 608 8400 damien.gorman@kablenet.com
Fax/Website	www.kablenet.com

KADENCE (UK) LTD

Title	**Industry Omnibus**
Coverage	Omnibus survey of various industry sectors including IT, HR, restaurants, SMEs, electronics, farmers, etc. based on telephone interviews.
Frequency	Quarterly.
Web facilities	Details of services on site.
Cost	On request.
Comments	
Address	Carlton House, London SW15 2BS
Tel./e-mail	0208 246 5400 mcoulter@kadence.com
Fax/Website	0208 246 5401 www.kadence.com

KEY NOTE PUBLICATIONS

Title	**Key Note Reports**
Coverage	A range of over 200 reports on UK markets and sectors, with many of the reports updated every 12 to 18 months. Each report follows a standard format with sections on market definition, market size, industry background, competitor analysis, SWOT analysis, buying behaviour, outside suppliers, current issues, forecasts and company profiles. Based on various sources including official statistics, trade association data, company reports, TGI data and, occasionally, commissioned research.
Frequency	Regular.
Web facilities	Free executive summaries, details of all reports and e-mail newsletter covering new reports on site.
Cost	£420; £480 for Key Note Plus reports.
Comments	
Address	Field House, 72 Oldfield Road, Hampton TW12 2HQ
Tel./e-mail	0208 481 8750 info@keynote.co.uk
Fax/Website	0208 783 0049 www.keynote.co.uk

KEY NOTE PUBLICATIONS

Title	**Key Note Market Reviews**
Coverage	These are reviews of general market sectors in the UK, such as food, drinks, catering, clothing, leisure and recreation and travel and tourism. Within each report, the market sector is broken down into its main segments. There is also a section profiling the major companies in the sector and, normally, some original consumer data. Most market reviews are updated regularly and there are approximately 40 titles in the series.
Frequency	Regular.
Web facilities	Free executive summaries, details of all reports and e-mail newsletter covering new reports on site.
Cost	£680.
Comments	
Address	Field House, 72 Oldfield Road, Hampton TW12 2HQ
Tel./e-mail	0208 481 8750 info@keynote.co.uk
Fax/Website	0208 783 0049 www.keynote.co.uk

KEY NOTE PUBLICATIONS

Title	**Top Markets**
Coverage	A digest of statistics and commentary on the top 150 markets covered in the MAPS market research report series. Each market summary has data on value, trade, brands, advertising and general trends.
Frequency	Annual.
Web facilities	Free executive summaries, details of all reports and e-mail newsletter covering new reports on site.
Cost	£695.
Comments	
Address	Field House, 72 Oldfield Road, Hampton TW12 2HQ
Tel./e-mail	0208 481 8710 info@keynote.co.uk
Fax/Website	0208 783 0049 www.keynote.co.uk

KEY NOTE PUBLICATIONS

Title	**Market Forecasts**
Coverage	Forecasts over a five-year period of trends in 150 markets covered in the MAPS market research report series.
Frequency	Annual.
Web facilities	Free executive summaries, details of all reports and e-mail newsletter covering new reports on site.
Cost	£695.
Comments	
Address	Field House, 72 Oldfield Road, Hampton TW12 2HQ
Tel./e-mail	0208 481 8710 info@keynote.co.uk
Fax/Website	0208 783 0049 www.keynote.co.uk

KING STURGE & CO

Title	**UK Industrial & Distribution Floorspace Today**
Coverage	Commentary on the industrial and distribution floorspace market with data sheets giving statistics by region.
Frequency	Three issues a year.
Web facilities	Reports can be freely viewed on website.
Cost	Free.
Comments	Pan-European and global reports also available.
Address	7 Stratford Place, London W1N 9AE
Tel./e-mail	0207 493 4933 mark.stupples@kingsturge.com
Fax/Website	0207 409 0469 www.kingsturge.co.uk

KING STURGE & CO

Title	**Office Markets**
Coverage	An annual review of the commercial property sector.
Frequency	Annual.
Web facilities	Reports can be freely viewed on website.
Cost	Free.
Comments	Pan-European and global reports also available.
Address	7 Stratford Place, London W1N 9AE
Tel./e-mail	0207 493 4933 mark.stupples@kingsturge.com
Fax/Website	0207 409 0469 www.kingsturge.co.uk

KNIGHT FRANK

Title	**Central London**
Coverage	Property development trends, including rents and floorspace, in central London.
Frequency	Quarterly.
Web facilities	Free access to all reports on site.
Cost	Free.
Comments	Other reports for towns and cities also available.
Address	20 Hanover Square, London W15 1HZ
Tel./e-mail	0207 629 8171 info@knightfrank.com
Fax/Website	0207 629 1610 www.knightfrank.com

KNIGHT FRANK

Title	**Retail Review**
Coverage	An overview of retail trends plus investment trends and a property overview.
Frequency	Twice a year.
Web facilities	Free access to all reports on site.
Cost	Free.
Comments	Other reports for towns and cities also available.
Address	20 Hanover Square, London W15 1HZ
Tel./e-mail	0207 629 8171 info@knightfrank.com
Fax/Website	0207 629 1610 www.knightfrank.com

KNIGHT FRANK

Title	**M25 Quarterly**
Coverage	A review of property trends around the M25 in the Greater London area.
Frequency	Quarterly.
Web facilities	Free access to all reports on site.
Cost	Free.
Comments	Other reports for towns and cities also available.
Address	20 Hanover Square, London W15 1HZ
Tel./e-mail	0207 629 8171 info@knightfrank.com
Fax/Website	0207 629 1610 www.knightfrank.com

KNIGHT FRANK

Title	**West End Offices Market Bulletin**
Coverage	A review of office developments, rents, yields etc. in central London.
Frequency	Quarterly.
Web facilities	Free access to all reports on the site.
Cost	Free.
Comments	Other reports for towns and cities also available.
Address	20 Hanover Square, London W15 1HZ
Tel./e-mail	0207 629 8171 info@knightfrank.com
Fax/Website	0207 629 1610 www.knightfrank.com

KNIGHT FRANK

Title	**City Office Bulletin**
Coverage	A review of office developments, rents, yields etc. in the City of London.
Frequency	Quarterly.
Web facilities	Free access to all reports on the site.
Cost	Free.
Comments	Other reports for towns and cities also available.
Address	20 Hanover Square, London W15 1HZ
Tel./e-mail	0207 629 8171 info@knightfrank.com
Fax/Website	0207 629 1610 www.knightfrank.com

KNIGHT FRANK

Title	**Residential Bulletin**
Coverage	A review of residential property developments in the UK.
Frequency	Monthly.
Web facilities	Free access to all reports on the site.
Cost	Free.
Comments	Other reports for towns and cities also available.
Address	20 Hanover Square, London W15 1HZ
Tel./e-mail	0207 629 8171 info@knightfrank.com
Fax/Website	0207 629 1610 www.knightfrank.com

KPMG

Title	**Survey of Directors' Compensation**
Coverage	Annual survey of pay and benefits of UK company directors based on survey by company.
Frequency	Annual.
Web facilities	Free copy of report on site.
Cost	Free.
Comments	
Address	8 Salisbury Square, London EC4Y 8BB
Tel./e-mail	0207 311 3000 georgina.simpkin@kpmg.co.uk
Fax/Website	0207 311 3311 www.kpmg.co.uk

KPMG

Title	**Executive Compensation Update**
Coverage	Commentary, news and statistics on salaries and benefits for directors and others.
Frequency	Quarterly.
Web facilities	Free copies of the reports on site.
Cost	Free.
Comments	
Address	8 Salisbury Square, London EC4Y 8BB
Tel./e-mail	0207 311 3000 georgina.simpkin@kpmg.co.uk
Fax/Website	0207 311 3311 www.kpmg.co.uk

	KPMG
Title	**Building Society Database**
Coverage	Mainly information on specific societies but there is also a statistical section with eight-year industry trends.
Frequency	Annual.
Web facilities	
Cost	On request.
Comments	
Address	8 Salisbury Square, London EC4Y 8BB
Tel./e-mail	0207 311 3000
Fax/Website	0207 311 3311

	LABOUR RESEARCH DEPARTMENT
Title	**Labour Research Fact Service**
Coverage	A weekly pamphlet containing news and statistics relating to the labour market. Based on various sources.
Frequency	Weekly.
Web facilities	Paid-for access to data on site plus some free data on pay and prices.
Cost	£61.
Comments	Also publishes a monthly journal, *Labour Research* and various other reports.
Address	78 Blackfriars Road, London SE1 8HF
Tel./e-mail	0207 928 3649 info@lrd.org.uk
Fax/Website	0207 928 0621 www.lrd.org.uk

	LABOUR RESEARCH DEPARTMENT
Title	**Workplace Report**
Coverage	Includes news and articles on bargaining issues plus *Bargaining – Key Statistics* with economic, labour market and earnings data.
Frequency	11 issues a year.
Web facilities	Paid-for access to data on site plus some free data on pay and prices.
Cost	£52.
Comments	Also publishes a monthly journal, *Labour Research* and various other reports.
Address	78 Blackfriars Road, London SE1 8HF
Tel./e-mail	0207 928 3649 info@lrd.org.uk
Fax/Website	0207 928 0621 www.lrd.org.uk

LAING & BUISSON PUBLICATIONS LTD

Title	**Health and Care Cover – UK Market Report**
Coverage	A review of the healthcare insurance market with details of market trends, market segments, suppliers, etc. Based on research by the company.
Frequency	Annual.
Web facilities	Free statistical pages covering hospitals, clinics, insurance and care homes on site.
Cost	£320.
Comments	
Address	29 Angel Gate, City Road, London EC1V 2PT
Tel./e-mail	0207 833 9123 info@laingbuisson.co.uk
Fax/Website	0207 833 9129 www.laingbuisson.co.uk

LAING & BUISSON PUBLICATIONS LTD

Title	**Laing's Healthcare Market Review**
Coverage	Analysis and statistics covering the private healthcare market with information on various sectors: acute healthcare services, medical insurance, mental health, primary medical care, and long-term care of the elderly. Based on research by the company.
Frequency	Annual.
Web facilities	Free statistical pages covering hospitals, clinics, insurance and care homes on site.
Cost	£295.
Comments	
Address	29 Angel Gate, City Road, London EC1V 2PT
Tel./e-mail	0207 833 9123 info@laingbuisson.co.uk
Fax/Website	0207 833 9129 www.laingbuisson.co.uk

LAING & BUISSON PUBLICATIONS LTD

Title	**Children's Nurseries: UK Market Sector Report**
Coverage	A review of the childrens' nursery market with details of market trends, market segments, suppliers, etc. Based on research by the company.
Frequency	Annual.
Web facilities	Free statistical pages covering hospitals, clinics, insurance and care homes on site.
Cost	£495.
Comments	
Address	29 Angel Gate, City Road, London EC1V 2PT
Tel./e-mail	0207 833 9123 info@laingbuisson.co.uk
Fax/Website	0207 833 9129 www.laingbuisson.co.uk

LAING & BUISSON PUBLICATIONS LTD

Title	**Care of Elderly People – UK Market Survey**
Coverage	A review of trends in the elderly healthcare market with data for market segments, suppliers, etc. Based on research by the company.
Frequency	Annual.
Web facilities	Free statistical pages covering hospitals, clinics, insurance and care homes on site.
Cost	£575.
Comments	
Address	29 Angel Gate, City Road, London EC1V 2PT
Tel./e-mail	0207 833 9123 info@laingbuisson.co.uk
Fax/Website	0207 833 9129 www.laingbuisson.co.uk

LEATHERHEAD FOOD RA

Title	**UK Food and Drinks Report**
Coverage	The report reviews the UK food market, industry and new product trends by sector. There are 17 food sectors covered in the report. Based on a combination of original research and various published sources.
Frequency	Annual.
Web facilities	General details of research reports on site plus paid-for access to market intelligence and other information on www.foodlineweb.com.
Cost	£659; £595 for members.
Comments	UK Foods and Drinks Report is usually published in April. Also publishes various one-off reports on the UK and European food industry.
Address	Randalls Road, Leatherhead KT22 7RY
Tel./e-mail	01372 376761 publications@lfra.co.uk
Fax/Website	01372 386228 www.lfra.co.uk

LEISURE INDUSTRIES RESEARCH CENTRE

Title	**Leisure Forecasts**
Coverage	Published in two volumes with the first volume covering leisure away from the home and the second volume relating to leisure in the home. Forecasts are given for five years ahead for consumer spending, prices and key market indicators. Based largely on the company's own research with some supporting commentary.
Frequency	Annual.
Web facilities	General details of statistics on site plus online ordering. E-mail alerts about new statistics.
Cost	£250; £200 with *Sport Market Forecasts* (next entry).
Comments	
Address	Unit 1, Sheffield Science Park, Howard Street, Sheffield S1 2LX
Tel./e-mail	0114 225 4578 lirc@shu.ac.uk
Fax/Website	0114 225 4488 www.shu.ac.uk/schools/slm/lirc

LEISURE INDUSTRIES RESEARCH CENTRE

Title	**Sport Market Forecasts**
Coverage	Detailed forecasts for specific sports sectors.
Frequency	Annual.
Web facilities	General details of statistics on site plus online ordering. E-mail alerts about new statistics.
Cost	£250; £200 with *Leisure Forecasts* (previous entry).
Comments	
Address	Unit 1, Sheffield Science Park, Howard Street, Sheffield S1 2LX
Tel./e-mail	0114 225 4578 lirc@shu.ac.uk
Fax/Website	0114 225 4488 www.shu.ac.uk/schools/slm/lirc

LEX SERVICE PLC

Title	**Lex Vehicle Leasing Report on Company Motoring**
Coverage	A report of detailed research on company car drivers, fleets and fleet managers.
Frequency	Annual.
Web facilities	Online ordering of statistics/publications on site.
Cost	£345.
Comments	
Address	Globe House, Globe Park, Marlow SL7 1YL
Tel./e-mail	0870 112 5500 marketing@lvl.co.uk
Fax/Website	0870 112 5660 www.lvl.co.uk

LIBRARY AND INFORMATION STATISTICS UNIT (LISU)

Title	**LISU Annual Library Statistics**
Coverage	A compendium of statistics on UK libraries including public libraries, university libraries, the national libraries and the book trade. Historical statistics are included for the last ten years and the data are based on returns to CIPFA, UFC and SCONUL supplemented by some special surveys.
Frequency	Annual.
Web facilities	Free download of report and data on the site.
Cost	£37.50.
Comments	LISU also publishes a range of occasional and one-off surveys of the library and publishing sectors.
Address	Loughborough University of Technology, Loughborough LE11 3TU
Tel./e-mail	01509 635680 lisu@lboro.ac.uk
Fax/Website	01509 635699 www.lboro.ac.uk/departments/dils/lisu/ publications/

LIBRARY AND INFORMATION STATISTICS UNIT (LISU)

Title	**Average Prices of British & US Academic Books**
Coverage	A survey of thousands of published titles with prices analysed by various subject categories and academic and calender year indexing.
Frequency	Twice yearly.
Web facilities	Publication details on site.
Cost	£30; £35 plus VAT for CD-ROM.
Comments	The survey is published in February and August each year. LISU also publishes a range of occasional and one-off surveys of the library and publishing sectors.
Address	Loughborough University of Technology, Loughborough LE11 3TU
Tel./e-mail	01509 635680 lisu@lboro.ac.uk
Fax/Website	01509 635699 www.lboro.ac.uk/departments/dils/lisu/ publications/

LIBRARY AND INFORMATION STATISTICS UNIT (LISU)

Title	**Public Library Materials Fund and Budget Survey**
Coverage	Originally concentrating on public library book funds, this survey now also covers audio and video material, service points, opening hours and staffing levels. Comparisons are presented between individual authorities responding to the survey and the latest year's budgets are compared to the previous year's.
Frequency	Annual.
Web facilities	Free download of the report on the site.
Cost	£32.50.
Comments	Published in July each year. LISU also publishes a range of occasional and one-off surveys of the library and publishing sectors.
Address	Loughborough University of Technology, Loughborough LE11 3TU
Tel./e-mail	01509 635680 lisu@lboro.ac.uk
Fax/Website	01509 635699 www.lboro.ac.uk/departments/dils/lisu/ publications/

LIBRARY AND INFORMATION STATISTICS UNIT (LISU)

Title	**Survey of Library Services to Schools and Children in the UK**
Coverage	An analysis of services based on a questionnaire survey carried out with guidance from AMDECL, SOCCEL and other groups of specialist librarians. It includes tables of detailed information by authority with explanatory comments, summaries and per capita indicators. The delegation effect of local management of schools on the Schools Library Service is monitored.
Frequency	Annual.
Web facilities	Free download of report on site.
Cost	£32.50.
Comments	LISU also publishes a range of occasional and one-off surveys of the library and publishing sectors.
Address	Loughborough University of Technology, Loughborough LE11 3TU
Tel./e-mail	01509 635680 lisu@lboro.ac.uk
Fax/Website	01509 635699 www.lboro.ac.uk/departments/dils/lisu/ publications/

LIVERPOOL MACROECONOMIC RESEARCH LTD

Title	**Quarterly Economic Bulletin**
Coverage	Quarterly commentary on economic trends supported by statistics and forecasts of future trends.
Frequency	Quarterly.
Web facilities	
Cost	£300; £80 per issue.
Comments	Published in March, June, October and December.
Address	Liverpool Macroeconomic Research Ltd, 5 Cable Road, Whiston, Liverpool L35 5AN
Tel./e-mail	0151 290 0194
Fax/Website	0151 290 0194

LLP LTD

Title	**Lloyds' Nautical Yearbook**
Coverage	Includes a section on the 'Year in Shipping', plus casualty statistics, port statistics and country information. Based on various sources.
Frequency	Annual.
Web facilities	Details of publications on site.
Cost	On request.
Comments	Publishes various regular statistical reports on international shipping trends.
Address	LLP Limited, Sheepen Place, Colchester CO3 3LP
Tel./e-mail	01206 772061
Fax/Website	01206 46273 www.llplimited.com

LOMBARD STREET RESEARCH

Title	**UK Economic Forecast**
Coverage	Quarterly forecasts and analysis of economic trends up to two years ahead. Based on company research.
Frequency	Quarterly.
Web facilities	General details and sample copies on site.
Cost	On request.
Comments	Available in hard copy of electronic format.
Address	38 Watling Street, London EC4M 9BR
Tel./e-mail	0207 382 5000 info@lombardstreetresearch.com
Fax/Website	0207 382 5929 www.lombardstreetresearch.com

LOMBARD STREET RESEARCH

Title	**Monthly Economic Review**
Coverage	News and analysis covering economic trends plus key data.
Frequency	Monthly.
Web facilities	General details and sample copies on site.
Cost	On request.
Comments	Available in hard copy of electronic format.
Address	38 Watling Street, London EC4M 9BR
Tel./e-mail	0207 382 5000 info@lombardstreetresearch.com
Fax/Website	0207 382 5929 www.lombardstreetresearch.com

LOMBARD STREET RESEARCH

Title	**Property Economics**
Coverage	News and analysis covering economic and property investment trends plus data on returns and yields.
Frequency	Monthly.
Web facilities	General details and sample copies on site.
Cost	On request.
Comments	Available in hard copy of electronic format.
Address	38 Watling Street, London EC4M 9BR
Tel./e-mail	0207 382 5000 info@lombardstreetresearch.com
Fax/Website	0207 382 5929 www.lombardstreetresearch.com

LOMBARD STREET RESEARCH

Title	**Portfolio Strategy**
Coverage	News and analysis aimed at asset managers plus key data covering liquidity measures, leading indicators, yields, returns.
Frequency	Monthly.
Web facilities	General details and sample copies on site.
Cost	On request.
Comments	Available in hard copy of electronic format.
Address	38 Watling Street, London EC4M 9BR
Tel./e-mail	0207 382 5000 info@lombardstreetresearch.com
Fax/Website	0207 382 5929 www.lombardstreetresearch.com

LONDON CHAMBER OF COMMERCE

Title	**The London Monitor**
Coverage	A review of economic and business trends in London including statistics on domestic business, investment, profits, exports, labour. Based on a survey of around 250 companies in the capital with additional data from official sources.
Frequency	Quarterly.
Web facilities	Free PDF reports on site.
Cost	Free.
Comments	
Address	33 Queen Street, London EC4R 1AP
Tel./e-mail	0207 248 4444 lc@londonchamber.co.uk
Fax/Website	0207 489 0391 www.londonchamber.co.uk

LONDON CHAMBER OF COMMERCE

Title	**Annual Review of the London Economy**
Coverage	A review of economic trends in the capital based on data from the chamber and other sources.
Frequency	Annual.
Web facilities	Free data on site.
Cost	Free.
Comments	
Address	33 Queen Street, London EC4R 1AP
Tel./e-mail	0207 248 4444 lc@londonchamber.co.uk
Fax/Website	0207 489 0391 www.londonchamber.co.uk

LONDON CORN CIRCULAR

Title	**Market Prices**
Coverage	Prices of cereals and various other crops with some forecasts of future prices.
Frequency	Weekly in a weekly journal.
Web facilities	
Cost	£80.
Comments	
Address	Palace Hall, Darthill Road, March PE35 8HP
Tel./e-mail	01733 560702
Fax/Website	

LONDON METAL EXCHANGE

Title	**LME Market Data**
Coverage	A regular market report including data on price movements, liquidity and volume. Based on the exchange's own data.
Frequency	Monthly.
Web facilities	Free price data on site with historical series.
Cost	On request.
Comments	
Address	56 Leadenhall Street, London EC3A 2BJ
Tel./e-mail	0207 264 5555 james.oliver@lme.co.uk
Fax/Website	0207 680 0505 www.lme.co.uk

LONDON STOCK EXCHANGE

Title	**Primary Market Fact Sheet**
Coverage	News, statistics on new issues, shares, equity values and market trends.
Frequency	Monthly.
Web facilities	All statistics can be viewed and downloaded from the site.
Cost	On request.
Comments	Historical statistics also on website.
Address	Stock Exchange, London EC2N 1HP
Tel./e-mail	0207 797 1000 products@londonstockexchange.com
Fax/Website	0891 437052 www.londonstockexchange.com

LONDON STOCK EXCHANGE

Title	**Secondary Market Fact Sheet**
Coverage	News, statistics on turnover, market movements, etc.
Frequency	Monthly.
Web facilities	All statistics can be viewed and downloaded from the site.
Cost	On request.
Comments	Historical statistics also on website.
Address	Stock Exchange, London EC2N 1HP
Tel./e-mail	0207 797 1000 products@londonstockexchange.com
Fax/Website	0891 437052 www.londonstockexchange.com

LONDON STOCK EXCHANGE

Title	**Trading Summary Fact Sheet**
Coverage	Trading data by security for all UK listed, FTSE UK index and AIM admitted companies.
Frequency	Monthly.
Web facilities	All statistics can be viewed and downloaded from the site.
Cost	On request.
Comments	Historical statistics also on website.
Address	Stock Exchange, London EC2N 1HP
Tel./e-mail	0207 797 1000 products@londonstockexchange.com
Fax/Website	0891 437052 www.londonstockexchange.com

LONDON STOCK EXCHANGE

Title	**AIM Market Statistics**
Coverage	Statistics covering trends in the recently established AIM market based on information maintained by the Stock Exchange.
Frequency	Monthly.
Web facilities	All statistics can be viewed and downloaded from the site.
Cost	On request.
Comments	Historical statistics also on website.
Address	Stock Exchange, London EC2N 1HP
Tel./e-mail	0207 797 1000 products@londonstockexchange.com
Fax/Website	0891 437052 www.londonstockexchange.com

LONDON STOCK EXCHANGE

Title	**Quarterly Fact File**
Coverage	A review of the exchange's market on a year-to-year basis.
Frequency	Quarterly.
Web facilities	All statistics can be viewed and downloaded free from the site.
Cost	On request.
Comments	Historical statistics are also available on the website.
Address	Stock Exchange, London EC2N 1HP
Tel./e-mail	0207 797 1000 products@londonstockexchange.com
Fax/Website	0891 437052 www.londonstockexchange.com

LONDON STOCK EXCHANGE

Title	**Quarterly Review**
Coverage	The publication contains a selection of key graphs and statistics which summarise the market's performance.
Frequency	Quarterly.
Web facilities	All statistics can be viewed and downloaded free from the site.
Cost	On request.
Comments	Historical statistics are also available on the website.
Address	Stock Exchange, London EC2N 1HP
Tel./e-mail	0207 797 1000 products@londonstockexchange.com
Fax/Website	0891 437052 www.londonstockexchange.com

MACMILLAN DAVIES HODES

Title	**The Value of Safety and Health**
Coverage	An annual survey of salaries and attitudes of health and safety practitioners.
Frequency	Annual.
Web facilities	
Cost	£75; £20 for members of the Institute of Occupational Safety and Health.
Comments	Produced in association with the Institute of Occupational Safety and Health.
Address	825a Wilmslow Road, Didsbury, Manchester M20 2RE
Tel./e-mail	0161 908 8330 HRSolutions@mdh.co.uk
Fax/Website	www.mdh.co.uk

MALTSTERS' ASSOCIATION OF GREAT BRITAIN

Title	**Malting Barley Purchases**
Coverage	Annual data on purchases by tonnage and barley varieties.
Frequency	Annual.
Web facilities	Free access to report on site.
Cost	Free.
Comments	
Address	31B Castle Gate, Newark NG24 1AZ
Tel./e-mail	01636 700781
Fax/Website	01636 701836 www.ukmalt.com

MANAGEMENT CONSULTANCIES ASSOCIATION

Title	**UK Consulting Industry**
Coverage	Detailed review of income by source and area, number of companies, employment, company types, company profiles, etc.
Frequency	Annual.
Web facilities	Free summary data on site.
Cost	£400; £250 for members.
Comments	Published by PMP (UK) Ltd, 15 Chiltern Business Centre, 63–65 Woodside Road, Amersham, HP6 6AA; telephone 01494 732830.
Address	49 Whitehall, London SW1A 2BX
Tel./e-mail	0207 321 3990 joy.hewgill@mca.org.uk
Fax/Website	0207 321 3991 www.mca.org.uk

MANAGEMENT CONSULTANCIES ASSOCIATION

Title	**Quarterly Survey**
Coverage	Surveys of member companies' turnover, workload trends.
Frequency	Quarterly.
Web facilities	Free summary statistics on site.
Cost	Free.
Comments	
Address	49 Whitehall, London SW1A 2BX
Tel./e-mail	0207 321 3990 joy.hewgill@mca.org.uk
Fax/Website	0207 321 3991 www.mca.org.uk

MANAGEMENT CONSULTANCY

Title	**Surveys**
Coverage	Regular surveys of the management consultancy sector with surveys of particular types of consultants and specific work areas. Based on various sources and some research by the journal.
Frequency	Regular in a monthly journal.
Web facilities	Free access to news and consultancy league tables on site.
Cost	On request.
Comments	Controlled circulation journal.
Address	VNU Business Publications, VNU House, 32–34 Broadwick Street, London W1A 2HG
Tel./e-mail	0207 316 9032 mc@vnu.co.uk
Fax/Website	0207 316 9250 www.managementconsultancy.co.uk

MANAGEMENT CONSULTANCY INFORMATION SERVICE

Title	**Management Consultancy Salary Survey**
Coverage	A survey of consultancy salaries across different functions, different consultancy sizes, etc.
Frequency	Every 18 months.
Web facilities	Free summary data on the site.
Cost	£30.
Comments	
Address	38 Blenheim Avenue, Gants Hill, Ilford IG2 6JQ
Tel./e-mail	0208 554 4695 annemallach@cwcom.net
Fax/Website	0208 554 4695 www.mcis.mcmail.com

MANAGEMENT CONSULTANCY INFORMATION SERVICE

Title	**Management Consultancy Fee Rate Survey**
Coverage	The survey analyses fees charged by management consultants ranging in size from sole practitioners to major international practices. The results are analysed by seven different practice areas and by four sector groups, as well as geographical variations, analysis by size of consultancy, fees charged for different levels of consultant, recruitment charges and terms of working. Based on original research.
Frequency	Every 18 months.
Web facilities	Free summary data on the site.
Cost	£30.
Comments	A relatively new survey, first published in 1992.
Address	38 Blenheim Avenue, Gants Hill, Ilford IG2 6JQ
Tel./e-mail	0208 554 4695 annemallach@cwcom.net
Fax/Website	0208 554 4695 www.mcis.mcmail.com

MANPOWER PLC

Title	**Employment Outlook Survey**
Coverage	Short-term forecasts of employment for specific sectors in manufacturing, services and the public sector based on the stated intentions of over 2000 companies and organisations. Data by region is included and a commentary accompanies the statistics.
Frequency	Quarterly.
Web facilities	The latest surveys are available free on the site.
Cost	Free.
Comments	
Address	52 High Holborn, London WC1V 6RL
Tel./e-mail	0207 831 6568 info@manpower.co.uk
Fax/Website	0207 404 1351 www.manpower.co.uk

MANUFACTURING CHEMIST

Title	**Aerosol Review**
Coverage	Listing of all aerosols filled in the UK and imported. Also lists all types of aerosols filled by company, brand name, type, etc. Based on non-official sources.
Frequency	Annual and as a separate item from the journal.
Web facilities	Free access to news on site.
Cost	On request.
Comments	
Address	Polygon Media Ltd, Tubs Hill House, Sevenoaks TN13 1BY
Tel./e-mail	01732 470025 hayshford@wilmington.co.uk
Fax/Website	01732 470070 www.manufacturing-chemist.info

MANUFACTURING TECHNOLOGIES ASSOCIATION

Title	**Basic Facts**
Coverage	Basic figures on production, sales, investment, imports, exports and consumption over a ten-year period. Also information on the leading export markets and leading import sources plus the UK's share of total world production and exports. Based on a mixture of Central government and non-official sources.
Frequency	Annual.
Web facilities	Free access to *Basic Facts* on site.
Cost	Free.
Comments	Produced in pocketbook format.
Address	62 Bayswater Road, London W2 3PS
Tel./e-mail	0207 298 6400 info@:mta.co.uk
Fax/Website	0207 298 6430 www.mta.org.uk

MANUFACTURING TECHNOLOGIES ASSOCIATION

Title	**MTA Trends Survey**
Coverage	Opinion survey of member companies (manufacturers, importers and suppliers) covering orders and business confidence.
Frequency	Quarterly.
Web facilities	Summary data in press release on site.
Cost	On request.
Comments	
Address	62 Bayswater Road, London W2 3PS
Tel./e-mail	0207 298 6400 info@:mta.co.uk
Fax/Website	0207 298 6430 www.mta.org.uk

MANUFACTURING TECHNOLOGIES ASSOCIATION

Title	**MTA Press Release**
Coverage	Review of machine tool import/export trends.
Frequency	Quarterly.
Web facilities	Free access to press release on site.
Cost	Free.
Comments	
Address	62 Bayswater Road, London W2 3PS
Tel./e-mail	0207 298 6400 info@:mta.co.uk
Fax/Website	0207 298 6430 www.mta.org.uk

MARKET & BUSINESS DEVELOPMENT (MBD)

Title	**MBD UK Market Research Reports**
Coverage	MBD publishes over 120 reports covering business to business, building, engineering and professional/office services markets and these are updated quarterly.
Frequency	Quarterly.
Web facilities	General details and sample pages on site.
Cost	£550.
Comments	
Address	Barnett House, 53 Fountain Street, Manchester M2 2AN
Tel./e-mail	0161 247 8600 enquiries@mbdltd.co.uk
Fax/Website	0161 247 8606 www.mbdltd.co.uk

MARKET ASSESSMENT INTERNATIONAL

Title	**Market Reports**
Coverage	Over 100 regular reports are published on UK consumer markets with data and analysis on market value, brands, market segments, consumers, advertising, companies, distribution and forecasts. Based on various sources.
Frequency	Regular.
Web facilities	Executive summaries of reports on site.
Cost	£799.
Comments	
Address	Field House, 72 Oldfield Road, Hampton TW12 2HQ
Tel./e-mail	0208 481 8710 info@keynote.co.uk
Fax/Website	0208 783 0049 www.keynote.co.uk

MARKET LOCATION LTD

Title	**Industry Analysis**
Coverage	Tables giving the distribution of industry by region and SIC classification. Based on Market Location's Primefile plus database of establishments.
Frequency	Regular.
Web facilities	General details of services on site.
Cost	On request.
Comments	
Address	1 Warwick Street, Leamington Spa CV32 5LW
Tel./e-mail	01926 450388 enquiries@marketlocation.com
Fax/Website	01926 430590 www.marketlocation.com

MARKET RESEARCH SCOTLAND

Title	**Scottish Consumer Omnibus**
Coverage	An omnibus survey based around a sample of 1000 consumers in Scotland.
Frequency	Monthly.
Web facilities	
Cost	On request.
Comments	
Address	9 Park Quadrant, Glasgow G3 6BS
Tel./e-mail	0141 332 5751
Fax/Website	0141 332 3035

MARKETING WEEK

Title	**Ball and Hoolahan Salary Survey**
Coverage	Volume 1 supplies key information on average salary levels by industry sector. Volume 2 supplies more detailed information on 11 different job titles from marketing director through to marketing executive.
Frequency	Annual.
Web facilities	
Cost	£129; £2.20 for single copy.
Comments	
Address	Centaur Communications, 50 Poland Street, London W1E 6JZ
Tel./e-mail	0207 970 4000
Fax/Website	0207 970 4392 www.marketing-week.co.uk

MDS TRANSMODAL

Title	**Overseas Trade Data**
Coverage	Detailed product information for imports and exports plus details of trading partners and port of entry and exit.
Frequency	Monthly.
Web facilities	General details of services on site.
Cost	Depends on amount of information required.
Comments	Available in various machine readable formats. The company also offers overseas trade forecasting services and is an agent for the International Passenger Survey.
Address	6 Hunter's Walk, Canal Street, Chester CH1 4EB
Tel./e-mail	01244 348301 queries@mdst.co.uk
Fax/Website	01244 348471 www.mdst.co.uk

MEAT AND LIVESTOCK COMMISSION

Title	**A Pocketful of Meat Facts 2---**
Coverage	Compilation of data on meat production, supplies, demand, consumption by type of meats. Based on various sources.
Frequency	Annual.
Web facilities	Free access to range of data on site.
Cost	Free.
Comments	Various other reports and surveys available by registering at www.mlceconomics.org.uk.
Address	Winterhill House, Snowdon Drive, Milton Keynes MK6 1AX
Tel./e-mail	01908 677577 contactus@mlc.org.uk
Fax/Website	01908 609221 www.mlc.org.uk

MEAT AND LIVESTOCK COMMISSION

Title	**UK Beef Market Trends**
Coverage	Annual historical data on supplies, imports, exports and consumption of beef.
Frequency	Annual.
Web facilities	Free access to data on site.
Cost	Free.
Comments	Various other reports and surveys available by registering at www.mlceconomics.org.uk.
Address	Winterhill House, Snowdon Drive, Milton Keynes MK6 1AX
Tel./e-mail	01908 677577 contactus@mlc.org.uk
Fax/Website	01908 609221 www.mlc.org.uk

MEAT AND LIVESTOCK COMMISSION

Title	**UK Beef Market Update**
Coverage	Regular commentary and data on beef supplies, prices, demand, etc.
Frequency	Regular.
Web facilities	Free access to data on site.
Cost	Free.
Comments	Various other reports and surveys available by registering at www. mlceconomics.org.uk.
Address	Winterhill House, Snowdon Drive, Milton Keynes MK6 1AX
Tel./e-mail	01908 677577 contactus@mlc.org.uk
Fax/Website	01908 609221 www.mlc.org.uk.

MEAT AND LIVESTOCK COMMISSION

Title	**UK Sheep Market Trends**
Coverage	Annual historical data on supplies, imports, exports and consumption of sheep meat.
Frequency	Annual.
Web facilities	Free access to data on site.
Cost	Free.
Comments	Various other reports and surveys available by registering at www. mlceconomics.org.uk.
Address	Winterhill House, Snowdon Drive, Milton Keynes MK6 1AX
Tel./e-mail	01908 677577 contactus@mlc.org.uk
Fax/Website	01908 609221 www.mlc.org.uk

MEAT AND LIVESTOCK COMMISSION

Title	**UK Pork Meat Trends**
Coverage	Annual historical data on supplies, imports, exports and consumption of pork.
Frequency	Annual.
Web facilities	Free access to data on site.
Cost	Free.
Comments	Various other reports and surveys available by registering at www. mlceconomics.org.uk.
Address	Winterhill House, Snowdon Drive, Milton Keynes MK6 1AX
Tel./e-mail	01908 677577 contactus@mlc.org.uk
Fax/Website	01908 609221 www.mlc.org.uk

MEAT AND LIVESTOCK COMMISSION

Title	**UK Bacon Meat Trends**
Coverage	Annual historical data on supplies, imports, exports and consumption of bacon.
Frequency	Annual.
Web facilities	Free access to data on site.
Cost	Free.
Comments	Various other reports and surveys available by registering at www.mlceconomics.org.uk.
Address	Winterhill House, Snowdon Drive, Milton Keynes MK6 1AX
Tel./e-mail	01908 677577 contactus@mlc.org.uk
Fax/Website	01908 609221 www.mlc.org.uk

MEAT TRADES JOURNAL

Title	**Market Prices**
Coverage	Wholesale and retail prices for different types of meat and livestock and the data usually refers to prices at the end of the previous week.
Frequency	Weekly in a weekly journal.
Web facilities	Free access to news on site.
Cost	On request.
Comments	
Address	William Reed Publishing, Broadford Park, Crawley RH11 9RT
Tel./e-mail	0800 652 6512 giles.pott@william-reed.co.uk
Fax/Website	www.mtj.co.uk

MEETINGS INDUSTRY ASSOCIATION

Title	**UK Conference Market Survey**
Coverage	Based on interviews with 300 corporate organisers and 300 association organisers of conferences, the survey looks at number of events held, delegate numbers, length of event, budgets, fees, locations, exhibitions with conferences, trade press used, etc.
Frequency	Annual.
Web facilities	General details and ordering facilities on site.
Cost	£165, £135 for members; £155 PDF version, £125 for members.
Comments	Also produces a quarterly trends survey but only available to members.
Address	PO Box 6984, Wellingborough NN29 7WU
Tel./e-mail	0845 230 5508 AngelaZ@mia-uk.org
Fax/Website	0845 230 7708 www.mia-uk.org

MEETINGS INDUSTRY ASSOCIATION

Title	**National Corporate Hospitality Survey**
Coverage	Based on interviews with buyers and recipients of corporate hospitality, the survey looks at types of hospitality, venues, budgets, reasons for arranging events, recipients' percepation of value of events, best type of events, etc.
Frequency	Regular.
Web facilities	General details on site.
Cost	On request.
Comments	Survey sponsored by Sodexho Prestige and further details from 0208 601 2013 or sales@corporatehospitality-online.co.uk. Also produces a quarterly trends survey but this is only available to members.
Address	PO Box 6984, Wellingborough NN29 7WU
Tel./e-mail	0845 230 5508 AngelaZ@mia-uk.org
Fax/Website	0845 230 7708 www.mia-uk.org

METAL BULLETIN PLC

Title	**Metal Bulletin Monthly**
Coverage	Monthly market reviews and forecasts plus news and prices.
Frequency	Monthly.
Web facilities	Paid for access to data on site.
Cost	Available free to an invited circulation list.
Comments	
Address	16 Lower Marsh, London SE1 7RJ
Tel./e-mail	0207 827 5297 ehayward@metalbulletin.com
Fax/Website	0207 827 5292 www.metalbulletin.com

METAL BULLETIN PLC

Title	**Metal Bulletin**
Coverage	Every issue contains 800 prices for metals, ferro-alloys, ores, steel, scrap.
Frequency	Weekly.
Web facilities	Paid for access to data on site.
Cost	£657.
Comments	A daily e-mail update service is also available. Various other market reports on metals and geographical markets.
Address	16 Lower Marsh, London SE1 7RJ
Tel./e-mail	0207 827 5297 ehayward@metalbulletin.com
Fax/Website	0207 827 5292 www.metalbulletin.com

METAL PACKAGING MANUFACTURERS' ASSOCIATION

Title	**MPA Industry Statistics**
Coverage	Data on sales of packaging materials, sales by end-user sector, sales by type of packaging, exports and employees. Based mainly on data collected by the association.
Frequency	Regular.
Web facilities	Free access to statistics on site.
Cost	Free.
Comments	
Address	Soane Point, 6–8 Market Place, Reading RG1 2EG
Tel./e-mail	0118 925 5520 enquiries@mpma.org.uk
Fax/Website	0118 925 5888 www.mpma.org.uk

MICHAEL PAGE

Title	**Salary Surveys**
Coverage	Regular salary surveys on various sectors: accountancy, banking, HR, legal, marketing, retailing, sales, taxation; technical, etc. Based on surveys of clients.
Frequency	Regular.
Web facilities	Free access to reports on site.
Cost	Free.
Comments	
Address	Victoria House, Southampton Row, London WC1B 4JB
Tel./e-mail	0207 831 2000 info@michaelpage.co.uk
Fax/Website	www.michaelpage.co.uk

MILLWARD BROWN

Title	**Northern Ireland Omnibus**
Coverage	A regular survey of 1100 adults in Northern Ireland based on face-to-face interviews in the home. Covers consumer markets for both products and services.
Frequency	Twice a month.
Web facilities	General details on the site.
Cost	On request.
Comments	Millward Brown took over Ulster Marketing Surveys in 2002.
Address	115 University Street, Belfast BT7 1HP
Tel./e-mail	02890 231060 enquiries@ums-research.com
Fax/Website	02890 243887 www.millwardbrown.com

MILLWARD BROWN

Title	**Northern Ireland Car Market**
Coverage	A review of the car market in Northern Ireland based on original research.
Frequency	Annual.
Web facilities	General details on the site.
Cost	£160.
Comments	Millward Brown took over Ulster Marketing Surveys in 2002.
Address	115 University Street, Belfast BT7 1HP
Tel./e-mail	02890 231060 enquiries@ums-research.com
Fax/Website	02890 243887 www.millwardbrown.com

MILLWARD BROWN

Title	**Internet Usage in Northern Ireland**
Coverage	A review of Internet usage and penetration in Northern Ireland based on original research.
Frequency	Annual.
Web facilities	General details on the site.
Cost	£80.
Comments	Millward Brown took over Ulster Marketing Surveys in 2002.
Address	115 University Street, Belfast BT7 1HP
Tel./e-mail	02890 231060 enquiries@ums-research.com
Fax/Website	02890 243887 www.millwardbrown.com

MINTEL INTERNATIONAL GROUP

Title	**Market Intelligence – Food and Drink**
Coverage	A series of regular reports on the UK food, drink sectors with detailed market data and forecasts in addition to key consumer trends.
Frequency	Monthly.
Web facilities	Details of all publications and press releases on site. Access to report contents for clients.
Cost	From £995 per report.
Comments	Special reports, services covering specific markets, ad hoc reports and analyses are also available.
Address	18–19 Long Lane, London EC1A 9HE
Tel./e-mail	0207 606 6000 info@mintel.com
Fax/Website	0207 606 5932 www.mintel.com

MINTEL INTERNATIONAL GROUP

Title	**Retail Intelligence**
Coverage	A series of regular reports on the UK retailing sector with basic retailing data updated regularly and specific reports updated every few years.
Frequency	Regular.
Web facilities	Details of all publications and press releases on site. Access to report contents for clients.
Cost	From £995 per report.
Comments	Special reports, services covering specific markets, ad hoc reports and analyses are also available.
Address	18–19 Long Lane, London EC1A 9HE
Tel./e-mail	0207 606 6000 info@mintel.com
Fax/Website	0207 606 5932 www.mintel.com

MINTEL INTERNATIONAL GROUP

Title	**Finance Intelligence**
Coverage	A series of regular reports on the UK financial services sector with basic data updated regularly and analytical articles updated every few years.
Frequency	Regular.
Web facilities	Details of all publications and press releases on site. Access to report contents for clients.
Cost	From £995 per report.
Comments	Special reports, services covering specific markets, ad hoc reports and analyses are also available.
Address	18–19 Long Lane, London EC1A 9HE
Tel./e-mail	0207 606 6000 info@mintel.com
Fax/Website	0207 606 5932 www.mintel.com

MINTEL INTERNATIONAL GROUP

Title	**Leisure Intelligence UK**
Coverage	A series of regular reports on the UK leisure sector with basic data updated regularly and analytical articles updated every few years.
Frequency	Regular.
Web facilities	Details of all publications and press releases on site. Access to report contents for clients.
Cost	From £995 per report.
Comments	Special reports, services covering specific markets, ad hoc reports and analyses are also available.
Address	18–19 Long Lane, London EC1A 9HE
Tel./e-mail	0207 606 6000 info@mintel.com
Fax/Website	0207 606 5932 www.mintel.com

MINTEL INTERNATIONAL GROUP

Title	**Market Intelligence – Essentials**
Coverage	A series of regular reports on UK non-food and drink consumer markets with detailed market data and forecasts in addition to key consumer trends.
Frequency	Monthly.
Web facilities	Details of all publications and press releases on site. Access to report contents for clients.
Cost	From £995 per report.
Comments	Special reports, series covering specific markets, ad hoc reports and analyses are also available.
Address	18–19 Long Lane, London EC1A 9HE
Tel./e-mail	0207 606 6000 info@mintel.com
Fax/Website	0207 606 5932 www.mintel.com

MONEYFACTS GROUP

Title	**Business Money Facts**
Coverage	A range of economic and monetary statistics including retail prices, annual inflation rates, average earnings, base rates, tax and price index, finance house base rates, commercial rents, employment statistics and house price data from the Halifax. Based on various official and non-official sources.
Frequency	Regular.
Web facilities	Details of publications on site.
Cost	£78.50.
Comments	
Address	Moneyfacts House, 66–70 Thorpe Road, Norwich NR1 1BJ
Tel./e-mail	0870 225 0476
Fax/Website	0870 225 0477 www.moneyfacts.co.uk

MONEYFACTS GROUP

Title	**Moneyfacts**
Coverage	A range of statistics on personal financial products and schemes.
Frequency	Monthly.
Web facilities	Details of publications on site.
Cost	£59.
Comments	
Address	Moneyfacts House, 66–70 Thorpe Road, Norwich NR1 1BJ
Tel./e-mail	0870 225 0476
Fax/Website	0870 225 0477 www.moneyfacts.co.uk

MONKS PARTNERSHIP

Title	**Management Pay UK**
Coverage	Pay and benefits of directors and managers in various industries and sectors. Also details of incentives, company cars. Based on the company's own research. Published in five separate publications: *Parent Board and Corporate; Divisions and Subsidiaries; Companies up to £100m; Annual and Long-Term Incentives; Pensions and Benefits.*
Frequency	Twice a year.
Web facilities	General details of publications on site.
Cost	Each report priced separately from £800 to £2000.
Comments	Other reports available on remuneration in specific sectors.
Address	The Mill House, Wendens Ambo, Saffron Walden CB11 4JX
Tel./e-mail	01799 54222 info@monkspartnership.com
Fax/Website	01799 541805 www.monkspartnership.com

MONKS PARTNERSHIP

Title	**Financial Sector City Pay Guide**
Coverage	A review of pay in the financial sector. Based on a survey by the company.
Frequency	Three times a year.
Web facilities	General details of publications on site.
Cost	£1200; £350 to participants.
Comments	Other reports available on remuneration in specific sectors.
Address	The Mill House, Wendens Ambo, Saffron Walden CB11 4JX
Tel./e-mail	01799 54222 info@monkspartnership.com
Fax/Website	01799 541805 www.monkspartnership.com

MONKS PARTNERSHIP

Title	**Survey of Non-Executive Director Practice and Fees**
Coverage	A survey of non-executive director salaries and benefits and other issues, based on a survey by the company. Latest survey covers 220 companies.
Frequency	Annual.
Web facilities	General details of publications on site.
Cost	£1200; £350 to participants.
Comments	Other reports available on remuneration in specific sectors.
Address	The Mill House, Wendens Ambo, Saffron Walden CB11 4JX
Tel./e-mail	01799 54222 info@monkspartnership.com
Fax/Website	01799 541805 www.monkspartnership.com

MONKS PARTNERSHIP

Title	**Company Car UK**
Coverage	Details of policies, benefits, changes based on a survey by the company.
Frequency	Annual.
Web facilities	General details of publications on site.
Cost	£660; £200 to participants.
Comments	Other reports available on remuneration in specific sectors.
Address	The Mill House, Wendens Ambo, Saffron Walden CB11 4JX
Tel./e-mail	01799 54222 info@monkspartnership.com
Fax/Website	01799 541805 www.monkspartnership.com

MORI

Title	**Deloitte/Ipsos MORI Delivery Index**
Coverage	Quarterly opinion survey of consumers asking for perceptions of economic conditions and government policy affecting the economy and related issues.
Frequency	Quarterly.
Web facilities	Free access to data on site.
Cost	Free.
Comments	Various other research services available and free access to basic survey data on site.
Address	MORI House, 79–81 Borough Street, London SE1 1FY
Tel./e-mail	0207 347 3000 mori@mori.com
Fax/Website	0207 347 3800 www.mori.com

MORI

Title	**General Public Omnibus**
Coverage	Weekly omnibus survey of a national sample of over 1000 adults.
Frequency	Weekly.
Web facilities	General details and free access to other data on site.
Cost	On request.
Comments	Various other research services available and free access to basic survey data on site.
Address	MORI House, 79–81 Borough Street, London SE1 1FY
Tel./e-mail	0207 347 3000 mori@mori.com
Fax/Website	0207 347 3800 www.mori.com

MORI

Title	**Social Research Review**
Coverage	A digest and analysis of some of the major polls and issues covered by MORI in the previous year.
Frequency	Annual.
Web facilities	Free access to report on site.
Cost	Free.
Comments	Various other research services available and free access to basic survey data on site.
Address	MORI House, 79–81 Borough Road, London SE1 1FY
Tel./e-mail	0207 347 3000 mori@mori.com
Fax/Website	0207 347 3800 www.mori.com

MORTGAGE FINANCE GAZETTE

Title	**Loans Figures and Figures/Indicators**
Coverage	Details of the number of mortgage loans by type of loan and other indicators of the housing market. Based on various sources.
Frequency	Monthly in a monthly journal.
Web facilities	
Cost	£54.
Comments	
Address	Charterhouse Communications Ltd, Arnold House, 36-41 Holywood Lane, London EC2A 3SF
Tel./e-mail	0207 827 5457
Fax/Website	0207 827 0567

MOTOR CYCLE INDUSTRY ASSOCIATION

Title	**Figures for Motorcycles, Mopeds and Scooters**
Coverage	A monthly review of new registrations by model, type, etc.
Frequency	Monthly.
Web facilities	Free access to data on site.
Cost	Free.
Comments	Published as a press release.
Address	Starley House, Eaton Road, Coventry CV6 2GH
Tel./e-mail	02476 250 800 mcia@mcia.co.uk
Fax/Website	02476 250 840 www.mcia.co.uk

MOTOR CYCLE INDUSTRY ASSOCIATION

Title	**Pocket Guide**
Coverage	Basic data on motorcycle production, registrations, etc.
Frequency	Regular.
Web facilities	Free access to data on site.
Cost	Free.
Comments	
Address	Starley House, Eaton Road, Coventry CV6 2GH
Tel./e-mail	02476 250 800 mcia@mcia.co.uk
Fax/Website	02476 250 840 www.mcia.co.uk

MOTOR CYCLE INDUSTRY ASSOCIATION

Title	**Motor Cycle Registration Information Service**
Coverage	A regularly updated service where clients can stipulate specific information required.
Frequency	Regular.
Web facilities	Some basic data on site.
Cost	On request.
Comments	
Address	Starley House, Eaton Road, Coventry CV6 2GH
Tel./e-mail	02476 250 800 mcia@mcia.co.uk
Fax/Website	02476 250 840 www.mcia.co.uk

MOTOR TRANSPORT

Title	**2--- Road Transport Market Survey**
Coverage	A survey of companies, vehicles, haulage trends in the road transport sector carried out for Motor Transport by NOP. The survey also includes comparative data for previous years.
Frequency	Annual in a weekly journal.
Web facilities	
Cost	£72; £2.50 for single copy.
Comments	
Address	Reed Business Information, Windsor Court, East Grinstead House, East Grinstead RH19 1XA
Tel./e-mail	01342 326972
Fax/Website	01342 335612 www.roadtransport.net

MOTOR TRANSPORT

Title	**Market Intelligence**
Coverage	Summary statistics and news covering vehicles and road transport with data collected from various sources.
Frequency	Weekly in a weekly journal.
Web facilities	
Cost	£72; £2.20 for single copy.
Comments	
Address	Reed Business Information, Windsor Court, East Grinstead House, East Grinstead RH19 1XA
Tel./e-mail	01342 326972
Fax/Website	01342 335612 www.roadtransport.net

MSI MARKETING RESEARCH FOR INDUSTRY

Title	**MSI Data Reports**
Coverage	MSI publishes over a 100 reports per year on UK consumer and industrial sectors and many of these are updated on a regular basis. Based primarily on research by the company supported by data from official non-official sources.
Frequency	Regular.
Web facilities	General details and ordering options on website.
Cost	£445–£545 depending on number of data units in each report.
Comments	
Address	Viscount House, River Dee Business Park, River Lane, Saltney, Chester CH4 8RH
Tel./e-mail	0800 195 6756 enquiries@msi-marketingresearch.co.uk
Fax/Website	0800 195 6757 www.msi-marketingresearch.co.uk

MUSHROOM GROWERS' ASSOCIATION

Title	**Industry Survey**
Coverage	Production and manpower figures for the sector plus a cost analysis, methods of growing and industry yield figures. Based on a survey of members and accompanied by a commentary.
Frequency	Annual.
Web facilities	
Cost	Free.
Comments	Primarily for members.
Address	PO Box 192, Stamford PE9 3ZT
Tel./e-mail	01780 722074
Fax/Website	01780 729006 www.mushroomgrowers.org

NATIONAL ASSOCIATION OF BRITISH AND IRISH MILLERS

Title	**NABIM Facts and Figures**
Coverage	A general overview of the milling and grain industries with key data.
Frequency	Annual.
Web facilities	Free access to PDF report on site.
Cost	Free.
Comments	
Address	21 Arlington Street, London SW1A 1RN
Tel./e-mail	0207 493 2521 info@nabim.org.uk
Fax/Website	0207 493 6785 www.nabim.org.uk

NATIONAL ASSOCIATION OF CIDER MAKERS

Title	**Industry Statistics**
Coverage	Data on sales, apples used, cider and perry sales, packaged and draught cider, imports, exports and consumption trends. Data for earlier years.
Frequency	Annual.
Web facilities	Free access to data on site.
Cost	Free.
Comments	Enquiries should be addressed to Simon Russell at the address below.
Address	Emma-Chris Way, Abbeywood Business Park, Filton, Bristol BS34 7JU
Tel./e-mail	0117 906 6565 srussell@freshwater-uk.com
Fax/Website	0117 940 2145 www.cideruk.com

NATIONAL ASSOCIATION OF ESTATE AGENTS

Title	**Market Trends**
Coverage	A review of trends in the housing market based on a survey of a sample of members, plus data from other sources.
Frequency	Monthly.
Web facilities	A general summary is available free on the site.
Cost	Free.
Comments	The survey is normally only available to members but some summary data on website.
Address	Arbon House, 21 Jury Street, Warwick CV34 4EH
Tel./e-mail	01926 496800 info@naea.co.uk
Fax/Website	01926 400953 www.naea.co.uk

NATIONAL ASSOCIATION OF PAPER MERCHANTS

Title	**Bad Debt Levels**
Coverage	A survey of levels of debt in the paper industry based on returns from members.
Frequency	Quarterly.
Web facilities	General summary on site.
Cost	On request.
Comments	
Address	PO Box 2850, Nottingham NG5 2WW
Tel./e-mail	0115 841 2129 info@napm.org.uk
Fax/Website	0115 841 0831 www.napm.org.uk

NATIONAL ASSOCIATION OF PAPER MERCHANTS

Title	**Merchanting Statistics**
Coverage	Detailed statistics on sales based on returns from member companies.
Frequency	Regular.
Web facilities	Some basic free statistics and member access to detailed data on the site.
Cost	On request.
Comments	
Address	PO Box 2850, Nottingham NG5 2WW
Tel./e-mail	0115 841 2129 info@napm.org.uk
Fax/Website	0115 841 0831 www.napm.org.uk

NATIONAL ASSOCIATION OF PENSION FUNDS

Title	**NAPF Annual Survey**
Coverage	A survey of various schemes with data on income, expenditure, size of fund, the nature of the schemes, benefits provided. It covers over 1100 pension schemes. The data are collected via a postal survey to all members of the association. A supporting commentary is included with the statistics.
Frequency	Annual.
Web facilities	Free summary statistics and paid-for access to detailed statistics on site. Online ordering facilities and e-mail alerts about new statistics.
Cost	£295.
Comments	Published in four parts.
Address	NIOC House, 4 Victoria Street, London SW1H 0NX
Tel./e-mail	0207 808 1300 publications@napf.co.uk
Fax/Website	0207 222 7585 www.napf.co.uk

NATIONAL ASSOCIATION OF STEEL STOCKHOLDERS

Title	**NASS Business Trends Survey**
Coverage	Monthly survey of members with analysis of prospects for the next three months.
Frequency	Monthly.
Web facilities	Some basic market information free on the site and details of statistics.
Cost	On request.
Comments	Usually only available to members.
Address	6th Floor, McLaren Building, Dale End, Birmingham B4 7LN
Tel./e-mail	0121 200 2288 info@nass.org.uk
Fax/Website	0121 236 7444 www.nass.org.uk

NATIONAL ASSOCIATION OF STEEL STOCKHOLDERS

Title	**NASS Trading Summary**
Coverage	Regular review of opening and closing stocks in the industry based on member's returns.
Frequency	Monthly.
Web facilities	
Cost	On request.
Comments	Usually only available to members.
Address	6th Floor, McLaren Building, Dale End, Birmingham B4 7LN
Tel./e-mail	0121 200 2288 info@nass.org.uk
Fax/Website	0121 236 7444 www.nass.org.uk

NATIONAL ASSOCIATION OF STEEL STOCKHOLDERS

Title	**NASS Forecast Trends**
Coverage	Forecasts for the demand, consumption and supply of steel.
Frequency	Twice a year.
Web facilities	
Cost	On request.
Comments	Usually only available to members.
Address	6th Floor, McLaren Building, Dale End, Birmingham B4 7LN
Tel./e-mail	0121 200 2288 info@nass.org.uk
Fax/Website	0121 236 7444 www.nass.org.uk

NATIONAL CENTRE FOR SOCIAL RESEARCH

Title	**British Social Attitudes**
Coverage	A survey of social values and attitudes in the UK in the 1980s and 1990s, based on interviews with approximately 3000 people. Supported by detailed analysis.
Frequency	Annual.
Web facilities	Details of all surveys on site.
Cost	£20.
Comments	
Address	35 Northampton Square, London ECV 0AX
Tel./e-mail	0207 250 1866 info@natcen.ac.uk
Fax/Website	0207 250 1524 www.natcen.ac.uk

NATIONAL COMPUTING CENTRE

Title	**Benchmark of IT Spending**
Coverage	A review of IT spending based on replies from over 200 organisations and representing total spending of over £700m.
Frequency	Annual.
Web facilities	Paid-for access to statistics and online ordering facilities on site.
Cost	£125.
Comments	
Address	Oxford House, Oxford Road, Manchester M1 7ED
Tel./e-mail	0161 228 6333 surveys@ncc.co.uk
Fax/Website	0161 242 2499 www.ncc.co.uk

NATIONAL COMPUTING CENTRE

Title	**Benchmark of Salaries and Employment Trends**
Coverage	An annual survey of the IT labour market based on replies from over 9000 IT specialists in almost 400 organisations.
Frequency	Annual.
Web facilities	Paid-for access to statistics on site. Online ordering facilities.
Cost	£330.
Comments	
Address	Oxford House, Oxford Road, Manchester M1 7ED
Tel./e-mail	0161 228 6333 surveys@ncc.co.uk
Fax/Website	0161 242 2499 www.ncc.co.uk

NATIONAL COMPUTING CENTRE

Title	**Salaries and Staff Issues in IT**
Coverage	A survey of salaries and benefits for 34 IT job titles based on questionnaires sent to 12 000 individuals in 600 organisations.
Frequency	Annual.
Web facilities	Paid-for access to statistics on site. Online ordering facilities.
Cost	£150.
Comments	
Address	Oxford House, Oxford Road, Manchester M1 7ED
Tel./e-mail	0161 228 6333 surveys@ncc.co.uk
Fax/Website	0161 242 2499 www.ncc.co.uk

NATIONAL COUNCIL FOR VOLUNTARY ORGANISATIONS (NCVO)

Title	**UK Voluntary Sector Almanac**
Coverage	A review of the voluntary sector with data on organisations, functions, expenditure, employment, charitable donations, etc.
Frequency	Regular.
Web facilities	General details on site.
Cost	£25; £17.50 for members.
Comments	
Address	Regent's Wharf, 8 All Saints Street, London N1 9RL
Tel./e-mail	0207 713 6161 ncvo@ncvo-vol.org.uk
Fax/Website	0207 713 6300 www.ncvo-vol.org.uk

NATIONAL COUNCIL FOR VOLUNTARY ORGANISATIONS (NCVO)

Title	**UK Giving**
Coverage	Annual data on trends in charitable donations and sponsorship. Based on data collected by the Council.
Frequency	Annual.
Web facilities	Free access to report on site.
Cost	Free.
Comments	
Address	Regent's Wharf, 8 All Saints Street, London N1 9RL
Tel./e-mail	0207 713 6161 ncvo@ncvo-vol.org.uk
Fax/Website	0207 713 6300 www.ncvo-vol.org.uk

NATIONAL ENVIRONMENT RESEARCH COUNCIL – BRITISH GEOLOGICAL SURVEY

Title	**Opencast Coalmining Statistics**
Coverage	Detailed statistics on production, mines operating, mines refused planning permission etc by mineral planning authority.
Frequency	Regular.
Web facilities	Free access to data on site.
Cost	Free.
Comments	Free basic statistics on site.
Address	Kingsley Dunham Centre, Keyworth, Nottingham NG12 5GG
Tel./e-mail	0115 936 3134 Enquiries@bgs.ac.uk
Fax/Website	0115 936 3276 www.bgs.ac.uk

NATIONAL ENVIRONMENT RESEARCH COUNCIL - BRITISH GEOLOGICAL SURVEY

Title	**UK Minerals Yearbook**
Coverage	A review of UK mineral production and consumption with sections for specific raw materials and products. Some historical data.
Frequency	Annual.
Web facilities	Free access to PDF report on site.
Cost	Free.
Comments	
Address	Kingsley Dunham Centre, Keyworth, Nottingham NG12 5GG
Tel./e-mail	0115 936 3134 Enquiries@bgs.ac.uk
Fax/Website	0115 936 3276 www.bgs.sc.uk

NATIONAL FARMERS' UNION

Title	**Facts on Farming**
Coverage	Data on farming structure, production, crops, livestock, etc.
Frequency	Regular.
Web facilities	Free access to data on site.
Cost	Free.
Comments	
Address	164 Shaftesbury Avenue, London WC2H 8HL
Tel./e-mail	0207 331 7200
Fax/Website	0207 331 7313 www.nfu.org.uk

NATIONAL FOUNDATION FOR EDUCATIONAL RESEARCH

Title	**National Survey of Trends in Primary Education**
Coverage	Based on responses from 600 primary school headteachers, the annual survey reviews pupil numbers and class sizes, curriculum developments, finances, new developments, etc.
Frequency	Annual.
Web facilities	Free digest of results on site for latest and previous years.
Cost	On request.
Comments	For the first time in 2004, the report was jointly sponsored by the Local Government Association.
Address	The Mere, Upton Park, Slough SL1 2DQ
Tel./e-mail	01753 637002 w.tury@nfer.ac.uk
Fax/Website	01753 637280 www.nfer.ac.uk

NATIONAL HOUSE BUILDING COUNCIL

Title	**New House-Building Statistics**
Coverage	Covers dwelling starts and completions, prices, market share of timber frame, first time buyers' ability to buy and some regional trends. Largely based on the council's own survey plus some central government data. Usually published two to three weeks after the quarter to which it relates and some historical data are included.
Frequency	Quarterly.
Web facilities	Free summary data from survey on site.
Cost	£50; £12.50 per issue.
Comments	
Address	Buildmark House, Chiltern Avenue, Amersham HP6 5AP
Tel./e-mail	01494 735249 info@nhbc.co.uk
Fax/Website	01494 735795 www.nhbc.co.uk

NATIONAL INSTITUTE OF ECONOMIC AND SOCIAL RESEARCH (NIESR)

Title	**National Institute Economic Review**
Coverage	General analysis of the UK and world economy with forecasts usually up to 18 months ahead. Special articles on relevant topics. A separate statistical section is included in each issue along with some tables in the text.
Frequency	Quarterly.
Web facilities	Free summary data and analysis on site plus paid-for access to detailed data.
Cost	£264 for institutions; £103 for individuals.
Comments	Publication available from Sage Publications, 6 Bonhill Street, London EC2A 4PU. Tel. 0207 324 8701. Also offers paid-for subscription access on the website to monthly GDP estimates.
Address	2 Dean Trench Street, Smith Square, London SW1P 3HE
Tel./e-mail	0207 222 7665 pubs@niesr.ac.uk
Fax/Website	0207 654 1900 www.niesr.ac.uk

NATIONAL READERSHIP SURVEY

Title	**National Readership Survey**
Coverage	Statistics on the readership of national newspapers and various consumer magazines based on a stratified random sample of over 28 000 individuals. Results are published a few months after the survey. Some commentary supports the text.
Frequency	Annual.
Web facilities	Top line survey data for newspapers, general magazines and women's magazines is free on the site. Also details of services, demographics, methodology, etc.
Cost	On request.
Comments	
Address	40 Parker Street, London WC2B 5PQ
Tel./e-mail	0207 242 8411 SteveMillington@nrs.co.uk
Fax/Website	0207 242 8303 www.nrs.co.uk

NATIONAL SPECIALIST CONTRACTORS COUNCIL

Title	**NSCC State of Trade Survey**
Coverage	Opinion survey of members covering workload, capacity, stocks, prices, margins, future likely trends.
Frequency	Regular.
Web facilities	Free PDF of survey on site.
Cost	Free.
Comments	Published the first *Payment Survey* in October 2005 covering payment by suppliers.
Address	School of the Built Environment, Northumbria University, Ellison Building, Newcastle-upon-Tyne NE1 8ST
Tel./e-mail	0191 227 4746 enquiries@nscc.org.uk
Fax/Website	0191 227 3167 www.nscc.org.uk

NATIONAL TYRE DISTRIBUTORS ASSOCIATION

Title	**TyreCheck 2---**
Coverage	An annual survey of member organisations and over 10 000 car inspections to check tyres.
Frequency	Annual.
Web facilities	Summary data from survey on site.
Cost	On request.
Comments	
Address	8 Temple Square, Aylesbury HP20 2QH
Tel./e-mail	0870 900 0600 info@ntda.co.uk
Fax/Website	0870 900 0610 www.ntda.co.uk

NATIONAL TYRE DISTRIBUTORS' ASSOCIATION

Title	**Tyre Statistics**
Coverage	Statistics on sales of new tyres, retreads, exhausts and batteries. Based on research by the association.
Frequency	Monthly.
Web facilities	General details on site.
Cost	On request.
Comments	Usually only available to members.
Address	8 Temple Square, Aylesbury HP20 2QH
Tel./e-mail	0870 900 0600 info@ntda.co.uk
Fax/Website	0870 900 0610 www.ntda.co.uk

NATIONWIDE

Title	**Monthly Review**
Coverage	A review of the UK housing market with commentary and statistics on house prices, types of houses purchased, mortgage lending, regional house prices and house prices by type of house. Based on data collected and analysed by the building society.
Frequency	Monthly.
Web facilities	Free access to latest data and historical data on site plus historical data.
Cost	Free.
Comments	Nationwide also has spreadsheets of house price data available back to 1952 for national data and back to 1973 for regional data. A guide to the house price methodology used by Nationwide is available free from the address below.
Address	Nationwide House, Pipers Way, Swindon SN38 1NW
Tel./e-mail	01793 455196
Fax/Website	01793 455903 www.nationwide.co.uk/hpi/

NATIONWIDE

Title	**Quarterly Review**
Coverage	Data on the housing market, including housing market forecasts and economic and consumer trends. Based on various sources.
Frequency	Quarterly.
Web facilities	Free access to latest data and historical data on site plus free access to historical data.
Cost	Free.
Comments	Nationwide also has spreadsheets of house price data available back to 1952 for national data and back to 1973 for regional data. A guide to the house price methodology used by Nationwide is available free from the address below.
Address	Nationwide House, Pipers Way, Swindon SN38 1NW
Tel./e-mail	01793 455196
Fax/Website	01793 455903 www.nationwide.co.uk/hpi/

NEMS MARKET RESEARCH

Title	**NEMS Omnibus Survey**
Coverage	Twice weekly telephone omnibus survey of a national sample of UK adults.
Frequency	Twice weekly.
Web facilities	General details on site.
Cost	On request.
Comments	
Address	22–23 Manor Way, Belasis Hall Technology Park, Billingham TS23 4HN
Tel./e-mail	01642 373355 info@nemsmr.co.uk
Fax/Website	01642 373350 www.nemsmr.co.uk

NEW POLICY INSTITUTE

Title	**Monitoring Poverty and Social Exclusion**
Coverage	A review of poverty trends which monitors 50 indicators of poverty and social exclusion.
Frequency	Annual.
Web facilities	Latest report available free on site.
Cost	Free.
Comments	Previously published by the Joseph Rowntree Foundation (see other entry, page 190). Updated poverty data available free at www.poverty.org.uk.
Address	109 Coppergate House, 16 Brune Street, London E1 7NJ
Tel./e-mail	0207 721 8421 info@npi.org.uk
Fax/Website	0207 721 8422 www.npi.org.uk

NEWSPAPER MARKETING AGENCY

Title	**Marketplace Facts**
Coverage	Regular statistics on readership, reach and advertising revenues for national newspapers.
Frequency	Regular.
Web facilities	Free access to data on site.
Cost	Free.
Comments	Also published advertising revenue data and free access on site.
Address	Empire House, 175 Piccadilly, London W1J 9EN
Tel./e-mail	0207 182 1700 enquiries@nmauk.co.uk
Fax/Website	0207 182 1711 www.nmauk.co.uk

NEWSPAPER SOCIETY

Title	**Annual Regional Press Survey Findings**
Coverage	Details of regional companies, turnover, revenues by sector, advertising and employment.
Frequency	Annual.
Web facilities	Free access to PDF on site plus other facts and figures.
Cost	Free.
Comments	
Address	Bloomsbury House, 74–77 Great Russell Street, London WC1B 3DA
Tel./e-mail	0207 636 7014 ns@newspapersoc.org.uk
Fax/Website	0207 631 5119 www.newspapersoc.org.uk

NORTHERN IRELAND CHAMBERS OF COMMERCE

Title	**Northern Ireland Business Monitor**
Coverage	A survey of business conditions in Northern Ireland, expectations for the future and business opinion on key issues. Based on a survey of member companies.
Frequency	Annual.
Web facilities	Free access to PDF report on site.
Cost	Free.
Comments	The 2004–2005 Monitor was the first of an annual series produced in association with BT.
Address	22 Great Victoria Street, Belfast BT2 7BJ
Tel./e-mail	0289 024 4113 mail@northernirelandchamber.com
Fax/Website	0289 024 7024 www.northernirelandchamber.com

NORTHERN IRELAND FOOD AND DRINK ASSOCIATION

Title	**Northern Ireland Food And Drink Handbook**
Coverage	Includes statistics on food market and industry, consumption and expenditure trends, grocery sales, forecasts, health and tourism.
Frequency	Annual.
Web facilities	Free access to handbook on site.
Cost	Free.
Comments	
Address	Quay Gate House, 15 Scrabo Street, Belfast BT5 4BD
Tel./e-mail	028 9045 2424 mbell@nifda.co.uk
Fax/Website	028 9045 3373 www.nifda.co.uk

NTC PUBLICATIONS LTD

Title	**Marketing Pocket Book**
Coverage	A statistical profile of the marketing, distribution and consumption of goods and services in the UK, with some additional data on Europe and other areas. Based on various sources, including official and market research publications.
Frequency	Annual.
Web facilities	Details and online ordering of most publications on site.
Cost	£24.
Comments	Published in association with the Advertising Association. A companion volume, *European Marketing Pocket Book*, is also available.
Address	Farm Road, Henley-on-Thames RG9 1EJ
Tel./e-mail	01491 411000 info@ntc.co.uk
Fax/Website	01491 571188 www.warc.com

NTC PUBLICATIONS LTD

Title	**Retail Pocket Book**
Coverage	Statistics on specific retail markets and the major retailers plus advertising trends and developments in retailing. A final section covers international retailing. Based on data collected from various sources.
Frequency	Annual.
Web facilities	Details and online ordering of most publications on site.
Cost	£32.
Comments	Published in association with Nielsen.
Address	Farm Road, Henley-on-Thames RG9 1EJ
Tel./e-mail	01491 411000 info@ntc.co.uk
Fax/Website	01491 571188 www.warc.com

NTC PUBLICATIONS LTD

Title	**UK Consumer Marketplace**
Coverage	A profile of Britain's towns, counties, products and consumer spending patterns based primarily on data collected by CACI (see other entry, page 62).
Frequency	Annual.
Web facilities	Details and online ordering of most publications on site.
Cost	£32.
Comments	Published in association with CACI.
Address	Farm Road, Henley-on-Thames RG9 1EJ
Tel./e-mail	01491 411000 info@ntc.co.uk
Fax/Website	01491 571188 www.warc.com

NTC PUBLICATIONS LTD

Title	**Lifestyle Pocket Book**
Coverage	Lifestyle data for the UK with sections on shopping habits, consumption patterns, leisure, holidays, media usage, personal finance, housing and households, transport, communications, employment, education, health, crime, economics and demographics. A final section provides some summary data on the rest of Europe. Based on various official and non-official sources.
Frequency	Annual.
Web facilities	Details and online ordering of most publications on site.
Cost	£24.
Comments	Published in association with the Advertising Association.
Address	Farm Road, Henley-on-Thames RG9 1EJ
Tel./e-mail	01491 411000 info@ntc.co.uk
Fax/Website	01491 571188 www.warc.com

NTC PUBLICATIONS LTD

Title	**Drink Pocket Book**
Coverage	Basic data on the drinks sector including general statistics on the market followed by sections on specific drinks and drink outlets. Some international data are included. Based on various sources but a strong reliance on data from Stats MR.
Frequency	Annual.
Web facilities	Details and online ordering of most publications on site.
Cost	£35.
Comments	Published in association with Stats MR.
Address	Farm Road, Henley-on-Thames RG9 1EJ
Tel./e-mail	01491 411000 info@ntc.co.uk
Fax/Website	01491 571188 www.warc.com

NTC PUBLICATIONS LTD

Title	**Media Pocket Book**
Coverage	A statistical profile of British commercial media. Coverage includes advertising spending by media and product category, circulation and readership data, publisher information, titles, stations, audiences, viewing, reach, indices of media rates and cover prices.
Frequency	Regular.
Web facilities	Details and online ordering of most publications on site.
Cost	£26.
Comments	
Address	Farm Road, Henley-on-Thames RG9 1EJ
Tel./e-mail	01491 411000 info@ntc.co.uk
Fax/Website	01491 571188 www.warc.com

NTC PUBLICATIONS LTD

Title	**Pensions Pocket Book**
Coverage	Statistics on pension schemes, the legal background and current pensions issues.
Frequency	Annual.
Web facilities	Details and online ordering of most publications on site.
Cost	£35.
Comments	Published in association with Hewitt Associates (see other entry).
Address	Farm Road, Henley-on-Thames RG9 1EJ
Tel./e-mail	01491 411000 info@ntc.co.uk
Fax/Website	01491 571188 www.ntc.co.uk

NTC PUBLICATIONS LTD

Title	**Insurance Pocket Book**
Coverage	Basic data on the insurance industry including an overview and detailed sections on life insurance, general insurance, London insurance market, specialised insurance, captives and the international market.
Frequency	Annual.
Web facilities	Details and online ordering of most publications on site.
Cost	£45.
Comments	Published in association with Towers Perrin Tillinghast.
Address	Farm Road, Henley-on-Thames RG9 1EJ
Tel./e-mail	01491 411000 info@ntc.co.uk
Fax/Website	01491 571188 www.ntc.co.uk

NTC PUBLICATIONS LTD

Title	**Financial Marketing Pocket Book**
Coverage	A guide to the UK personal finance sector covering personal incomes, wealth and savings, consumers' expenditure, personal investments, life assurance, general insurance, credit, mortgages, banking, credit cards and advertising.
Frequency	Annual.
Web facilities	Details and online ordering of most publications on site.
Cost	£40.
Comments	Published in association with Gfk NOP.
Address	Farm Road, Henley-on-Thames RG9 1EJ
Tel./e-mail	01491 411000 info@ntc.co.uk
Fax/Website	01491 571188 www.ntc.co.uk

OPINION LEADER RESEARCH

Title	**Opinion Leader Panel**
Coverage	A panel survey of over 100 key opinion leaders such as directors in industry, politicians, media, trade unionists, city analysts, etc.
Frequency	Monthly.
Web facilities	Details on site.
Cost	On request.
Comments	
Address	5th Floor, Holborn Gate, 330 High Holborn, London WC1V 7QG
Tel./e-mail	0207 861 3080 enquiries@opinionleader.co.uk
Fax/Website	0207 861 3081 www.opinionleader.co.uk

OUT OF HOME GROUP

Title	**Out of Home Statistics**
Coverage	Range of statistics from various sources on out of home eating and catering, plus details of employment and industry trends.
Frequency	Regular.
Web facilities	Free access to data on site.
Cost	Free.
Comments	The group is part of the Food and Drink Federation.
Address	Federation House, 6 Catherine Street, London WC2B 5JJ
Tel./e-mail	0207 836 2460 outofhome@fdf.org.uk
Fax/Website	0207 836 0580 www.outofhome.org

OUTDOOR ADVERTISING ASSOCIATION

Title	**Figures and Market Data**
Coverage	Summary data on the outdoor advertising sector including expenditure, sector advertising, types of posters, numbers of sites, share of advertising, etc.
Frequency	Regular.
Web facilities	Free access to data on site.
Cost	Free.
Comments	
Address	Summit House, 27 Sale Place, London W2 1YR
Tel./e-mail	0207 973 0315 enquiries@oaa.org.uk
Fax/Website	0207 973 0318 www.oaa.org.uk

OVUM

Title	**Market Trends**
Coverage	A report on the software and computing services industry including forecasts. Split into four sections: software services, software support services, project services and outsourcing. Based largely on research by the company.
Frequency	Annual.
Web facilities	General details of research surveys on site plus paid-for access to detailed data. News on site.
Cost	£2350.
Comments	
Address	Cardinal Tower, 12 Farringdon Road, London EC1M 3HS
Tel./e-mail	0207 551 9039 mail@ovumholway.com
Fax/Website	www.ovumholway.com

OXFORD ECONOMIC FORECASTING LTD

Title	**UK Economic Outlook**
Coverage	Detailed forecasts of the UK economy, along with other major world economies. Summary articles and features on trends.
Frequency	Quarterly.
Web facilities	Summary data, details of all publications and paid-for online access on site.
Cost	£200 per issue.
Comments	
Address	Abbey House, 121 St Aldates, Oxford OX1 1HB
Tel./e-mail	01865 268900 mailbox@oef.com
Fax/Website	01865 268906 www.oef.com

OXFORD ECONOMIC FORECASTING LTD

Title	**UK Industrial Prospects**
Coverage	An analysis, with forecasts, of 70 UK sectors based on a model developed by the company.
Frequency	Twice yearly.
Web facilities	Summary data, details of all publications and paid-for online access to data on site.
Cost	£650 per issue.
Comments	
Address	Abbey House, 121 St Aldates, Oxford OX1 1HB
Tel./e-mail	01865 268900 mailbox@oef.co.uk
Fax/Website	01865 268906 www.oef.com

OXFORD ECONOMIC FORECASTING LTD

Title	**UK Regional Prospects**
Coverage	An analysis, with forecasts, of the economies of 13 Government Standard Office regions.
Frequency	Twice yearly.
Web facilities	Summary data, details of all publications and paid-for online access to data on site.
Cost	£900 per issue.
Comments	
Address	Abbey House, 121 St Aldates, Oxford OX1 1HB
Tel./e-mail	01865 268900 mailbox@oef.co.uk
Fax/Website	01865 268906 www.oef.com

OXFORD ECONOMIC FORECASTING LTD

Title	**UK Consumer Outlook**
Coverage	An analysis, with forecasts, of trends in 50 consumer sectors.
Frequency	Twice yearly.
Web facilities	Summary data, details of all publications and paid-for online access to data on site.
Cost	£600 per issue.
Comments	
Address	Abbey House, 121 St Aldates, Oxford OX1 1HB
Tel./e-mail	01865 268900 mailbox@oef.co.uk
Fax/Website	01865 268906 www.oef.com

OXFORD ECONOMIC FORECASTING LTD

Title	**UK Weekly Brief**
Coverage	A review of key economic trends based on various sources.
Frequency	Weekly.
Web facilities	Summary data, details of all publications and paid-for online access to data on site.
Cost	£15 per issue.
Comments	
Address	Abbey House, 121 St Aldates, Oxford OX1 1HB
Tel./e-mail	01865 268900 mailbox@oef.co.uk
Fax/Website	01865 268906 www.oef.com

PACKAGING FEDERATION

Title	**PF UK Market Report**
Coverage	Annual data on packaging by type, products packaged, manufacturing, employment, packaging materials, production and recycling. Two years' worth of data on site.
Frequency	Annual.
Web facilities	Free access to data on site.
Cost	Free.
Comments	
Address	Vigilant House, 120 Wilton Road, London SW1V 1JZ
Tel./e-mail	0207 808 7217 iandent@packagingfedn.co.uk
Fax/Website	0207 808 7218 www.packagingfedn.co.uk

PASSENGER SHIPPING ASSOCIATION

Title	**Annual Cruise Review**
Coverage	Review of cruising trends by destination, type, etc. based on research undertaken by research agency IRN Research (see other entry, page 186).
Frequency	Annual.
Web facilities	Free access to report on site.
Cost	Free.
Comments	
Address	4th Floor, Walmar House, 288–292 Regent Street, London W1R 5HE
Tel./e-mail	0207 436 2449 press@discover-cruises.co.uk
Fax/Website	0207 636 9206 www.cruiseinformationservice.co.uk

PERIODICAL PUBLISHERS ASSOCIATION

Title	**Data and Trends**
Coverage	Detailed statistics on production, sales, trade, titles, prices, etc. available on site.
Frequency	Regular.
Web facilities	Free access to data on site.
Cost	Free.
Comments	
Address	28 Kingsway, London WC2B 6JR
Tel./e-mail	0207 404 4166 info@ppa.co.uk
Fax/Website	0207 404 4167 www.ppamarketing.net

PERIODICAL PUBLISHERS ASSOCIATION

Title	**The Magazine Handbook 2**---
Coverage	A compilation of data on the journal sector based on various sources. Statistics on the industry, circulation, advertising, readership, profitability, new media and exports. Sections on both the consumer and business press.
Frequency	Annual.
Web facilities	
Cost	£25; £15 for members.
Comments	Also publishes various research reports on the magazine sector.
Address	28 Kingsway, London WC2B 6JR
Tel./e-mail	0207 404 4166 info@ppa.co.uk
Fax/Website	0207 404 4167 www.ppa.co.uk

PET FOOD MANUFACTURERS' ASSOCIATION

Title	**Pet Ownership**
Coverage	Statistics on pet ownership broken down by type of pet and demographics of owners. Also historical data.
Frequency	Regular.
Web facilities	The data are published on the site and is available free.
Cost	Free.
Comments	Also some basic market data available free on the site.
Address	20 Bedford Street, Covent Garden, London WC2E 9HP
Tel./e-mail	0207 379 9009 info@pfma.org.uk
Fax/Website	0207 379 8008 www.pfma.com

PETROLEUM ARGUS LPG WORLD

Title	**Petroleum Argus Fundamentals**
Coverage	Statistical analysis of the petroleum sector with data on prices, output, trade and consumption.
Frequency	Monthly.
Web facilities	
Cost	On request.
Comments	
Address	93 Shepperton Road, London N1 3DF
Tel./e-mail	0207 359 8792 lpgw@petroleumargus.com
Fax/Website	0207 359 6661 www.petroleumargus.com

PETROLEUM ECONOMIST

Title	**Markets**
Coverage	Tables covering oil prices, world production and tanker freight rates based on various sources.
Frequency	Monthly in a monthly journal.
Web facilities	
Cost	£365.
Comments	Also publishes regular statistics on world oil trends.
Address	PO Box 105, Baird House, 15-17 St Cross Street, London EC1N 8VW
Tel./e-mail	0207 831 5588 petecon@petroleum-economist.com
Fax/Website	0207 831 4567 www.petroleum-economist.com

PETROLEUM ECONOMIST

Title	**UK North Sea Survey**
Coverage	Statistics on North Sea oil fields with data on reserves, ownership, production, etc. Compiled from a variety of sources.
Frequency	Annual in a monthly journal.
Web facilities	
Cost	£365.
Comments	Also contains regular statistics on world oil trends.
Address	PO Box 105, Baird House, 15-17 St Cross Street, London EC1N 8VW
Tel./e-mail	0207 831 5588 petecon@petroleum-economist.com
Fax/Website	0207 831 4567 www.petroleum-economist.com

PETROLEUM TIMES

Title	**Petroleum Times Energy Report**
Coverage	Provides pump prices for petrol in various towns and cities in the UK. Based on the journal's own survey with some supporting text.
Frequency	Twice a month.
Web facilities	
Cost	£195 per annum.
Comments	
Address	Nexus Media Ltd, Nexus House, Azalea Drive, Swanley BR8 8HY
Tel./e-mail	01322 660070
Fax/Website	01322 667633 www.atelier.net/energyreport

PHARMACEUTICAL JOURNAL

Title	**Retail Sales Index for Chemists**
Coverage	General figures on the sales trends in total and for specific products sold in chemists. Based on central government data.
Frequency	Weekly.
Web facilities	
Cost	£99.
Comments	Other statistics published occasionally.
Address	1 Lambeth High Street, London SE1 7JN
Tel./e-mail	0207 735 9141 editor@pharmj.com
Fax/Website	0207 572 2505 www.pharmj.com

PHOTO IMAGING COUNCIL

Title	**UK Market Figures 2---**
Coverage	Data on camera sales by type for the last two years based on data from research agency Gfk.
Frequency	Annual.
Web facilities	Free access to basic data on site plus industry overview data.
Cost	Free.
Comments	
Address	Orbital House, 85 Croydon Road, Caterham CR3 6PD
Tel./e-mail	01883 334497 pic@admin.co.uk
Fax/Website	www.pic.uk.net

PHOTO MARKETING ASSOCIATION INTERNATIONAL (UK) LTD

Title	**2--- Industry Trends Report**
Coverage	A review of consumer and market trends in the sector based on original market research.
Frequency	Annual.
Web facilities	General details on site and members can download copies of report. Also spreadsheet of industry data by country available free to others on site.
Cost	On request.
Comments	Usually only available to members.
Address	Wisteria House, 28 Fulling Mill Lane, Welwyn AL6 9N5
Tel./e-mail	0870 240 4542 mmcnaught@pmai.org
Fax/Website	01438 716 572 www.pmai.org/international/united_kimgdom

	PKF
Title	**The Football Survey**
Coverage	A annual survey of the financial directors of UK football companies.
Frequency	Annual.
Web facilities	Free access to this and many other reports on site.
Cost	Free.
Comments	
Address	Farringdon Place, 30 Farringdon Road, London EC1M 3AP
Tel./e-mail	0207 065 0000 info@pkf.co.uk
Fax/Website	0207 065 0650 www.pkf.co.uk

	PKF
Title	**Hotel Britain**
Coverage	A review of the operating and financial characteristics of a sample of around 825 hotels from AA five star to two star. Details of occupancy rates, revenues, costs and expenses with data for the latest year and the previous year. Some supporting text.
Frequency	Annual.
Web facilities	Free access to this and many other reports on site.
Cost	Free.
Comments	
Address	Farringdon Place, 30 Farringdon Road, London EC1M 3AP
Tel./e-mail	0207 065 0000 hotels@uk.pkf.com
Fax/Website	0207 065 0650 www.pkf.co.uk

	PKF
Title	**SME Index**
Coverage	A review of the performance of the SME sector focusing on financial trends. Based on a survey by the company.
Frequency	Quarterly.
Web facilities	Free access to this and many other reports on the site.
Cost	Free.
Comments	
Address	Farringdon Place, 30 Farringdon Road, London EC1M 3AP
Tel./e-mail	0207 065 0000 info@uk.pkf.com
Fax/Website	0207 065 0650 www.pkf.co.uk

POINT OF PURCHASE ADVERTISING INTERNATIONAL UK AND IRELAND

Title	**POPAI Members Survey**
Coverage	Opinion survey of members covering turnover, business confidence, future trends, etc.
Frequency	Quarterly.
Web facilities	General details on site.
Cost	On request.
Comments	
Address	Devonshire House, Lutterworth LE17 4AG
Tel./e-mail	01455 554848 info@popai.co.uk
Fax/Website	01455 554421 www.popai.co.uk

POSTAR

Title	**Postar**
Coverage	Postar audience research measures the effectiveness of outdoor advertising through travel and other surveys.
Frequency	Regular.
Web facilities	General details plus some basic data on site.
Cost	On request.
Comments	
Address	Summit House, 27 Sale Place, London W2 1YR
Tel./e-mail	0207 479 9700 info@postar.co.uk
Fax/Website	0207 706 7143 www.postar.co.uk

PPL RESEARCH LTD

Title	**Board Market Digest**
Coverage	A monthly review of market trends for buyers and suppliers of packaging papers and boards.
Frequency	Monthly.
Web facilities	General details on site.
Cost	£270; £320 plus VAT for electronic version.
Comments	
Address	PO Box 2002, Watford WD25 9ZT
Tel./e-mail	01923 894777 enquiries@pplresearch.co.uk
Fax/Website	01923 894888 www.pplresearch.co.uk

PPL RESEARCH LTD

Title	**UK Preview**
Coverage	The *UK Preview* includes demand and price forecasts for the UK paper and board market.
Frequency	Twice yearly.
Web facilities	General details on site.
Cost	£699 per issue (either hardcopy or electronic).
Comments	
Address	PO Box 2002, Watford WD25 9ZT
Tel./e-mail	01923 894777 enquiries@pplresearch.co.uk
Fax/Website	01923 894888 www.pplresearch.co.uk

PPL RESEARCH LTD

Title	**Paper Market Digest**
Coverage	Monthly digest which includes statistics on market trends and prices.
Frequency	Monthly.
Web facilities	General details on site.
Cost	£270; £320 plus VAT for electronic version.
Comments	
Address	PO Box 2002, Watford WD25 9ZT
Tel./e-mail	01923 894777 enquiries@pplresearch.co.uk
Fax/Website	01923 894888 www.pplresearch.co.uk

PREMIER BRANDS

Title	**Hot Beverages Handbook**
Coverage	A two-volume report on specific hot drinks segments, e.g. tea, coffee, milk-based drinks, etc based mainly on commissioned research.
Frequency	Annual.
Web facilities	
Cost	Free
Comments	Monthly hot beverage market updates.
Address	PO Box 8, Moreton, Wirral CH46 8XF
Tel./e-mail	0151 522 4000
Fax/Website	0151 522 4020 www.premierbrands.com

PRE-SCHOOL LEARNING ALLIANCE

Title	**Members Survey**
Coverage	Facts and figures on pre-school play based on data collected by the association from members and covering staffing, facilities, funding, children.
Frequency	Annual.
Web facilities	Free access to report on site.
Cost	Free.
Comments	Also publishes an annual report.
Address	69 Kings Cross Road, London WC1X 9LL
Tel./e-mail	0207 833 0991 pla@pre-school.org.uk
Fax/Website	0207 837 4942 www.pre-school.org.uk

PRICE WATERHOUSE COOPERS

Title	**UK Economic Outlook**
Coverage	Analysis, commentary and data on UK economic trends based on various sources.
Frequency	Three times a year.
Web facilities	Free access to data on site.
Cost	Free.
Comments	Publishes various other market and strategic reports.
Address	Southwark Towers, 32 London Bridge Street, London SE1 9SY
Tel./e-mail	0207 583 5000
Fax/Website	0207 822 4562 www.pw.com/uk

PRICE WATERHOUSE COOPERS

Title	**Executive Compensation: Review of the Year**
Coverage	Based on a survey by the company and an analysis of trends in executive salaries.
Frequency	Annual.
Web facilities	Free access to data on site.
Cost	Free.
Comments	Publishes various other market and strategic reports.
Address	Southwark Towers, 32 London Bridge Street, London SE1 9SY
Tel./e-mail	0207 583 5000
Fax/Website	0207 822 4562 www.pw.com/uk

PROCESSING AND PACKAGING MACHINERY ASSOCIATION (PPMA)

Title	**UK Imports and Exports of Packaging Machinery**
Coverage	Brief commentary and graphs showing exports and imports over a three-year period. The figures are produced from Customs and Excise sources and separate intra-EU and extra-EU trade.
Frequency	Annual.
Web facilities	
Cost	Free.
Comments	
Address	New Progress House, 34 Stafford Road, Wallington SM6 9AA
Tel./e-mail	0208 773 8111 admin:ppma.co.uk
Fax/Website	0208 773 0022 www.ppma.co.uk

PROPERTY INTELLIGENCE PLC

Title	**Retail Demand Report**
Coverage	An annual review of trends in the retail property market covering over 1000 retail centres.
Frequency	Annual.
Web facilities	Free PDF of the report on the site.
Cost	Free.
Comments	Property Intelligence PLC offers various property and related databases.
Address	Portman House, 2 Portman Street, London W1H 6EB
Tel./e-mail	0207 839 7684 info@focusnet.co.uk
Fax/Website	0207 491 7821 www.focusnet.co.uk

PROPERTY INTELLIGENCE PLC

Title	**Commercial Auction Guide Analysis**
Coverage	A regular review benchmarking prices of commercial property at auctions around the UK.
Frequency	Twice yearly.
Web facilities	Free PDF of the report on site.
Cost	Free.
Comments	Property Intelligence PLC offers various property and related databases.
Address	Portman House, 2 Portman Street, London W1H 6EB
Tel./e-mail	0207 839 7684 info@focusnet.co.uk
Fax/Website	0207 491 7821 www.focusnet.co.uk

PROPERTY INTELLIGENCE PLC

Title	**London Office Market Report**
Coverage	Regular review of trends in London office properties including rents, revenues, etc.
Frequency	Quarterly.
Web facilities	Free PDF of report on site.
Cost	Free.
Comments	Property Intelligence PLC offers various property and related databases.
Address	Portman House, 2 Portman Street, London W1H 6EB
Tel./e-mail	0207 839 7684 info@focusnet.co.uk
Fax/Website	0207 491 7821 www.focusnet.co.uk

PROPRIETARY ASSOCIATION OF GREAT BRITAIN

Title	**OTC Industry Growth**
Coverage	Sales of over-the-counter (OTC) products by core product categories and specific items. Also an analysis of the data.
Frequency	Annual.
Web facilities	Free access to reports for last four years on site.
Cost	Free.
Comments	Produced in association with IRI.
Address	Vernon House, Sicilian Avenue, London WC1A 2QS
Tel./e-mail	0207 242 8331 info@pagb.co.uk
Fax/Website	0207 405 7719 www.pagb.org.uk

PUBLIC RELATIONS CONSULTANTS ASSOCIATION

Title	**Benchmarking Survey**
Coverage	Survey of industry growth trends, new business, employment trends, etc. Based on survey by the association.
Frequency	Annual.
Web facilities	General details on site.
Cost	On request.
Comments	Also publish a regular *Agency Barometer*, an opinion survey of key issues.
Address	Willow House, Willow Place, London SW1 1JH
Tel./e-mail	0207 233 6026 pressoffice@prca.org.uk
Fax/Website	0207 828 4797 www.prca.org.uk

PUBLISHERS' ASSOCIATION

Title	**University Library Spending on Books, Journals and Electronic Resources**
Coverage	An annual review of university library spending on various information resources based on a survey by the association.
Frequency	Annual.
Web facilities	Free access to report on site. Also key statistics free on site under 'Market Information' pages.
Cost	Free.
Comments	Also publishes various one-off reports.
Address	29B Montague Street, London WC1B 5DW
Tel./e-mail	0207 691 9191 mail@publishers.org.uk
Fax/Website	0207 691 9199 www.publishers.org.uk

PUBLISHERS' ASSOCIATION

Title	**CAAP Student Survey: Student Information Sources and Book Buying Behaviour**
Coverage	An annual review of spending by students on books and other information resources based on a survey by the association.
Frequency	Annual.
Web facilities	Detailed data only available to members but free access to key statistics on site.
Cost	On request.
Comments	Report only available to members. Also publishes various one-off reports.
Address	29B Montague Street, London WC1B 5DW
Tel./e-mail	0207 691 9191 mail@publishers.org.uk
Fax/Website	0207 691 9199 www.publishers.org.uk

PUBLISHERS' ASSOCIATION

Title	**School Book Spending in the UK**
Coverage	Annual analysis of spending on books by sector, type, etc. based on a survey by the association.
Frequency	Annual.
Web facilities	Available free on the site. Also key statistics free on site under 'Key Facts and Figures' pages.
Cost	Free.
Comments	Also publishes various one-off reports.
Address	29B Montague Street, London WC1B 5DW
Tel./e-mail	0207 691 9191 7474 mail@publishers.org.uk
Fax/Website	0207 691 9199 www.publishers.org.uk

PURCON CONSULTANTS LTD

Title	**Purcon Salary Survey**
Coverage	A salary survey prepared from the Purcon Register which has records of over 10 000 candidates for jobs in purchasing and supply. Also includes data on bonuses and company cars.
Frequency	Quarterly.
Web facilities	Online ordering facilities on site.
Cost	£300; £100 per issue.
Comments	
Address	Prospect House, Repton Place, Amersham HP7 9LP
Tel./e-mail	01494 737300 info@purcon.co.uk
Fax/Website	01494 737333 www.purcon.co.uk

QUARRY PRODUCTS' ASSOCIATION

Title	**Aggregate Sales Trends**
Coverage	Statistics on the production and use of core products, crushed rock, sand and gravel, asphalt and ready mixed concrete.
Frequency	Quarterly.
Web facilities	Basic data and commentary every quarter free on site.
Cost	On request.
Comments	More detailed statistics are available to members.
Address	38–44 Gillingham Street, London SW1V 1AU
Tel./e-mail	0207 963 8000 info@qpa.org
Fax/Website	0207 963 8001 www.qpa.org

RAC PLC

Title	**RAC Report on Motoring**
Coverage	A survey of over 1000 motorists examining issues such as motor car dependency, ownership, safety, driving offences, etc.
Frequency	Annual.
Web facilities	Executive summary, general conclusions and ordering facilities on site.
Cost	£250.
Comments	
Address	RAC House, 1 Forest Road, Feltham TW13 7RR
Tel./e-mail	0208 917 2708 icarpenter@rac.co.uk
Fax/Website	0208 917 2608 www.rac.co.uk

RADIO ADVERTISING BUREAU

Title	**Quarterly Marketplace Report**
Coverage	Audience and revenue results for the commercial radio sector based on research by RAB.
Frequency	Quarterly.
Web facilities	Free access to data and analysis on site, plus news and charts on the market bringing together data from various sources.
Cost	Free.
Comments	
Address	The Radiocentre, 72 Shaftesbury Avenue, London W1D 5DU
Tel./e-mail	0207 306 2500 websupport@rab.co.uk
Fax/Website	www.rab.co.uk

RADIO JOINT AUDIENCE RESEARCH (RAJAR)

Title	**Radio Audience Listening**
Coverage	Audience figures for BBC radio and national and local commercial radio.
Frequency	Quarterly.
Web facilities	Free summary data from the quarterly surveys on the site. Also paid-for access to detailed data for subscribers.
Cost	£1100.
Comments	
Address	Paramount House, 162-170 Wardour Street, London W1F 8ZX
Tel./e-mail	0207 292 9040 info@rajar.co.uk
Fax/Website	0207 292 9041 www.rajar.co.uk

RECRUITMENT & EMPLOYMENT CONFEDERATION

Title	**Recruitment Industry Survey**
Coverage	UK sales by the recruitment industry and total industry turnover. Also data broken down by temporary/permament workers. Based on a survey by the federation.
Frequency	Annual.
Web facilities	Free summary on site and online ordering facilities.
Cost	£110 (£100 electronic copy); £80 for members (£40 electronic).
Comments	
Address	36–38 Mortimer Street, London W1N 7RG
Tel./e-mail	0207 462 3260 info@rec.uk.com
Fax/Website	0207 255 2878 www.rec.uk.com

REED PERSONNEL SERVICES

Title	**Reed Market Index**
Coverage	A review of trends in the jobs market with separate indices for temporary employment and permanent employment. Based on information obtained by the company.
Frequency	Monthly.
Web facilities	Free access to report on site.
Cost	Free.
Comments	
Address	6th Floor, Tolworth Tower, Ewell Road, Tolworth KT6 7EL
Tel./e-mail	0208 399 5221
Fax/Website	0208 399 4930 www.reed.co.uk

RESEARCH NOW!

Title	**UK Online Panel**
Coverage	Regular online panel survey of UK consumers with results on spending, lifestyles, behaviour, etc.
Frequency	Regular.
Web facilities	General details on site.
Cost	On request.
Comments	
Address	66 South Lambeth Road, London SW8 1RL
Tel./e-mail	0207 091 7800 www.researchnow.co.uk
Fax/Website	0207 091 7801 services@researchnow.co.uk

RMIF LTD

Title	**New Car Sales by County**
Coverage	A regional and county breakdown of new car sales, in units, for the latest year with the percentage change over the previous year. Sales are broken down into total cars and company cars.
Frequency	Annual.
Web facilities	Free basic statistics on site.
Cost	Free.
Comments	RMIF is the Retail Motor Industry Federation.
Address	201 Great Portland Street, London W1N 6AB
Tel./e-mail	0207 580 9122
Fax/Website	0207 580 6376 www.rmif.co.uk

RMIF LTD

Title	**Monthly Statistics**
Coverage	Monthly figures for new car sales, in units, with a breakdown between total cars and company cars.
Frequency	Monthly.
Web facilities	Free basic statistics on site.
Cost	Free.
Comments	RMIF is the Retail Motor Industry Federation.
Address	201 Great Portland Street, London W1N 6AB
Tel./e-mail	0207 580 9122
Fax/Website	0207 580 6376 www.rmif.co.uk

ROBERT WALTERS

Title	**Salary Survey 2---**
Coverage	Detailed report and database searchable by sector (various professional services sectors) giving salary levels, changes and general trends and issues.
Frequency	Regular.
Web facilities	Free access to data on site.
Cost	Free.
Comments	
Address	9–10 St Andrews Square, Edinburgh EH2 2AF
Tel./e-mail	0131 718 6025 edinburgh@robertwalters.com
Fax/Website	0131 718 6100 www.robertwalters.com

ROYAL BANK OF SCOTLAND PLC

Title	**Monthly UK Economic Update**
Coverage	A review of general economic trends and analysis of key economic issues.
Frequency	Monthly.
Web facilities	Free access to data on site.
Cost	Free.
Comments	Also publishes some UK regional surveys.
Address	42 St Andrew Square, Edinburgh EH2 2YE
Tel./e-mail	0131 523 2393 economics@rbs.co.uk
Fax/Website	0131 556 8555 www.royalbankscot.co.uk

ROYAL BANK OF SCOTLAND PLC

Title	**Royal Bank of Scotland Oil and Gas Index**
Coverage	Data on production from North Sea oil fields and the average daily value of oil production based on a telephone survey of oil field operators. An analysis of the statistics is also included.
Frequency	Monthly.
Web facilities	Free access to data on site.
Cost	Free.
Comments	Produced in association with BBC Radio Scotland. Also publishes some UK regional surveys.
Address	42 St Andrew Square, Edinburgh EH2 2YE
Tel./e-mail	0131 523 2393 economics@rbs.co.uk
Fax/Website	0131 556 8555 www.royalbankscot.co.uk

ROYAL BANK OF SCOTLAND PLC

Title	**Scottish Retail Sales Monitor**
Coverage	A monthly review of retail sales in Scotland based on data collected by the bank.
Frequency	Monthly.
Web facilities	Free access to data on the site.
Cost	Free.
Comments	Also publishes some UK regional surveys.
Address	42 St Andrew Square, Edinburgh EH2 2YE
Tel./e-mail	0131 523 2393 economics@rbs.co.uk
Fax/Website	0131 556 8555 www.royalbankscot.co.uk

ROYAL INSTITUTION OF CHARTERED SURVEYORS

Title	**Construction Market Survey**
Coverage	A quarterly review of construction and housing trends based on a combination of official and non-official data.
Frequency	Quarterly.
Web facilities	Free access to report on site.
Cost	Free.
Comments	
Address	Surveyor House, Westwood Way, Coventry CV4 8JE
Tel./e-mail	0870 333 1600 contactrics@rics.org
Fax/Website	0870 334 3811 www.rics.org

ROYAL INSTITUTION OF CHARTERED SURVEYORS

Title	**Housing Market Report**
Coverage	National figures and regional data each month for various types and ages of property. Shows the trends in prices over the previous three months and includes comments on the market situation from estate agents.
Frequency	Monthly.
Web facilities	Free access to report on site.
Cost	Free.
Comments	
Address	Surveyor House, Westwood Way, Coventry CV4 8JE
Tel./e-mail	0870 333 1600 contactrics@rics.org
Fax/Website	0870 334 3811 www.rics.org

ROYAL SOCIETY FOR THE PREVENTION OF ACCIDENTS

Title	**Home and Leisure Accidents Surveillance Web Database**
Coverage	Statistics on accidents in the home and external areas.
Frequency	Regular.
Web facilities	General details on site.
Cost	Free.
Comments	Regular data not collected since 2003 but ROSPA staff can answer specific enquiries.
Address	Edgbaston Park, 353 Bristol Road, Birmingham B5 7ST
Tel./e-mail	0121 248 2066 help@rospa.co.uk
Fax/Website	0121 248 2011 www.rospa.co.uk

RYDEN

Title	**Ryden Property Review**
Coverage	A review of economic trends in Scotland, with forecasts, is followed by a commentary on the Scottish property market covering Edinburgh, Glasgow, Aberdeen and Dundee. Specific sections on shops and industrial and warehouse property. Based primarily on data from the company.
Frequency	Twice yearly.
Web facilities	Free access to the report on site.
Cost	Free.
Comments	
Address	46 Castle Street, Edinburgh EH2 3BN
Tel./e-mail	0131 225 6612
Fax/Website	0131 225 5766 www.ryden.co.uk

SALARY SURVEY PUBLICATIONS

Title	**Survey of Appointments' Data and Trends**
Coverage	A generic series title for various surveys of salaries and appointments in a range of sectors including IT, human resources personnel. Most surveys are based on an analysis of advertisements in the press and actual salary data.
Frequency	Regular.
Web facilities	
Cost	On request – typical prices are £295–£325 per survey.
Comments	
Address	7 High Street, Lambourn RG17 8XL
Tel./e-mail	01488 72705 ssp@easynet.co.uk
Fax/Website	

SCONUL

Title	**UK Higher Education Library Management Statistics**
Coverage	An annual review of management data based on sample returns from SCONUL members.
Frequency	Annual.
Web facilities	Member access to statistics and online ordering facilities on site.
Cost	On request.
Comments	Member access to SCONUL Library Statistics: Trends Analysis on website.
Address	102 Euston Street, London NW1 2HA
Tel./e-mail	0207 387 0317 info@sconul.ac.uk
Fax/Website	0207 383 3197 www.sconul.ac.uk

SCONUL

Title	**SCONUL Annual Library Statistics**
Coverage	Expenditure and operational trends based on the annual returns from SCONUL libraries. A small amount of text is included.
Frequency	Annual.
Web facilities	Member access to statistics and online ordering facilities on site.
Cost	£40.
Comments	Member access to SCONUL Library Statistics: Trends Analysis on website.
Address	102 Euston Street, London NW1 2HA
Tel./e-mail	0207 387 0317 info@sconul.ac.uk
Fax/Website	0207 383 3197 www.sconul.ac.uk

SCOTCH WHISKY ASSOCIATION

Title	**Scotch Whisky Exports**
Coverage	Detailed analysis of export values and volumes and key country destinations.
Frequency	Twice yearly.
Web facilities	General summary in press release on site.
Cost	On request.
Comments	
Address	20 Atholl Crescent, Edinburgh EH3 8HF
Tel./e-mail	0131 222 9330 contact@swa.org.uk
Fax/Website	www.scotch-whisky.org.uk

SCOTCH WHISKY ASSOCIATION

Title	**Scotch Whisky Statistics**
Coverage	Figures on the activities of the industry including production, exports, stocks and duty paid. Figures for some previous years also given. Based mainly on Central government statistics with a small amount of original data.
Frequency	Annual.
Web facilities	Free access to data on site on 'Enquiries' page.
Cost	Free.
Comments	
Address	20 Atholl Crescent, Edinburgh EH3 8HF
Tel./e-mail	0131 222 9330 contact@swa.org.uk
Fax/Website	www.scotch-whisky.org.uk

SCOTCH WHISKY ASSOCIATION

Title	**Scotch at a Glance**
Coverage	A breakdown of the top export markets and UK markets for whisky.l
Frequency	Annual.
Web facilities	Free access to data on site.
Cost	Free.
Comments	
Address	20 Atholl Crescent, Edinburgh EH3 8HF
Tel./e-mail	0131 222 9330 contact@swa.org.uk
Fax/Website	www.scotch-whisky.org.uk

SCOTTISH COUNCIL DEVELOPMENT AND INDUSTRY

Title	**Survey of Oil and Gas Industry**
Coverage	Analysis and data on sales, activity, Scottish and UK activity, exports, etc.
Frequency	Annual.
Web facilities	Free access to report on site.
Cost	Free.
Comments	
Address	23 Chester Street, Edinburgh EH3 7AD
Tel./e-mail	0131 225 7911 enquiries@scdi.org.uk
Fax/Website	0131 220 2116 www.scdi.org.uk

SCOTTISH COUNCIL DEVELOPMENT AND INDUSTRY

Title	**Survey of Scottish Manufactured Exports**
Coverage	A regular survey of manufacturing sector exports.
Frequency	Annual.
Web facilities	General details and some free data on site.
Cost	Free.
Comments	
Address	23 Chester Street, Edinburgh EH3 7AD
Tel./e-mail	0131 225 7911 enquiries@scdi.org.uk
Fax/Website	0131 220 2116 www.scdi.org.uk

SCOTTISH NEWSPAPER PUBLISHERS ASSOCIATION

Title	**Facts and Figures**
Coverage	Data on readership profiles for various types of newspapers in Scotland.
Frequency	Annual
Web facilities	Free access to data on site.
Cost	Free.
Comments	
Address	48 Palmerston Place, Edinburgh EH12 5DE
Tel./e-mail	0131 220 4353 info@snpa.org.uk
Fax/Website	0131 220 4344 www.snpa.org.uk

SEAFISH

Title	**United Kingdom Fish Industry Annual Statistics**
Coverage	A compendium of data including landings and aquaculture production, fleet size, trade in fish and fish products, fish processing, household purchases of fish, catering sector. Historical data for at least six years is included in some tables.
Frequency	Annual.
Web facilities	General details plus free summary statistics and online ordering facilities on site.
Cost	£5.
Comments	Also publishes a *European Supplies Bulletin* with statistics on specific European countries.
Address	18 Logie Mill, Logie Green Road, Edinburgh EH7 4HG
Tel./e-mail	0131 558 3331 seafish@seafish.co.uk
Fax/Website	0131 558 1442 www.seafish.co.uk

SEAFISH

Title	**United Kingdom Seafood Industry Annual Statistics**
Coverage	Detailed statistics from production stages through to supplies and consumption. Based mainly on Central government sources.
Frequency	Annual.
Web facilities	General details plus free summary data and online ordering facilities on site.
Cost	£35; £10 per issue.
Comments	Also publishes a *European Supplies Bulletin* with statistics on specific European countries.
Address	18 Logie Mill, Logie Green Road, Edinburgh EH7 4HG
Tel./e-mail	0131 558 3331 seafish@seafish.co.uk
Fax/Website	0131 558 1442 www.seafish.co.uk

SEAFISH

Title	**Household Fish Consumption in Great Britain**
Coverage	Analysis of sales by species for household consumption, split into fresh/chilled and frozen sales. The statistics are taken from a sample survey of households and comparable data for the previous year is given. Some text supports the data.
Frequency	Quarterly.
Web facilities	General details plus some free summary statistics and online ordering facilities on site.
Cost	£75; £20 per issue.
Comments	Also publishes a European Supplies Bulletin with statistics on specific European countries.
Address	18 Logie Mill, Logie Green Road, Edinburgh EH7 4HG
Tel./e-mail	0131 558 3331 seafish@seafish.co.uk
Fax/Website	0131 558 1442 www.seafish.co.uk

SEAFISH

Title	**UK Trade Bulletin**
Coverage	Quantity and value of imports and exports of fish intended for human consumption. The latest month's figures with the year to date and comparative figures for the previous year. Based on central government data.
Frequency	Monthly.
Web facilities	General details plus some free summary statistics and online ordering facilities on site.
Cost	£35; £5 per issue.
Comments	Also publishes a *European Supplies Bulletin* with statistics on specific European countries.
Address	18 Logie Mill, Logie Green Road, Edinburgh EH7 4HG
Tel./e-mail	0131 558 3331 seafish@seafish.co.uk
Fax/Website	0131 558 1442 www.seafish.co.uk

SEAFISH

Title	**United Kingdom Fish Catering Sector Handbook**
Coverage	Published in the same format as the *Fish Industry Annual Statistics*, the booklet considers 10 sub-sectors of the catering market in detail. Data on total tonnage of fish, the most popular species, distribution channels, type of product.
Frequency	Regular.
Web facilities	General details plus free summary statistics and online ordering facilities on site.
Cost	£5.
Comments	Also publishes a *European Supplies Bulletin* with statistics on specific European countries.
Address	18 Logie Mill, Logie Green Road, Edinburgh EH7 4HG
Tel./e-mail	0131 558 3331 seafish@seafish.co.uk
Fax/Website	0131 558 1442 www.seafish.co.uk

SEAFOOD SCOTLAND

Title	**Scottish Seafood Industry – Key Facts and Figures**
Coverage	Overview and data on the seafood sector covering catches, operators, species, etc. Based on various sources.
Frequency	Regular.
Web facilities	Free PDF of data on site.
Cost	Free.
Comments	
Address	18 Logie Mill, Logie Green Road, Edinburgh EH7 4HG
Tel./e-mail	0131 557 9344 enquiries@seafoodscotland.org
Fax/Website	0131 557 9344 www.seafoodscotland.org

SEWELLS INTERNATIONAL

Title	**BCA Used Car Market Report**
Coverage	A regular review of the used car market with details of sales, prices, networks, etc.
Frequency	Annual.
Web facilities	Publication details and online ordering facilities on site.
Cost	£175.
Comments	
Address	EMAP Automotive, Peterborough Business Park, Peterborough PE2 6EA
Tel./e-mail	01733 468 254
Fax/Website	01733 468 349 www.sewells.co.uk

SEWELLS INTERNATIONAL

Title	**UK Servicing and Repair Report**
Coverage	Statistics on levels and types of servicing and repairs for vehicles.
Frequency	Annual.
Web facilities	Publication details and online ordering facilities on site.
Cost	£175.
Comments	
Address	EMAP Automotive, Peterborough Business Park, Peterborough PE2 6EA
Tel./e-mail	01733 468 254
Fax/Website	01733 468 349 www.sewells.co.uk

SEWELLS INTERNATIONAL

Title	**Franchise Networks**
Coverage	Statistics on car distribution networks, commercial vehicle distribution networks, dealer groups and petrol retailing.
Frequency	Annual.
Web facilities	Publication details and online ordering facilities on site.
Cost	£175.
Comments	
Address	EMAP Automotive, Peterborough Business Park, Peterborough PE2 6EA
Tel./e-mail	01733 468 254
Fax/Website	01733 468 349 www.sewells.co.uk

SEWELLS INTERNATIONAL

Title	**Retail Motor Industry Pay Guide**
Coverage	A survey of 15 000 dealers and garages with data for 26 franchise dealer jobs. Based on the company's own research.
Frequency	Annual.
Web facilities	Publication details and online ordering facilities on site.
Cost	£94.95.
Comments	
Address	EMAP Automotive, Peterborough Business Park, Peterborough PE2 6EA
Tel./e-mail	01733 468 254
Fax/Website	01733 468 349 www.sewells.co.uk

SHARWOOD & CO LTD

Title	**Ethnic Foods Market Review**
Coverage	An analysis of trends in the ethnic foods market with data on total sales, sales by market sector (e.g. Chinese, Indian etc.), sales by type of product, household penetration and brand shares. Based on research commissioned by the company.
Frequency	Annual.
Web facilities	
Cost	Free.
Comments	
Address	J A Sharwood & Co Ltd, Egham TW20 9QG
Tel./e-mail	01784 473000
Fax/Website	

SHAWS' PRICE GUIDES LTD

Title	**Shaws' Retail Price Guide**
Coverage	Fair selling prices, recommended by the manufacturers or by the editors, for 13 000 products divided into various categories, e.g. groceries, household, medicines, tobacco, etc. Based on regular surveys carried out by the company.
Frequency	Monthly.
Web facilities	
Cost	£18.50.
Comments	
Address	Baden House, 7 St Peters Place, Brighton BN1 6TB
Tel./e-mail	01273 680041
Fax/Website	01273 606588

SILK ASSOCIATION OF GREAT BRITAIN

Title	**Imports and Exports**
Coverage	Quarterly detailed import and export data based on information from Customs and Excise.
Frequency	Quarterly.
Web facilities	Some basic free industry data on the site.
Cost	On request.
Comments	Usually only available to members.
Address	5 Portland Place, London W1N 3AA
Tel./e-mail	0207 636 7788 sagb@dial.pipex.com
Fax/Website	0207 636 7788 www.silk.org.uk

SILK ASSOCIATION OF GREAT BRITAIN

Title	**Serica**
Coverage	Mainly news and comment on the silk industry but it includes some statistics, mainly imports and exports.
Frequency	Six issues per year.
Web facilities	Some basic free industry data on the site.
Cost	On request.
Comments	
Address	5 Portland Place, London W1N 3AA
Tel./e-mail	0207 636 7788 sagb@dial.pipex.com
Fax/Website	0207 636 7788 www.silk.org.uk

SMALL BUSINESS RESEARCH TRUST

Title	**Quarterly Survey of Small Businesses in Britain**
Coverage	A survey of small businesses in the UK, 95% of which employ fewer than 50 people. Information on turnover, employment, sales, exports and business problems plus features on the sector.
Frequency	Quarterly.
Web facilities	General details of publications on site and link to University of Liverpool Management School.
Cost	On request.
Comments	Published be the University of Liverpool Management School in association with HSBC.
Address	Business Gateway, University of Liverpool, Foresight Centre, 3 Brownlow Street, Liverpool L69 3GL
Tel./e-mail	08450 700654 business@liverpool.ac.uk
Fax/Website	www.sbrt.ac.uk

SOCIETY OF BUSINESS ECONOMISTS

Title	**Business Economists' Salary Survey**
Coverage	Basic salaries and benefits by employment type, age and sex. Based on a sample of society members. A commentary supports the data.
Frequency	Annual.
Web facilities	Free access to survey on site.
Cost	Free.
Comments	
Address	Dean House, Vernham Dean andover SP11 0JZ
Tel./e-mail	01264 737552
Fax/Website	0207 900 2585 www.sbe.co.uk

SOCIETY OF BUSINESS ECONOMISTS

Title	**SBE Surveys**
Coverage	Regular surveus on key economic topics and issues based on an opinion survey of a sample of members.
Frequency	Regular.
Web facilities	Free access to the surveys on the site.
Cost	Free.
Comments	E-mailed to members and others.
Address	Dean House, Vernham Dean andover SP11 0JZ
Tel./e-mail	01264 737552
Fax/Website	0207 900 2585 www.sbe.co.uk

SOCIETY OF COUNTY TREASURERS

Title	**Standard Spending Indicators**
Coverage	Statistics on spending on particular services by local authorities in England. Based on returns from the local authorities.
Frequency	Annual.
Web facilities	Details of publications and some basic data freely available on site.
Cost	£40 to members; £50 to local authorities, libraries and universities
Comments	Produced in association with the Society of Municipal Treasurers.
Address	Financial Planning, Somerset County Council, County Hall, Taunton TA1 4DY
Tel./e-mail	01823 355295 fss@somerset.gov.uk
Fax/Website	01823 355554 www.sctnet.org.uk

SOCIETY OF INFORMATION TECHNOLOGY MANAGEMENT

Title	**IT Trends Survey**
Coverage	Annual survey of e-government trends, investment, expenditiure and customer access.
Frequency	Annual.
Web facilities	Free executive summary on site.
Cost	£300 (£450 report and data); £250 for members (£400 report and data).
Comments	
Address	PO Box 121, Northampton NN4 6TG
Tel./e-mail	01604 674800 enquiries@socitm.gov.uk
Fax/Website	www.socitm.gov.uk

SOCIETY OF MOTOR MANUFACTUERERS' AND TRADERS (SMMT)

Title	**UK New Vehicle Production Data**
Coverage	Monthly data on new vehicle production by brand, type, model etc.
Frequency	Monthly.
Web facilities	General details of publications plus free downloadable *UK Motor Industry Facts* on site.
Cost	On request.
Comments	Also publishes monthly and annual statistics for other European countries and the world market.
Address	Automotive Data Services, Forbes House, Halkin Street, London SW1X 7DS
Tel./e-mail	0207 235 7000 parcweb@smmt.co.uk
Fax/Website	0207 235 7112 www.smmt.co.uk

SOCIETY OF MOTOR MANUFACTURERS AND TRADERS (SMMT)

Title	**Used Vehicle Statistics**
Coverage	Sales and other data covering used vehicles and based on the society's own survey.
Frequency	Quarterly.
Web facilities	General details of publications plus free downloadable *UK Market Industry Facts* on site.
Cost	On request.
Comments	Also publishes monthly and annual statistics for European countries and the world market.
Address	Automotive Data Services, Forbes House, Halkin Street, London SW1X 7DS
Tel./e-mail	0207 235 7000 parcweb@smmt.co.uk
Fax/Website	0207 235 7112 www.smmt.co.uk

SOCIETY OF MOTOR MANUFACTURERS' AND TRADERS (SMMT)

Title	**SMMT Monthly Statistical Review**
Coverage	Production and registrations of motor vehicles by manufacturer and model plus imports and exports of products of the motor industry. Less frequent special tables such as forecasts and the annual motor vehicle census. Based on a combination of central government data and the society's own survey.
Frequency	Monthly.
Web facilities	General details of publications plus free downloadable *UK Motor Industry Facts* on site.
Cost	£200; £150 for members.
Comments	Also publishes monthly and annual statistics for European countries and the world market.
Address	Automotive Data Services, Forbes House, Halkin Street, London SW1X 7DS
Tel./e-mail	0207 235 7000 parcweb@smmt.co.uk
Fax/Website	0207 235 7112 www.smmt.co.uk

SOCIETY OF MOTOR MANUFACTURERS AND TRADERS (SMMT)

Title	**UK New Vehicles Registrations**
Coverage	Monthly statistics plus individual tailored reports on vehicle registrations. Data available by model, manufacturer, location, etc.
Frequency	Monthly.
Web facilities	General details of publications plus free downloadable *UK Motor Industry Facts* on site.
Cost	Price depends on the nature of the information required.
Comments	Also publishes monthly and annual statistics for other European countries and the world market.
Address	Automotive Data Services, Forbes House, Halkin Street, London SW1X 7DS
Tel./e-mail	0207 235 7000 parcweb@smmt.co.uk
Fax/Website	0207 235 7112 www.smmt.co.uk

SOCIETY OF MOTOR MANUFACTURERS AND TRADERS (SMMT)

Title	**Vehicles in Use – Motorparc Statistics Service**
Coverage	A service based on the annual census of motor vehicles carried out by the government agency, DVLA. Covers vehicles by type, ranges, colour, market segment, etc.
Frequency	Regular.
Web facilities	General details of publications plus free downloadable *UK Motor Industry Facts* on site.
Cost	Price depends on the nature of the information required.
Comments	Also publishes monthly and annual statistics for other European countries and the world market.
Address	Automotive Data Services, Forbes House, Halkin Street, London SW1X 7DS
Tel./e-mail	0207 235 7000 parcweb@smmt.co.uk
Fax/Website	0207 235 7112 www.smmt.co.uk

SODEXHO

Title	**Sodexho School Meals Survey**
Coverage	A survey of eating habits of children at school,covering meals and snacks, etc. Based on commissioned research.
Frequency	Regular.
Web facilities	Free PDF of report on site.
Cost	Free.
Comments	
Address	Solar House, Kingsway Street, Stevenage SG1 2OA
Tel./e-mail	01483 341400
Fax/Website	01483 341541 www.sodexho.co.uk

SOIL ASSOCIATION

Title	**Organic Market Report**
Coverage	Detailed data on organic food production, supply and consumption.
Frequency	Annual.
Web facilities	Free access to executive summary on the site.
Cost	£100.
Comments	Other reports produced and details on website.
Address	Bristol House, 40–56 Victoria Street, Bristol BS1 6BY
Tel./e-mail	0117 314 5000 info@soilassociation.org
Fax/Website	0117 314 5001 www.soilassociation.org

SOIL ASSOCIATION

Title	**Organic Food and Farm Report**
Coverage	Data and analysis of organic food and farming trends based on data from the association.
Frequency	Regular.
Web facilities	Free access to summary data on site.
Cost	£100.
Comments	Other reports produced and details on website.
Address	Bristol House, 40–56 Victoria Street, Bristol BS1 6BY
Tel./e-mail	0117 314 5000 info@soilassociation.org
Fax/Website	0117 314 5001 www.soilassociation.org

SPON PRESS

Title	**Spon's Architects' and Builders' Price Book**
Coverage	Prices of materials, prices for measured work and rates of wages. Based mainly on Spon's own surveys with additional data from other non-official sources.
Frequency	Annual.
Web facilities	General details and online ordering facilities on site.
Cost	£130.
Comments	
Address	2 Park Square, Milton Park, Abingdon OX14 4RN
Tel./e-mail	0207 017 6672 9855 Tony.Moore@tandf.co.uk
Fax/Website	0207 017 6702 2300 www.pricebooks.co.uk

SPON PRESS

Title	**Spon's Civil Engineering and Highway Works Price Book**
Coverage	Prices and costs of building, services, engineering, external work, landscaping, etc. Based on Spon's own surveys and other non-official sources.
Frequency	Annual.
Web facilities	General details and online ordering facilities on site.
Cost	£130.
Comments	
Address	2 Park Square, Milton Park, Abingdon OX14 4RN
Tel./e-mail	0207 017 6672 Tony.Moore@tandf.co.uk
Fax/Website	0207 017 6702 www.pricebooks.co.uk

SPON PRESS

Title	**Spon's Landscape and External Works Price Book**
Coverage	Prices and costs covering hard and soft landscapes and external works generally. Based on Spon's own surveys and some other non-official data.
Frequency	Annual.
Web facilities	General details and online ordering facilities on site.
Cost	£95.
Comments	
Address	2 Park Square, Milton Park, Abingdon OX14 4RN
Tel./e-mail	0207 017 6672 Tony.Moore@tandf.co.uk
Fax/Website	0207 017 6702 www.pricebooks.co.uk

SPON PRESS

Title	**Spon's Mechanical and Electrical Services Price Book**
Coverage	Prices and costs of heating, lighting, ventilation, air conditioning and other service items in industrial and commercial property. Based on Spon's own surveys plus other non-official sources.
Frequency	Annual.
Web facilities	General details and online ordering facilities on site.
Cost	£125.
Comments	
Address	2 Park Square, Milton Park, Abingdon OX14 4RN
Tel./e-mail	0207 017 6672 Tony.Moore@tandf.co.uk
Fax/Website	0207 017 6702 www.pricebooks.co.uk

SPORTS MARKETING SURVEYS

Title	**UK Sponsorship Market**
Coverage	Data and commentary on market size, sponsors, public attitudes to sponsorship, importance of sponsorship, branding, etc. Based largely on original research.
Frequency	Regular.
Web facilities	General details on site.
Cost	£300.
Comments	
Address	The Courtyard, Wisley GU23 6QL
Tel./e-mail	01932 350600 info@sportsmarketingsurveys.com
Fax/Website	01932 350375 www.sportsmarketingsurveys.com

SPORTS MARKETING SURVEYS

Title	**Sports Syndicated Surveys**
Coverage	Various syndicated surveys on a range of sports including running, football, golf, racing, fitness.
Frequency	Regular.
Web facilities	General details of services and some summary data on site.
Cost	On request.
Comments	
Address	The Courtyard, Wisley GU23 6QL
Tel./e-mail	01932 350600 info@sportsmarketingsurveys.com
Fax/Website	01932 350375 www.sportsmarketingsurveys.com

STATIONERY TRADE REVIEW

Title	**Reference Book and Buyers' Guide**
Coverage	The annual handbook for the stationery industry which includes an overview of the market and trends in the previous year. Includes market information on business machines, social stationery and office products. Based on the journal's regular survey of manufacturers.
Frequency	Annual.
Web facilities	
Cost	£45.
Comments	
Address	Nexus Media Ltd, Nexus House, Azalea Drive, Swanley BR8 8HY
Tel./e-mail	01322 660070 alison.bowles@nexusmedia.com
Fax/Website	01322 667633 www.nexusmedia.com

STATISTICS ON TOURISM AND RESEARCH (Star UK)

Title	**Sightseeing in the UK**
Coverage	Details of attractions and sites visited by number of tourists and key trends.
Frequency	Annual.
Web facilities	Basic tourism facts and details of publications on website.
Cost	£45.
Comments	Star UK is the liaison group for national tourist boards in the UK.
Address	Research Department, Thames Tower, Black's Road, Hammersmith, London W6 9EL
Tel./e-mail	0208 846 9000
Fax/Website	0208 563 0302 www.staruk.org.uk

STATISTICS ON TOURISM AND RESEARCH (Star UK)

Title	**The UK Tourist Statistics**
Coverage	An annual report based on the United Kingdom Tourism Survey (UKTS). Data includes the volume of UK residents' tourism, characteristics of their trips and the people taking them. Subjects covered include purpose of trip, destinations, types of transport, accommodation used, categories of tourist spending. Also includes historical data.
Frequency	Annual.
Web facilities	Basic tourism facts and details of publications available on website.
Cost	£95.
Comments	Star UK is the liaison group for national tourist boards in the UK.
Address	Research Department, Thames Tower, Black's Road, Hammersmith, London W6 9EL
Tel./e-mail	0208 846 9000
Fax/Website	0208 563 0302 www.staruk.org.uk

STATISTICS ON TOURISM AND RESEARCH (Star UK)

Title	**Visits to Tourist Attractions**
Coverage	Gives details of attendances at tourist attractions in the UK, seasonal opening, ownership and information on free admission. Attractions include historic houses, gardens, museums and art galleries, wildlife attractions, country parks, steam railways and workplaces.
Frequency	Annual.
Web facilities	Basic tourism facts and details of publications available on website.
Cost	£26.
Comments	Star UK is the liaison group for national tourist boards in the UK.
Address	Research Department, Thames Tower, Black's Road, Hammersmith, London W6 9EL
Tel./e-mail	0208 846 9000
Fax/Website	0208 563 0302 www.staruk.org.uk

STATISTICS ON TOURISM AND RESEARCH (Star UK)

Title	**UK Occupancy Survey**
Coverage	Statistics relating to national occupancy levels in serviced accommodation, seasonal variations, regional differences, types of accommodation and length of stay.
Frequency	Regular.
Web facilities	Basic tourism facts and details of publications available on website
Cost	£35.
Comments	Star UK is the liaison group for national tourist boards in the UK.
Address	Research Department, Thames Tower, Black's Road, Hammersmith, London W6 9EL
Tel./e-mail	0208 846 9000
Fax/Website	0208 563 0302 www.staruk.org.uk

STATISTICS ON TOURISM AND RESEARCH (Star UK)

Title	**UKTS 2----**
Coverage	Annual data from the UK tourism survey.
Frequency	Annual.
Web facilities	Free on the website.
Cost	Free.
Comments	Star UK is the liaison group for national tourist boards in the UK.
Address	Research Department, Thames Tower, Black's Road, Hammersmith, London W6 9EL
Tel./e-mail	0208 846 9000
Fax/Website	0208 563 0302 www.staruk.org.uk

STATISTICS ON TOURISM AND RESEARCH (Star UK)

Title	**UK Tourism Facts**
Coverage	General compilation of basic tourism statistics collected from various sources.
Frequency	Annual.
Web facilities	Free on the website.
Cost	Free.
Comments	Star UK is the liaison group for national tourist boards in the UK.
Address	Research Department, Thames Tower, Black's Road, Hammersmith, London W6 9EL
Tel./e-mail	0208 846 9000
Fax/Website	0208 563 0302 www.staruk.org.uk

SURVEY RESEARCH ASSOCIATES

Title	**SRA Omnibus Survey**
Coverage	A multi-client survey covering various topics and based on a sample size of 1500 adults. Interviews are carried out in the home.
Frequency	Twice a month.
Web facilities	
Cost	On request.
Comments	
Address	Tower House, Southampton Street, London WC2E 7HN
Tel./e-mail	0207 612 0369
Fax/Website	0207 612 0361

SYNOVATE

Title	**Omnicar**
Coverage	A monthly motoring omnibus survey based on a sample of 1000 motorists. Analysis of purchases, services, DIY, insurance, number of cars in household, engine size, make, model, etc.
Frequency	Monthly.
Web facilities	General details of surveys on site.
Cost	On request.
Comments	
Address	Mount Offham, Offham, West Malling ME19 5PG
Tel./e-mail	01732 874150 darren.wallond@synovate.com
Fax/Website	01732 875100 www.synovate.com

SYSTEM THREE SCOTLAND

Title	**Scottish Opinion Survey**
Coverage	A regular survey monitoring opinion, marketing and advertising activity in Scotland. Based on a sample of 1000 adults.
Frequency	Monthly.
Web facilities	
Cost	On request.
Comments	
Address	6 Hill Street, Edinburgh EH2 3JZ
Tel./e-mail	0131 220 1178
Fax/Website	0131 220 1181

TAS PUBLICATIONS AND EVENTS LTD

Title	**Bus Industry Monitor**
Coverage	A four-volume report with individual volumes on the market, public spending and support, investment and fleet analysis, industry performance.
Frequency	Annual.
Web facilities	General details of publications and online ordering facilities, on site.
Cost	£299.
Comments	
Address	Ross Holme, West End, Long Preston, Skipton BD23 4QL
Tel./e-mail	01729 840756 info@tas-passtrans.co.uk
Fax/Website	01729 840705 www.tas-passtrans.co.uk

TAS PUBLICATIONS AND EVENTS LTD

Title	**Rail Industry Monitor**
Coverage	A review of rail industry trends including the market, public spending and investment, vehicles and equipment and industry performance.
Frequency	Annual.
Web facilities	General details of publications and online ordering facilities, on site.
Cost	£235.
Comments	
Address	Ross Holme, West End, Long Preston, Skipton BD23 4QL
Tel./e-mail	01729 840756 info@tas-passtrans.co.uk
Fax/Website	01729 840705 www.tas-passtrans.co.uk

TAS PUBLICATIONS AND EVENTS LTD

Title	**Rapid Transport Monitor**
Coverage	A review of rapid transport trends published in various volumes: market trends, planning and finance, operating systems, planned systems.
Frequency	Annual.
Web facilities	General details of publications and online ordering facilities on site.
Cost	£175.
Comments	
Address	Ross Holme, West End, Long Preston, Skipton BD23 4QL
Tel./e-mail	01729 840756 info@tas-passtrans.co.uk
Fax/Website	01729 840705 www.tas-passtrans.co.uk

TELECOMMUNICATIONS INDUSTRY ASSOCIATION

Title	**Telecommunication Yearbook**
Coverage	Statistics on the industry based primarily on research by the association.
Frequency	Regular.
Web facilities	General details of publications, news and online ordering facilities on site.
Cost	£70.
Comments	Usually only available to members but requests from others considered. Price refers to non-member price.
Address	Douglas House, 32–34 Simpson Road, Fenny Stratford, Milton Keynes MK1 1BQ
Tel./e-mail	01908 645000 info@tia.org.uk
Fax/Website	01908 632263 www.tia.org.uk

TELMAR INFORMATION SERVICES AND SOFTWARE SOLUTIONS

Title	**Telmar Databases**
Coverage	Telmar has access to various media and consumer databases containing statistics.
Frequency	Continuous.
Web facilities	General details on site.
Cost	On request and depending on the nature and range of information required.
Comments	
Address	46 Chagford Street, London NW1 6EB
Tel./e-mail	0207 569 7500 info@telmar.co.uk
Fax/Website	0207 569 7501 www.telmar.co.uk

THE GROCER

Title	**Grocer Price List**
Coverage	A supplement usually produced on the first Saturday of each month giving detailed prices for various foods and grocery products.
Frequency	Monthly supplement to a weekly journal.
Web facilities	
Cost	£45; £1.30 per issue.
Comments	*The Grocer* also has regular market surveys of the main food and non-food markets.
Address	William Reed Publishing Ltd, Broadfield Park, Crawley RH11 9RT
Tel./e-mail	01293 610259 grocer.editorial@william-reed.co.uk
Fax/Website	01293 610333 www.william-reed.co.uk

THE GROCER

Title	**Market Figures**
Coverage	Prices of various foods including vegetables, meat, salad, cheese, egg, butter, lard, etc. Based on various non-official sources with some supporting text.
Frequency	Weekly in a weekly journal.
Web facilities	
Cost	£45; £1.30 per issue.
Comments	*The Grocer* also has regular market surveys of the main food and non-food markets.
Address	William Reed Publishing Ltd, Broadfield Park, Crawley RH11 9RT
Tel./e-mail	01293 610259 grocer.editorial@william-reed.co.uk
Fax/Website	01293 610333 www.william-reed.co.uk

THE HBC LTD

Title	**UK Housewares Datapack**
Coverage	Market information on 85 product sectors classified as non-electrical housewares used in the kitchen. Over 900 pages of analysis and data based on research by the company.
Frequency	Annual.
Web facilities	
Cost	£2950.
Comments	Also undertakes commissioned research on the housewares sector. Previously known as the Housewares Business Centre.
Address	45 Parkfield Road, Coleshill, Birmingham B46 3LD
Tel./e-mail	01675 464216 hbc@easynet.co.uk
Fax/Website	01675 467524

THE HBC LTD

Title	**Home Facts & Fotos: Consumer Lifestyle**
Coverage	Data and a photographic report on home design, decorating and colour.
Frequency	Annual.
Web facilities	
Cost	£1750.
Comments	
Address	45 Parkfield Road, Coleshill, Birmingham B46 3LD
Tel./e-mail	01675 464216 hbc@easynet.co.uk
Fax/Website	01675 467524

THE LAW SOCIETY

Title	**Trends in the Solicitor's Profession: Annual Statistical Report**
Coverage	Detailed statistics covering qualified solicitors, recruitment and training of solictors, admission to the rolls, law firms and offices.
Frequency	Annual.
Web facilities	Free access to summary and full PDF report on site.
Cost	£20 (hard copy).
Comments	Previous year's reports and summaries also freely available on site.
Address	113 Chancery Lane, London WC2A 1PL
Tel./e-mail	0207 320 5623 EnquiriesSRU@lawsociety.org.uk
Fax/Website	0207 316 5642 www.research.lawsociety.org.uk

THE LAW SOCIETY

Title	**Facts Sheets**
Coverage	Fact sheets covering various topics and mainly updated annually. Topics cover solicitor numbers, type of work undertaken, minority ethnic group solicitors, law firms, women solicitors.
Frequency	Annual.
Web facilities	Free access to fact sheets on site.
Cost	Free.
Comments	
Address	113 Chancery Lane, London WC2A 1PL
Tel./e-mail	0207 320 5623 EnquiriesSRU@lawsociety.org.uk
Fax/Website	0207 316 5642 www.research.lawsociety.org.uk

TIMBER TRADES JOURNAL

Title	**Markets**
Coverage	Various statistics on timber and wood consumption, trade, prices, etc. Different statistics appear each week and based on various sources.
Frequency	Weekly in a weekly journal.
Web facilities	Free access to market reports and news on site.
Cost	£129.
Comments	
Address	Polygon Media Ltd, Tubs Hill House, London Road, Sevenoaks TN13 1BY
Tel./e-mail	01732 470042
Fax/Website	01732 470049 www.worldwidewood.com

TNS

Title	**Omnimed**
Coverage	A weekly omnibus survey of practising GPs to cover drugs use, attitudes to topical issues, etc.
Frequency	Weekly.
Web facilities	Services details and some summary data on site.
Cost	On request.
Comments	Various other research services available.
Address	Westgate, London W5 1UA
Tel./e-mail	0208 967 0007 research@tns-global.com
Fax/Website	0208 967 4060 www.tns-global.com

TNS

Title	**Online Kids**
Coverage	A monthly online omnibus surveying a sample of children aged 8 to 14.
Frequency	Monthly.
Web facilities	Services details and some summary data on site.
Cost	On request.
Comments	Various other research services available.
Address	Westgate, London W5 1UA
Tel./e-mail	0208 967 0007 research@tns-global.com
Fax/Website	0208 967 4060 www.tns-global.com

TNS

Title	**Pharmacy Omnibus**
Coverage	A monthly omnibus survey of a sample of retail pharmacists covering products, trading, topical issues, etc.
Frequency	Monthly.
Web facilities	Services details and some summary data on site.
Cost	On request.
Comments	Various other research services available.
Address	Westgate, London W5 1UA
Tel./e-mail	0208 967 0007 research@tns-global.com
Fax/Website	0208 967 4060 www.tns-global.com

TNS

Title	**RSGB Omnibus**
Coverage	General weekly consumer omnibus based on a sample of 2000 adults.
Frequency	Weekly.
Web facilities	Services details and some summary data on site.
Cost	On request.
Comments	Various other research services available.
Address	Westgate, London W5 1UA
Tel./e-mail	0208 967 0007 research@tns-global.com
Fax/Website	0208 967 4060 www.tns-global.com

TNS

Title	**Omnimas**
Coverage	Omnibus survey based on a sample of 2000 adults every week. Face-to-face interviews in the home.
Frequency	Weekly.
Web facilities	Services details and some summary data on site.
Cost	On request.
Comments	Various other research services available.
Address	Westgate, London W5 1UA
Tel./e-mail	0208 967 0007 research@tns-global.com
Fax/Website	0208 967 4060 www.tns-global.com

TNS

Title	**BusinessLine**
Coverage	Quarterly omnibus survey based on a sample of MDs and directors in companies with over 50 employees.
Frequency	Quarterly.
Web facilities	Services details and some summary data on site.
Cost	On request.
Comments	Various other research services available.
Address	Westgate, London W5 1UA
Tel./e-mail	0208 967 0007 research@tns-global.com
Fax/Website	0208 967 4060 www.tns-global.com

TNS

Title	**High Net Worth Omnibus**
Coverage	Monthly omnibus survey based on a sample of 1000 individuals and covering purchases and behaviour.
Frequency	Monthly.
Web facilities	Services details and some summary data on site.
Cost	On request.
Comments	Various other research services available.
Address	Westgate, London W5 1UA
Tel./e-mail	0208 967 0007 research@tns-global.com
Fax/Website	0208 967 4060 www.tns-global.com

TNS

Title	**Online Bus**
Coverage	Weekly online omnibus survey of 1000 adults covering spending, product use, etc.
Frequency	Weekly.
Web facilities	Services details and some summary data on site.
Cost	On request.
Comments	Various other research services available.
Address	Westgate, London W5 1UA
Tel./e-mail	0208 967 0007 research@tns-global.com
Fax/Website	0208 967 4060 www.tns-global.com

TNS

Title	**PhoneBus**
Coverage	Weekly telephone omnibus survey of between 1000 and 2000 adults covering spending, product use, etc.
Frequency	Weekly.
Web facilities	Services details and some summary data on site.
Cost	On request.
Comments	Various other research services available.
Address	Westgate, London W5 1UA
Tel./e-mail	0208 967 0007 research@tns-global.com
Fax/Website	0208 967 4060 www.tns-global.com

TNS TRAVEL AND TOURISM

Title	**UK Occupancy Survey for Serviced Accommodation**
Coverage	Occupancy rates for hotels, guesthouses and bed and breakfast establishments based on a regular sample survey.
Frequency	Monthly.
Web facilities	Free access to summary data on Statistics on Tourism and Research site (see entry under this heading for details, page 277–9).
Cost	Free.
Comments	
Address	19 Atholl Crescent, Edinburgh EH3 8HQ
Tel./e-mail	0131 656 4000 occsurvey@tns-global.com
Fax/Website	0131 656 4001 www.tns-global.com

TOBACCO ALLIANCE

Title	**Annual Economic Survey of Tobacco Alliance Members**
Coverage	Analysis and data on counterfeiting and tobacco smuggling.
Frequency	Annual.
Web facilities	Free access to data on site plus annual price data.
Cost	Free.
Comments	
Address	12 Bergham Mews, Blythe Road, London W14 0HN
Tel./e-mail	0800 008 282 joe.brice@tobaccoalliance.org.uk
Fax/Website	www.tobaccoalliance.org.uk

TOBACCO MANUFACTURERS' ASSOCIATION

Title	**Tobacco Statistics**
Coverage	Statistics and commentary on the tobacco industry with data covering the market, taxes, employment, revenue, prices and smoking prevalence. Based on various sources.
Frequency	Regular.
Web facilities	Free access to data on site.
Cost	Free.
Comments	
Address	5th Floor, Burwood House, 14–16 Caxton Street, London SW1H O2B
Tel./e-mail	0207 544 0108 information@the-tma.org.uk
Fax/Website	0207 544 0117 www.the-tma.org.uk

TOY RETAILERS ASSOCIATION

Title	**Toy Sales Statistics**
Coverage	Two years of annual data for toy sales and sales by category and outlets.
Frequency	Annual.
Web facilities	Free access to data on site under 'Marketing' pages.
Cost	Free.
Comments	
Address	Gainsborough Waterfront Enterprise Park, Lea Road, Gainsborough DN21 1LX
Tel./e-mail	08707 537437 enquiries@toyretailersassociation.co.uk
Fax/Website	08707 060042 www.toyretailersassociation.co.uk

UNITED KINGDOM ASSOCIATION OF ONLINE PUBLISHERS

Title	**AOP Census**
Coverage	Annual bechmarking survey of AOP members covering turnover, revenue models, page impressions, future trends and comments on key issues affecting the industry.
Frequency	Annual.
Web facilities	Free press release from survey on site.
Cost	Free for members.
Comments	
Address	Queens House, 28 Kingsway, London WC2B 6JR
Tel./e-mail	0207 404 4166 lisa.quinlan@ukaop.org.uk
Fax/Website	0207 404 4167 www.ukaop.org.uk

UNITED KINGDOM DATA ARCHIVE

Title	**UK Data Archive**
Coverage	The archive holds surveys from various official and non-official sources including all the major ONS continuous surveys such as the Family Expenditure Survey, General Household Survey, National Food Survey plus many non-official surveys from organisations such as NOP, Gallup, Research Services, etc.
Frequency	Continuous.
Web facilities	Details and news of data sources on site.
Cost	On request.
Comments	
Address	Wivenhoe Park, University of Essex, Colchester CO4 3SO
Tel./e-mail	01206 872143 help@esds.ac.uk
Fax/Website	01206 872003 www.data-archive.ac.uk

UNITED KINGDOM FILM COUNCIL

Title	**Annual Review & Statistical Yearbook**
Coverage	Data includes film audiences, demographics, film earnings, distribution trends, screens and top films.
Frequency	Annual.
Web facilities	Free access to recent year's reports on site.
Cost	Free.
Comments	
Address	10 Little Portland Street, London W1W 7JG
Tel./e-mail	0207 861 7861 info@ukfilmcouncil.org.uk
Fax/Website	0207 861 7862 www.ukfilmcouncil.org.uk

UNITED KINGDOM FILM COUNCIL

Title	**Research and Statistics Bulletin**
Coverage	General data on film admissions and box office plus specialist areas covered in specific issues, e.g. films on television, DVDs, etc.
Frequency	Twice yearly.
Web facilities	Free access to last few years' bulletins on site.
Cost	Free.
Comments	
Address	10 Little Portland Street, London W1W 7JG
Tel./e-mail	0207 861 7861 info@ukfilmcouncil.org.uk
Fax/Website	0207 861 7862 www.ukfilmcouncil.org.uk

UNITED KINGDOM ONSHORE PIPELINE OPERATORS ASSOCIATION

Title	**UKOPA Pipeline Product Loss Incidents**
Coverage	Regular historical series of data on product and pipeline losses and incidents.
Frequency	Regular.
Web facilities	Free access to report on site.
Cost	Free.
Comments	At the time of preparing this directory, the latest series covers 1962 to 2004.
Address	Ripley Road, Ambergate, Derby DE56 2FZ
Tel./e-mail	01773 852 003 phill.jones@ukopa.co.uk
Fax/Website	01773 856 456 www.ukopa.co.uk

UNITED KINGDOM PETROLEUM INDUSTRY ASSOCIATION

Title	**UKPIA Statistical Review**
Coverage	Compilation of statistics on refineries, fuels, prices, filling stations, energy use, etc. Data collected from various sources.
Frequency	Annual.
Web facilities	Free access to PDF report on site.
Cost	Free.
Comments	
Address	9 Kingsway, London WC2B 6XF
Tel./e-mail	0207 240 0289 info@ukpia.com
Fax/Website	www.ukpia.com

UNITED KINGDOM STEEL ASSOCIATION

Title	**UK Steel Key Statistics 2---**
Coverage	Data on demand, end user sectors, prices, trade, UK deliveries, energy consumption. Historical data in many tables.
Frequency	Annual.
Web facilities	Free access to data on site.
Cost	Free.
Comments	
Address	Broadway House, Tothill Street, London SW1H 9NQ
Tel./e-mail	0207 222 7777 enquiries@uksteel.org.uk
Fax/Website	0207 222 2782 www.uksteel.org.uk

UNIVERSITY OF DURHAM BUSINESS SCHOOL

Title	**Small Business Trends**
Coverage	Detailed analysis and statistics on SMEs with sections on general trends, SMEs by industrial and service sector and future trends. Based on an analysis of various sources.
Frequency	Every two years.
Web facilities	
Cost	On request.
Comments	
Address	Mill Hill Lane, Durham DH1 3LB
Tel./e-mail	0191 374 2211
Fax/Website	0191 374 3748

UNIVERSITY OF NOTTINGHAM BUSINESS SCHOOL, CENTRE FOR MANAGEMENT BUY-OUT RESEARCH

Title	**Exit**
Coverage	Statistics and analysis on buy-out exits in the UK.
Frequency	Regular.
Web facilities	Free access to PDF on the site.
Cost	Free.
Comments	The centre was founded by Deloitte & Touche and Barclays Private Equity Ltd.
Address	University of Nottingham, Jubilee Campus, Wollaton Road, Nottingham NG8 1BB
Tel./e-mail	0115 9515493 margaret.burdett@nottingham.ac.uk
Fax/Website	0115 9515204 www.cmbor.org

UNIVERSITY OF NOTTINGHAM BUSINESS SCHOOL, CENTRE FOR MANAGEMENT BUY-OUT RESEARCH

Title	**Management Buy-Out Quarterly Review**
Coverage	A market overview and commentary on recent market trends with some statistics on buy-outs.
Frequency	Quarterly.
Web facilities	
Cost	£500; £150 per issue.
Comments	The centre was founded by Deloitte & Touche and Barclays Private Equity Ltd.
Address	University of Nottingham, Jubilee Campus, Wollaton Road, Nottingham NG8 1BB
Tel./e-mail	0115 9515493 margaret.burdett@nottingham.ac.uk
Fax/Website	0115 9515204 www.cmbor.org

UNIVERSITY OF READING, DEPARTMENT OF AGRICULTURE AND FOOD ECONOMICS

Title	**Farm Business Data**
Coverage	Based partly on a survey carried out by the university and summaries of other surveys, the report analyses performance trends in the farming sector.
Frequency	Annual.
Web facilities	General details on site.
Cost	£20.
Comments	
Address	4 Earley Gate, Whiteknights Road, Reading RG6 6AR
Tel./e-mail	0118 378 7426 c.m.bradshaw@reading.ac.uk
Fax/Website	0118 378 5034 www.apd.rdg.ac.uk

UNIVERSITY OF READING, DEPARTMENT OF AGRICULTURE AND FOOD ECONOMICS

Title	**Horticultural Business Data**
Coverage	Analysis and statistics for three business groups – glasshouse holdings, vegetable and mixed horticultural holdings and fruit holdings. Based largely on the university's survey supplemented by some central government data.
Frequency	Annual.
Web facilities	General details on site.
Cost	£16.
Comments	
Address	4 Earley Gate, Whiteknights Road, Reading RG6 6AR
Tel./e-mail	0118 378 7426 c.m.bradshaw@reading.ac.uk
Fax/Website	0118 378 85034 www.apd.rdg.ac.uk

UNIVERSITY OF WARWICK, INSTITUTE FOR EMPLOYMENT RESEARCH

Title	**IER Bulletin**
Coverage	Contains regular data and analysis on labour market trends and general economic trends with features on specific aspects of the labour market. Includes regional, sector data and some forecasts of employment trends.
Frequency	Six times a year.
Web facilities	Free access to PDFs of reports on site.
Cost	Free.
Comments	
Address	University of Warwick, Gibbett Hill Road, Coventry CV4 7AL
Tel./e-mail	02476 523284 ier@warwick.ac.uk
Fax/Website	02476 524241 www.warwick.ac.uk/ier

UNIVERSITY OF YORK, CENTRE FOR HOUSING POLICY

Title	**University of York Index of Private Rents and Yields**
Coverage	Statistics on average rents and yields with regional data and data for local authority areas. There is also a Valuations Index and a Transactions Index.
Frequency	Quarterly.
Web facilities	General details of statistics on site.
Cost	£200.
Comments	Published in partnership with the Association of Residential Letting Agents and other agents, Halifax and the Rent Officer Service.
Address	University of York, York YO10 5DD
Tel./e-mail	01904 433691 jd19@york.ac.uk
Fax/Website	01904 432318 www.york.ac.uk/inst/chp/

VERDICT RESEARCH LTD

Title	**Verdict on Womenswear Retailing**
Coverage	Analysis and statistics on market trends and value, consumer spending, key players and the issues affecting the sector. Based on a combination of published data and original research.
Frequency	Annual.
Web facilities	General details of all publications, paid-for online access to research and free executive summaries on site.
Cost	£1650.
Comments	
Address	Charles House, 108–110 Finchley Road, London NW3 5JJ
Tel./e-mail	0207 675 7701 retail@verdict.co.uk
Fax/Website	0207 675 7702 www.verdict.co.uk

VERDICT RESEARCH LTD

Title	**Verdict on Childrenswear Retailers**
Coverage	Analysis and statistics on market trends and value, consumer spending, key players and the issues affecting the sector. Based on a combination of published data and original research.
Frequency	Annual.
Web facilities	General details of all publications, paid-for online access to research and free executive summaries.
Cost	£1650.
Comments	
Address	Charles House, 108-110 Finchley Road, London NW3 5JJ
Tel./e-mail	0207 675 7701 retail@verdict.co.uk
Fax/Website	0207 675 7702 www.verdict.co.uk

VERDICT RESEARCH LTD

Title	**Retail Futures**
Coverage	A series of reports on 8 retail sectors with forecasts of retailing trends (up to 8 quarters) and trends for last 8 quarters.
Frequency	Quarterly.
Web facilities	General details of all publications, paid for online access to research and free executive summaries on site.
Cost	On request.
Comments	
Address	Charles House, 108-110 Finchley Road, London NW3 5JJ
Tel./e-mail	0207 675 7701 retail@verdict.co.uk
Fax/Website	0207 675 7702 www.verdict.co.uk

VERDICT RESEARCH LTD

Title	**Verdict on Grocery Retailing**
Coverage	Analysis and statistics on market trends and value, consumer spending, key players and the issues affecting the sector. Based on a combination of published data and original research.
Frequency	Annual.
Web facilities	General details of all publications, paid for online access to research and free executive summaries.
Cost	£1650.
Comments	
Address	Charles House, 108–110 Finchley Road, London NW3 5JJ
Tel./e-mail	0207 675 7701 retail@verdict.co.uk
Fax/Website	0207 675 7702 www.verdict.co.uk

VERDICT RESEARCH LTD

Title	**Verdict on Homewares Retailers**
Coverage	Analysis and statistics on market trends and value, consumer spending, key players and the issues affecting the sector. Based on a combination of published data and original research.
Frequency	Annual.
Web facilities	General details of all publications, paid-for online access to research and free executive summaries on site.
Cost	£1650.
Comments	
Address	Charles House, 108–110 Finchley Road, London NW3 5JJ
Tel./e-mail	0207 675 7701 retail@verdict.co.uk
Fax/Website	0207 675 7702 www.verdict.co.uk

VERDICT RESEARCH LTD

Title	**Verdict on e-Retail**
Coverage	Analysis and statistics on market trends and value, consumer spending, key players and the issues affecting the sector. Based on a combination of published data and original research.
Frequency	Annual.
Web facilities	General details of all research, paid-for online access to research and free executive summaries on site.
Cost	£1650.
Comments	
Address	Charles House, 108–110 Finchley Road, London NW3 5JJ
Tel./e-mail	0207 675 7701 retail@verdict.co.uk
Fax/Website	0207 675 7702 www.verdict.co.uk

VERDICT RESEARCH LTD

Title	**Verdict on Value Clothing**
Coverage	Analysis and statistics on market trends and value, consumer spending, key players and the issues affecting the sector. Based on a combination of published data and original research.
Frequency	Annual.
Web facilities	General details of all publications, paid-for online access to research and free executive summaries on site.
Cost	£1650.
Comments	
Address	Charles House, 108–110 Finchley Road, London NW3 5JJ
Tel./e-mail	0207 675 7701 retail@verdict.co.uk
Fax/Website	0207 675 7702 www.verdict.co.uk

VERDICT RESEARCH LTD

Title	**Verdict on Footwear Retailers**
Coverage	Analysis and statistics on market trends and value, consumer spending, key players and the issues affecting the sector. Based on a combination of published data and original research.
Frequency	Annual.
Web facilities	General details of all publications, paid-for online access to research and free executive summaries on site.
Cost	£1650.
Comments	
Address	Charles House, 108–110 Finchley Road, London NW3 5JJ
Tel./e-mail	0207 675 7701 retail@verdict.co.uk
Fax/Website	0207 675 7702 www.verdict.co.uk

VERDICT RESEARCH LTD

Title	**Verdict on Department Stores**
Coverage	Analysis and statistics on market trends and value, consumer spending, key players and the issues affecting the sector. Based on a combination of published data and original research.
Frequency	Annual.
Web facilities	General details of all publications, paid-for online access to research and free executive summaries on site.
Cost	£1650-
Comments	
Address	Charles House, 108–110 Finchley Road, London NW3 5JJ
Tel./e-mail	0207 675 7701 retail@verdict.co.uk
Fax/Website	0207 675 7702 www.verdict.co.uk

VERDICT RESEARCH LTD

Title	**Verdict on Home Deliveries and Fulfilment**
Coverage	Analysis and statistics on market trends and value, consumer spending, key players and the issues affecting the sector. Based on a combination of published data and original research.
Frequency	Annual.
Web facilities	General details of all publications, paid-for online access to research and free executive summaries on site.
Cost	£1650.
Comments	
Address	Charles House, 108–110 Finchley Road, London NW3 5JJ
Tel./e-mail	0207 675 7701 retail@verdict.co.uk
Fax/Website	0207 675 7702 www.verdict.co.uk

VERDICT RESEARCH LTD

Title	**Verdict on Electrical Retailers**
Coverage	Analysis and statistics on market trends and value, consumer spending, key players and the issues affecting the sector. Based on a combination of published data and original research.
Frequency	Annual.
Web facilities	General details of all publications, paid-for online access to research and free executive summaries on site.
Cost	£1650.
Comments	
Address	Charles House, 108–110 Finchley Road, London NW3 5JJ
Tel./e-mail	0207 675 7701 retail@verdict.co.uk
Fax/Website	0207 675 7702 www.verdict.co.uk

VERDICT RESEARCH LTD

Title	**Verdict on DIY and Gardening**
Coverage	Analysis and statistics on market trends and value, consumer spending, key players and the issues affecting the sector. Based on a combination of published data and original research.
Frequency	Annual.
Web facilities	General details of all publications, paid-for online access to research and free executive summaries on site.
Cost	£1650.
Comments	
Address	Charles House, 108–110 Finchley Road, London NW3 5JJ
Tel./e-mail	0207 675 7701 retail@verdict.co.uk
Fax/Website	0207 675 7702 www.verdict.co.uk

VERDICT RESEARCH LTD

Title	**Verdict on Furniture and Floor Coverings Retailers**
Coverage	Analysis and statistics on market trends and value, consumer spending, key players and the issues affecting the sector. Based on a combination of published data and original research.
Frequency	Annual.
Web facilities	General details of all publications, paid-for online access to research and free executive summaries on site.
Cost	£1650.
Comments	
Address	Charles House, 108–110 Finchley Road, London NW3 5JJ
Tel./e-mail	0207 675 7701 retail@verdict.co.uk
Fax/Website	0207 675 7702 www.verdict.co.uk

VERDICT RESEARCH LTD

Title	**Verdict on Out of Town Retailing**
Coverage	Analysis and statistics on sector trends and value, consumer spending, key players and the issues affecting the sector. Based on a combination of published data and original research.
Frequency	Annual.
Web facilities	General details of all publications, paid-for online access to research and free executive summaries on site.
Cost	£1650.
Comments	
Address	Charles House, 108–110 Finchley Road, London NW3 5JJ
Tel./e-mail	0207 675 7701 retail@verdict.co.uk
Fax/Website	0207 675 7702 www.verdict.co.uk

VERDICT RESEARCH LTD

Title	**Verdict on Menswear Retailing**
Coverage	Analysis and statistics on market trends and value, consumer spending, key players and the key issues affecting the sector. Based on a combination of published data and original research.
Frequency	Annual.
Web facilities	General details of all publications, paid-for online access to research and free executive summaries on site.
Cost	£1650.
Comments	
Address	Charles House, 108-110 Finchley Road, London NW3 5JJ
Tel./e-mail	0207 675 7701 retail@verdict.co.uk
Fax/Website	0207 675 7702 www.verdict.co.uk

VERDICT RESEARCH LTD

Title	**Verdict on Music and Video Retailers**
Coverage	Analysis and statistics on market trends and value, consumer spending, key players and the issues affecting the sector. Based on a combination of published data and original research.
Frequency	Annual.
Web facilities	General details of all publications, paid-for online access to research and free executive summaries on site.
Cost	£1650.
Comments	
Address	Charles House, 108–110 Finchley Road, London NW3 5JJ
Tel./e-mail	0207 675 7701 retail@verdict.co.uk
Fax/Website	0207 675 7702 www.verdict.co.uk

VERDICT RESEARCH LTD

Title	**Verdict on Health and Beauty Retailing**
Coverage	Analysis and statistics on consumer trends, consumer spending, key players and the issues affecting the sector. Based on a combination of published data and original research.
Frequency	Annual.
Web facilities	General details of all publications, paid-for online access to research and free executive summaries on site.
Cost	£1650.
Comments	
Address	Charles House, 108–110 Finchley Road, London NW3 5JJ
Tel./e-mail	0207 675 7701 retail@verdict.co.uk
Fax/Website	0207 675 7702 www.verdict.co.uk

VERDICT RESEARCH LTD

Title	**Verdict on Neighbourhood Retailing**
Coverage	Analysis and statistics on market trends and value, consumer spending, key players and the issues affecting the sector. Based on a combination of published data and original research.
Frequency	Annual.
Web facilities	General details of all publications, paid-for online access to research and free executive summaries on site.
Cost	£1650.
Comments	
Address	Charles House, 108–110 Finchley Road, London NW3 5JJ
Tel./e-mail	0207 675 7701 retail@verdict.co.uk
Fax/Website	0207 675 7702 www.verdict.co.uk

VISIT BRITAIN

Title	**Inbound Tourism Statistics and Research**
Coverage	Various reports and files covering numbers of inbound tourists (monthly), countries of origin, historical trends, etc.
Frequency	Monthly.
Web facilities	Free access to reports on site.
Cost	Free.
Comments	
Address	Research Department, Thames Tower, Black's Road, Hammersmith, London W6 9EL
Tel./e-mail	0208 846 9000 blvcinfo@visitbritain.org
Fax/Website	0208 563 0302 www.visitbritain.com/research

VISIT BRITAIN

Title	**Domestic Tourism Statistics and Research**
Coverage	Various reports and files covering number of overnight trips, value of tourism, occupancy levels, trips to visitor attractions, etc.
Frequency	Monthly.
Web facilities	Free access to data on site.
Cost	Free.
Comments	
Address	Research Department, Thames Tower, Black's Road, Hammersmith, London W6 9EL
Tel./e-mail	0208 846 9000 blvcinfo@visitbritain.org
Fax/Website	0208 563 0302 www.visitbritain.com/research.

VISIT BRITAIN

Title	**Business Confidence Monitor**
Coverage	Opinion surveys of tourism businesses arranged in three sectors: accommodation, attractions, transport.
Frequency	Quarterly.
Web facilities	
Cost	On request.
Comments	Conducted for Visit Britain by MEW Research/BDRC. See also entry headed Statistics and Tourism Research for more tourism sources (page 277–9).
Address	Research Department, Thames Tower, Black's Road, Hammersmith, London W6 9EL
Tel./e-mail	0208 846 9000
Fax/Website	0208 563 0302 www.tourismtrade.org.uk

WALLCOVERING MANUFACTURERS ASSOCIATION OF GREAT BRITAIN

Title	**Annual Statistics**
Coverage	Data on the UK wallcoverings sector based on an analysis of returns from member companies.
Frequency	Annual.
Web facilities	
Cost	Free.
Comments	Usually only available to members but plans to offer a summary version to the public for a fee.
Address	James House, Bridge Street, Leatherhead KT22 7EP
Tel./e-mail	01372 360660 alison.brown@bcf.co.uk
Fax/Website	01372 376069

WATER UK

Title	**Waterfacts 2---**
Coverage	Compilation of data including details of operators, financial performances, environmental data, distribution, supplies, leaks, rainfall and climate. Data collected from various sources.
Frequency	Annual.
Web facilities	Free access to report on site.
Cost	Free.
Comments	
Address	1 Queen Anne's Gate, London SW1H 9BT
Tel./e-mail	0207 344 1844 info@water.org.uk
Fax/Website	0207 344 1866 www.water.org.uk

WATSON WYATT WORLDWIDE

Title	**Employment and Salary Surveys**
Coverage	Various surveys of employment and earnings in sectors such as corporate services, architecture, IT, etc.
Frequency	Regular.
Web facilities	
Cost	On request.
Comments	
Address	Park Gate, 21 Tothill Street, London SW1H 9LL
Tel./e-mail	0207 222 8037 customerservice@eu.watsonwyatt.com
Fax/Website	www.watsonwyatt.com

WEATHERALL GREEN AND SMITH

Title	**South East Office Market**
Coverage	Details of rates for offices in the south-east. Based on data collected by the company.
Frequency	Annual.
Web facilities	Free access to all reports on site.
Cost	Free.
Comments	Various ad hoc and international reports also available.
Address	90 Chancery Lane, London WC2A 1EU
Tel./e-mail	0207 338 4000 monitor@atisreal.com
Fax/Website	0207 831 2564 www.weatheralls.co.uk

WEATHERALL GREEN AND SMITH

Title	**London Office Market**
Coverage	Details of rates for premium offices in areas of London. Based on data collected by the company.
Frequency	Quarterly.
Web facilities	Free access to reports on site.
Cost	Free.
Comments	Various ad hoc and international reports also available.
Address	90 Chancery Lane, London WC2A 1EU
Tel./e-mail	0207 738 4000 monitor@atisreal.com
Fax/Website	0207 831 2564 www.weatheralls.co.uk

WEATHERALL GREEN AND SMITH

Title	**House View**
Coverage	Overview of trends in the housing market plus forecasts. Based on research by the company.
Frequency	Quarterly.
Web facilities	Free access to reports on site.
Cost	Free.
Comments	Various ad hoc and international reports also available.
Address	90 Chancery Lane, London WC2A 1EU
Tel./e-mail	0207 738 4000 monitor@atisreal.com
Fax/Website	0207 831 2564 www.weatheralls.co.uk

WHITBREAD BEER COMPANY

Title	**Whitbread On-Trade Market Report**
Coverage	Commentary and statistics on the on-trade market for alcoholic drinks. Based primarily on commissioned research.
Frequency	Annual.
Web facilities	
Cost	Free.
Comments	
Address	Porter Tun House, Capability Green, Luton LU1 3LW
Tel./e-mail	01582 391166
Fax/Website	01582 397397 www.whitbread.co.uk

WHITBREAD BEER COMPANY

Title	**Whitbread Take-Home Market Report**
Coverage	Commentary and statistics on the take-home market for alcoholic drinks with data on market size, brands, outlets and current trends. Based primarily on commissioned research.
Frequency	Annual.
Web facilities	
Cost	Free.
Comments	
Address	Porter Tun House, Capability Green, Luton LU1 3LW
Tel./e-mail	01582 391166
Fax/Website	01582 397397 www.whitbread.co.uk

WILLIAMS DE BROE

Title	**Weekly Economic Indicators**
Coverage	Weekly data on UK economic trends with regular forecasts for the main economic indicators.
Frequency	Weekly.
Web facilities	
Cost	Free.
Comments	
Address	6 Broadgate, London EC2M 2RP
Tel./e-mail	0207 588 7511 david.smith@wdebroe.com
Fax/Website	0207 410 9932 www.wdebroe.com

WILLIAMS DE BROE

Title	**Quarterly Interest Rate Outlook**
Coverage	Detailed review of interest rates and the UK economic and financial outlook.
Frequency	Quarterly.
Web facilities	
Cost	Free.
Comments	
Address	6 Broadgate, London EC2M 2RP
Tel./e-mail	0207 588 7511 david.smith@wdebroe.com
Fax/Website	0207 410 9932 www.wdebroe.com

WORLD TEXTILE PUBLICATIONS

Title	**The Wool Market**
Coverage	Statistics on the prices of wool based on data collected by the journal.
Frequency	Monthly in a monthly journal.
Web facilities	Details of publications and online ordering facilities on site.
Cost	£80.
Comments	
Address	World Textile Publications Ltd, Perkin House, 1 Longlands Street, Bradford BD1 2TP
Tel./e-mail	01274 378800 info@world-textile.net
Fax/Website	01274 378811 www.world-textile.net

WORLD TEXTILE PUBLICATIONS

Title	**Weekly Market Report**
Coverage	A weekly summary of prices and news relating to the wool market.
Frequency	Weekly.
Web facilities	Details of publications and online ordering facilities on site.
Cost	£175.
Comments	Published every Thursday.
Address	World Textile Publications Ltd, Perkin House, 1 Longlands Street, Bradford BD1 2TP
Tel./e-mail	01274 378800 info@world-textile.net
Fax/Website	01274 378811 www.world-textile.net

YOUGOV LTD

Title	**YouGov Prosperity Index**
Coverage	Based on quarterly survey of a sample of UK adults online. Results cover current and expected financial situation of households, perceptions of economy, living standards.
Frequency	Quarterly.
Web facilities	Results of this survey and basic results from other surveys on site.
Cost	Free.
Comments	
Address	1 West Smithfield, London EC1A 9JU
Tel./e-mail	0207 618 3010 info@yougov.com
Fax/Website	0207 618 3025 www.yougov.com

YOUTH RESEARCH GROUP

Title	**YORG Survey**
Coverage	A survey of six- to 16-year-olds in the UK and other European countries. Based on a sample of around 7000 and the survey is conducted by the company each school term.
Frequency	Annual.
Web facilities	General details and some summary data on site.
Cost	On request.
Comments	
Address	4 Pinetrees, Portsmouth Road, Esher KT10 9LF
Tel./e-mail	01372 468554 yorg@supanet.com
Fax/Website	01372 469788 www.yorg.com

Title Index

Subject Index

Join our e-mail newsletter

Gower is widely recognized as one of the world's leading publishers on management and business practice. Its programmes range from 1000-page handbooks through practical manuals to popular paperbacks. These cover all the main functions of management: human resource development, sales and marketing, project management, finance, etc. Gower also produces training videos and activities manuals on a wide range of management skills.

As our list is constantly developing you may find it difficult to keep abreast of new titles. With this in mind we offer a free e-mail news service, approximately once every two months, which provides a brief overview of the most recent titles and links into our catalogue, should you wish to read more or see sample pages.

To sign up to this service, send your request via e-mail to **info@gowerpub.com**. Please put your e-mail address in the body of the e-mail as confirmation of your agreement to receive information in this way.

GOWER